9/10

The
Days of our
Lives

THE TRUE STORY OF ONE
FAMILY'S DREAM
AND THE UNTOLD HISTORY OF
DAYS OF OUR LIVES

KEN CORDAY

EXECUTIVE PRODUCER OF *DAYS OF OUR LIVES*

Days of our Lives
Publications

791.45
COR

Published by Sourcebooks, Inc.

P.O. Box 4410, Naperville, Illinois 60567-4410

(630) 961-3900

Fax: (630) 961-2168

www.sourcebooks.com

Library of Congress Cataloging-in-Publication Data

Corday, Ken.

   The days of our lives : the true story of one family's dream and the untold history of Days of our lives / by Ken Corday.

      p. cm.

1. Days of our lives (Television program) I. Title.

   PN1992.77.D38C67 2010

   791.45'72—dc22

                              2010001457

Printed and bound in the United States of America.

SB 10 9 8 7 6 5 4 3 2

For Ted, Betty, and Chris

In order to know where you're going,
it's good to remember where you have been.

—Mark Mahon
Strength and Honour

Contents

Prologue ix

Foreword. xv

1 . Providence and the Past 1

2 . The New Pioneers 7

3 . Fat Cans and Superbombs .13

4 . Betty 17

5 . My Back Pages 21

6 . The Move 37

7 . How the West Was One 49

8 . The Beginning and the End 59

9 . He Speaks in Riddles, Metaphors, and Clichés 69

10. Coming of Age. 75

11. Brother Eagle, Sister Sky 97

12. Gone to an Hour 101

13. The Once and Future King 107

14. Do or Die. 113

15. Not So Fast, You Lucky Dog! 117

16. The Glory Years. 125

17. There She Goes 137

18. The Hourglass Ladies. 147

19. There He Goes. 163

20. I Need a Hero 169

21. The Gay Nineties. 179

22. "The Barbarians Are at the Leveraged Gate". 183

23. "Bang! You're Alive". 187

24. Behind the Scenes 193

25. "Forty Years, Ten Thousand Episodes,
     and Growing". 205

26. The Dirtiest Half Dozen. .209

27. Life after Forty. 223

28. Life Support. 231

Epilogue. 241

Special Thanks 249

Biography of Ken Corday 251

PROLOGUE

Still dressed in her nightgown, the old woman slowly climbed the stairs to the roof of her Manhattan apartment building. In a dream that was rapidly becoming a nightmare, she had left the confines of the twelfth floor and the pain of another long, despairing weekend to reach her destination at last. It was a clear, bitterly cold Monday morning. She had not eaten in three days, but she had been drinking all the while.

She looked down from the top of the building, fourteen floors to the street below, Central Park West, and thought that she had chosen the right time and place to do the deed (as much as anyone really thinks in such a moment). Cars were starting to pile up at the stoplight on the corner of Ninety-first Street, but there was still little foot traffic. She looked down and, knowing the street was clear, walked to the edge of the roof without hesitation and jumped.

∞

At exactly the same time on that winter morning, a fourth-grade boy, late for school, emerged from the building's lobby and made the most fateful turn of his life. He walked out from under the entry awning and felt the sudden rush of freezing air numb his face. He was aware that something else was not right…something above him had gone haywire. He looked up as he was about to reach the corner, and what he saw indelibly changed his life.

A naked blur of skin and hair whooshed by as she passed him and landed headfirst on the car parked nearest to him. She left most of herself in a splatter of red and pink and gray, and some of herself on his nicely pressed school blazer, white shirt, and tie. He stopped and couldn't move. Moments like this seem to move frame by frame, over in a matter of seconds, but then they last an eternity. She was dead, immediately out of her pain, but his had just begun.

As the police and ambulance sirens began to be heard in the distance, he stood mesmerized. The doorman found him and ushered him back inside. The boy went up to his apartment and rang the doorbell.

My mother and I answered the door. We looked out on a face of shock, one that had aged years in the minutes since my older brother had left for school. He explained what had happened. It was only after noticing the residue on his clothes that our mother stopped doubting his story, which at first had seemed to be another excuse for truancy. She ran to the front window of the apartment to see the truth for herself. The truth was hideous.

Spread out over a large bloody circle were the remains of the jumper, now covered by a dark gray New York City Morgue blanket. Even from the fifth floor, the smell of the disinfectant and street cleaner was pungent and sweet at the same time. Like cold cream mixed with Lysol…a smell that would forever haunt us. For the rest of our lives, those smells would stop us and remind us of "the incident," as our mother later referred to it in psychiatrists' offices all over Manhattan.

"Oh, God, Chris…Christ Jesus." She hugged him close to her.

"Are you all right?" she asked. Of course he wasn't, as he recounted

the entire experience without really saying what he felt. He was emotionally scarred for life.

Our mother, for one of only a few times in her forty years, was dumbstruck, without any words or, for that matter, comprehension. What had
happened to her elder son? Why had this nightmare been visited on
him, he who was in need of care, love, nurturing, and above all else,
really in need of being dealt some new, good cards?

A lot of expectations had been placed on my brother as the firstborn
son. But he was always a problem child, tormented by God knows what
and always in need of better experiences. He seemed to live under his own
storm cloud, and my mother, my father, and I never truly understood why.
He was bright and talented but was never really happy with his soul.

Later that same week, my brother came home from school early.
Our mother had made him attend in spite of "the incident" and the
memory that she so desperately wanted to go away. He was doing nothing but staring at the walls when I bounced in, impervious and unaware
of his newly inflicted psychological wound.

"How about we go take our new saucers to the park?" I asked. He
shrugged and kept on staring at the wall. "Come on…Mom's not going
to be home until later, and the doorman will walk us across the street
and into the park…"

"Okay…all right." So we changed into snow pants and got everything ready for an afternoon's fun.

Central Park in March can be a wondrous place, especially after a
fresh snow, the kind we had gotten a few days after the suicide. The
snowdrifts piled their way up the sides of the old stone walls lining the
park and were the perfect landing zone for any child's frolic. We were
barely in the park when we thanked the doorman who had escorted us
and then headed out on our own.

Our destination was the reservoir that lies closest to the West Side, between Eighty-sixth Street and Ninety-sixth Street, and that is home to not only New York City's ducks in the spring, but also to the thousands of joggers and walkers who circumnavigate the park's peripheral cinder track every day of the year. The reservoir is flanked on all sides by gently sloping hills and small wooded areas dating back to the seventeenth century. We arrived at our favorite hill within minutes and busied ourselves with joining the mob of other children riding their sleds and saucers down and back, over and over.

During one of our forays back up the hill, we, or really my brother, encountered some bigger boys, also from the Upper West Side. They were obviously not neighborhood kids, judging from their dress and their pronounced New York accents, and they had a very unfriendly air about them.

Much as an angry dog sees fear in a passerby on the street, these three strangers were looking for trouble, and once again my brother found himself in the right place at the wrong time. After trying to block the way up the hill, they advanced on him, closing rank slowly. Then the obscenities started: "Hey, Jew boy, why don't you go home to Mama?" "Hey, punk, we're going to kick your ass!"

Before he knew it, my brother was at the bottom of a pile and being pummeled by all three delinquents, all the while being asked if he wanted more or would shout uncle. Every time he tried to get that word out, they filled his mouth with dirty snow and the beating continued. I stood in shock, too afraid to help and too amazed to run. I could not believe my big brother, three and a half years older, was being so degraded. Even more so, I could not believe it was really happening so soon after the other "incident."

Our mother had told us we were baptized in St. Patrick's Cathedral. We had never seen the inside of a synagogue, worn a yarmulke, or spoken a word of Hebrew. We were "fallen-away" Catholics living a reformed life in an Episcopalian school environment. Why would anyone mistake us for being Jewish? Maybe it was because of my brother's dark black hair and large nose. Maybe he was just another scapegoat. Whatever the reason, these thugs had found a soft target and succeeded in reducing another middle-class city kid to a new level of low self-esteem.

Even more so, this had shown me, for the first time, that big brothers have feet of clay.

Later, as we slowly retreated in silence to Central Park West, unspoken pity passed from younger to older brother. But he just kept wiping his bloody nose and checking his chipped front tooth, more concerned about what our mother would say regarding the cost of the dental repair than what change this had created in my perception of him as an everlasting protector. I could only watch what was happening to him. I was powerless to help or change him, and I was the one who was crying.

FOREWORD

In 1971 I walked up to the door of an old redwood cottage in the Santa Cruz Mountains and knocked four times. A woman answered the door. She was in her late seventies and had a distinguished air about her and a twinkle in her eye. She was a psychic from the old country, Czechoslovakia or Romania, and her name was Janice Volkmer.

She invited me in. She was tiny and spoke with a very heavy accent. Her home was furnished with old-world bric-a-brac and oversized furniture. I immediately felt at ease. We made small talk for only a moment. She asked me if I was comfortable having a reading with her. I told her I was.

She sat me down across from her at a large dining-room table. She had a wall-to-wall mirror behind her that made the small room appear twice as large, much as she seemed twice as large once we sat down. She asked me my birth date, and then she took my hands in hers, turned my palms up, and gasped as she looked at them.

She said, "You have a simian crease, a line that runs straight across the middle of both hands, and it is extremely rare." She told me it represented my head line and was a sure sign of either a one-pointed genius or a homicidal maniac. I knew I was neither brilliant nor a killer, but she continued.

"This simian crease means you will do only one thing well for your entire life, and you will succeed if you don't fight or fear it." Then she said, "Your heart will be broken once, but you will live a long life after that, with one marriage and three children." Then her words seemed to trail off as she started reading tarot cards and spelling out their details of my near future. But the bit about the simian crease had given me the chills.

I said good-bye to her after what I thought was about twenty minutes. As I walked to my car, I looked at my watch and noticed that two hours had passed since I knocked on her door. I had gone into her old cottage, time seemed to have stopped, and she had seen my future.

When she said I would do one thing well my whole life, I was sure that she meant I would become the famous rock 'n' roll drummer I dreamed of being. She was right, but I wasn't.

∞

In 1985 *Days of our Lives* celebrated its twentieth anniversary at the Beverly Hills Hotel. In the years following my visit to the Santa Cruz psychic, I had discovered the true meaning of her vision for me, but the great promise and its potential had not completely revealed themselves.

I had changed horses midstream and at the age of thirty found myself in a brave new world that was not of drums and rock 'n' roll, but was still entertainment. I had landed in Soap Operaville instead of Woodstock, and I had unwittingly grown first accustomed and then later comfortable with my new digs. I had arrived, and I had seen the writing on the wall. But I had not yet conquered.

On that lovely night in early November, I escorted my mother to the *Days of our Lives* party. She was then seventy-three years old, and her health was failing. I was thirty-four years old and just starting to hit my stride as a composer and a producer. My father, Ted Corday, had created the show, and since the age of fifty-four, my mother had raised it.

I had proposed to my future wife, Sherry Williams, only a few months before. As we were seated at the head table, I introduced this lovely brunette lady with big, beautiful green eyes to all the guests at the table, and together, we both surprised my mother by showing her Sherry's engagement ring. My mother was ecstatic, and both women were charmed by each other's presence. I saw in Sherry so many qualities that I had loved about my mother. Strange how men find wives that have many of the qualities they admire in their mothers.

The festivities that night were spectacular. Great food, network speeches that weren't too long, a few very funny celebrity guests—and a hilarious reel of outtakes from the past twenty years. Everyone had a splendid time. Even my mother, with her emphysema and shackled by her portable oxygen tank, relished the gaiety. And she and my future wife seemed to have taken more of a shine to each other than ever before. Betty Corday had a daughter-in-law to be.

Soon the evening came to a close, and the fun was over. I was driving my mother home when she casually mentioned, in her erudite Bostonian manner, that she thought the time had come.

"Ken," she said. "I know you adore writing your music, and I think you're doing a wonderful job helping with producing the show, but you're still learning."

"Uh-oh," I thought. "Here it comes...the motherly advice."

She continued. "I'm not talking about learning the difference between camera one and camera two, or how to take a meeting with the network, or dealing with a difficult actor or producer, or any of that day-to-day sort of thing.

"No. What I mean is that you're still learning the magic of the show—that which breathes life into it—and on which it lives and thrives, or without which it withers and dies. Story. Story. Story. Nothing more.

Nothing less. That's why people want to watch the show—to see their story. And that talent, knowing a great story from a good one, and a good story from a bad one, is what made your father and Irna Phillips and Bill Bell great. It's what's kept us on the air for the last twenty years."

I was really listening to her then. She seemed to be imparting some sacred, secret, yet simple wisdom to me, and she was doing so with her own special purpose.

She continued. "You know I'm getting tired of running the show, and my health is not all that great." Which was quite the understatement, but my mother was a gifted and soft-spoken queen of the understatement. Then came the words that I had not expected to hear that night, or anytime in the near future, but that had always loomed larger than life somewhere in the back of my mind ready to be said and heard.

"I think it might be time for you to take over."

There was a long, very pregnant pause. The silence was palpable. I was not shocked, but I was speechless. Then she broke the ice again.

"Think about it. Think it over. You know I think you'll be great, but you have to want to do it because you love the show and the business, not for me or the money."

I said, "Okay. I'll think about it. Thanks. I love you, and I'm proud you think I can handle such a huge task, but I'm not sure." I was debating this all in my mind at the same time she was saying it. I was conflicted…honored by her request but not yet sure I wanted to commit to such an important responsibility.

So she went on.

"Think about it like you would think about any good story," she said. "They all have a beginning, a middle, and an end. How will this make your life and your story better and different? What can you bring to it that will make it better and keep it going for another twenty years?"

I thought she was kidding. Another twenty years? I'd be over fifty by then. How could she see such a future for me or for the show?

But Betty Corday, like her husband, my father, Ted Corday, knew a good story and had an uncanny sense of the future. And even if I didn't, she saw me as a central character in the story of the show's future.

She had, in her subtle, loving, Old Irish way, passed me the mantle in a casual conversation on the way home from the show's twentieth anniversary party. I think she knew, much as my father had twenty years before, that the time was right.

It was going to be up to me. All I had to do was continue the legacy, the successful story behind the successful story, for her, for myself, and, most of all, for millions of faithful viewers.

"What should I do?" I thought, as I drove into the night. Where would the decision to take this path lead me? I knew it would change my life forever.

As I pondered what the next twenty or more years of my life would be like, I began to envision both great success and failure. This was my father's legacy and my mother's blood, sweat, and tears. No was not an option.

∾

This is the story of one family: our dreams, our past, and our greatest achievement—the American dream realized in the tragedies and the ultimate success of what could happen only once in many lifetimes. It is also my own personal story, the story of my life and my brother's life and how they intertwined with our parents' lives and the *Days of our Lives*.

This is the story of the Corday family, my family, starting in the roots of immigrant America and finally arriving at a place that can only be considered heaven on earth, the creation of the Disneyland of daytime television, *Days of our Lives*. Spanning two centuries and culminating in the fruition of the longest-running drama in the illustrious history of NBC Television, this is the truth behind what millions of Americans have enjoyed for forty-four amazing years.

I am Ken Corday, and these are the days of our lives.

CHAPTER 1

PROVIDENCE AND THE PAST

The union of Ted and Betty Corday produced my brother, Chris, and me, and their journey together also gave birth to *Days of our Lives*, but like any good journey, this one has a particularly peculiar and fabled path.

The marriage in 1942 of my parents, Ted and Betty, was the first marriage outside the faith in either family, ever. Dating back more than one hundred years, and probably even more, both families had the traditional understanding that interfaith marriages were not only unacceptable but absolutely wrong, and they resulted in the couple's being ostracized by the family. Marry a Jew, and your children might never get to heaven! Marry a Christian, and the Jewish family might forever regard you as dead. They might never speak your name again.

Regardless, it was 1942. The Second World War had begun for America the day after Pearl Harbor, and the entire human force of America was drawn up in the greatest global conflict of the century. So for Ted and Betty, two young New Yorkers working in the theater and facing Ted's induction into the army in April 1942, it became obvious that since they were totally in love with each other, the time had come to change the orthodoxy of years of sacred religious principles and get married. They did—three days before Ted was to report to boot camp. It was a simple ceremony in front of a justice of the peace in Manhattan with their two best friends in attendance, and that was that. Three days later the honeymoon ended, and off to war Ted went.

∞

Though Ted met Betty in New York, she was not a lifetime New Yorker by any means. Betty Corday's ancestry dated back to the late seventeenth century in Plymouth, Massachusetts. Her great-great-grandfather, times ten, was John Carver, the first governor of that colony of English settlers. Governor Carver died of sunstroke six months after taking office, leaving a wife and two children. Betty could claim she was a descendant of that first Pilgrim colonist. She could also trace her lineage to the *Mayflower*, the Daughters of the American Revolution, and a piece of Boston proper.

Her birthplace in Boston was near the home of Joseph P. Kennedy and all of his soon-to-be famous children. Her parents were John and Martha Shay. Martha's maiden name was also Shea; the different spelling owed to her more Southern Irish or Catholic ancestry, as opposed to her husband, who was, in fact, an Orangeman, one of Northern Irish stock and a Protestant.

Martha didn't tell her parents that she was marrying a Protestant until long after their marriage vows had been taken in one of Boston's finest Catholic churches. What did it matter anyway? John Shay practiced Catholicism with the same fervor and devotion as any other parishioner, even though he had never converted nor taken first communion as a Roman Catholic.

They had two daughters: Betty, the elder, was born on March 21, 1912, and Martha Jean was to follow three years later. Betty Shay's first crush, when she was seventeen, was on the eldest of the Kennedy boys, Joe Jr. She was soon to have her coming-out as a Boston debutante, and she dreamt he was the perfect match, as well as the love of her life. But Betty's father lost everything in the stock-market crash of 1929 that started the Great Depression.

Almost overnight in 1929, the Shay family moved from the top of Boston society to the dregs of the lower middle class. They took up residency in the suburb of Waltham, southwest of Boston. John Shay went from being a hugely successful investment banker to being bankrupt. He was forced to sell what little was not mortgaged and move his family to a small two-bedroom house in what was then considered "the sticks." Betty went from being a Boston deb to being a junior in a public high school.

At seventeen, Betty had learned her lesson well and would never, for the rest of her life, make an investment in anything other than government-insured, AAA-rated Treasury bills, which, in later years, showed many a skeptic how brilliant her investment strategy was, however hard learned.

Fresh out of high school at the age of nineteen, Betty decided to move to New York City against her parents' wishes. It was 1932, and Manhattan, even in the Great Depression, held promise for a young woman who wanted to be an actress on Broadway but, more importantly, also had the typing skills necessary to get a job doing entry-level secretarial work. And she did get secretarial work. However, for the next ten years, all through her twenties, this ravishing "black Irish" beauty would court the city, dating, but inevitably rejecting, all suitors while she kept her virtue. She wanted to be an actress more than anything. First she typed, and then she edited, all the while learning the rules of the show-business game.

One day, on a cattle call for the upcoming production of *Tortilla Flat*, she met its director, Ted Corday, and was swept off her feet. Ted was sitting in the middle rows of a theater during the auditions, as most directors do. When Betty came on stage, Ted told his assistant, "See that girl? I'm going to marry her." Just like that. The rest was history.

Although she was wrong for the part, she was right for him. Over the next decades, their future would be forged by the stage, by the radio airwaves, and finally by television. Betty was a pioneer in spirit and not afraid of the future.

∽

Ted was the eldest boy of six children, born to David and Katy Cohen in 1908 in Winnipeg, Canada, at the stroke of midnight one very cold night between May 7 and May 8. His parents had met some ten years earlier in England and had decided to set sail for the New World (that being Canada, for anyone of English descent). David and Katy Cohen's ancestry could be traced much further back than England, though, and the fabled story that accompanied it was absolutely preposterous.

The Cohens originally came from a small city in Lithuania called Kovna. The family Cohen was all part of the religious hierarchy in a community of peaceful and intellectual Jews. The eldest of the great-grandfathers was a rabbi in this city of merchants and scholars. He was a deeply religious man who had followed the tradition of his grandfathers by studying the Talmud and the Torah and then becoming a rabbi.

As the story goes, in 1812 Napoleon had conquered all of Western Europe except Britain, and the French army was making its way through Eastern Europe with only one goal in mind: the occupation of Russia and its crown jewel, Moscow, with all of its riches.

On his way there, Napoleon traversed the northern route through the Baltic States to the west of Russia. While his massive armies were en route, they passed through Lithuania. The city of Kovna, being a small center of Jewish passivism in a neutral country, proved to be a good stopping place to replenish the Grande Armée and to take stock…or perhaps leave some "resources" behind for later.

Great moments in history, whether personal or popular, are always born from great opportunities.

For the Rabbi Cohen, opportunity came knocking on a cold Friday night. It is said that the great Napoleon himself (but more likely, a group of soldiers led by one of his colonels) greeted the shocked Rabbi brusquely, then ordered him to fling open his cellar posthaste so as to provide storage for a large number of sealed barrels. Under the cover of darkness and with the assistance of the Rabbi Cohen, the French Army's "resources of food" were cellared away. Once the French contingent was satisfied that their provisions were safely secured, they instructed the compliant Rabbi that on no account was he to disturb them—the barrels were to be left untouched until the French returned to retrieve them after their victorious Russian Campaign. They got no argument from great-great-great grandfather. The next day, Napoleon's army vanished from Kovna, as if it had never been there. Unfortunately for the little Emperor Napoleon, the French forces met with great resistance from the Russians as they entered and slowly made their way hundreds of miles eastward toward Moscow.

By early winter the French forces were routed and forced to retreat, but not via the northern route through the Baltics and Lithuania by which they had come. The fierce Russian winter had made that impossible. Napoleon's army had to turn tail and take the southern route out of Russia.

Napoleon returned to France broken, beaten, and later banished to the island of Elba. But the loss of Russia eventually became a huge gain for the family Cohen of Kovna, Lithuania.

After enough time had passed and the Rabbi was quite sure that the French troops were not going to return to recapture their "resources," he decided to open what, for all he knew, were barrels filled with food. Instead, lo and behold, he found them to be loaded with treasure.

The barrels contained a multitude of gold coins, totaling more than he could even value. The Rabbi Cohen gave pause only long enough to round up his family, including his youngest son, Issac, and move far away from Kovna. After all, villagers can be suspicious of a family's sudden windfall of wealth. So they carefully stole away and left Kovna and Lithuania behind (not an inexpensive proposition). Following a stop in a town called "Kaeden" where, as lore would have it, they acquired a fair amount of land, the family Cohen eventually landed in South Africa, in the new British provinces...far away from any Europeans who might question their heritage or doubt their newfound prosperity.

A wealthy two generations later, Issac's son David Cohen, the "black sheep" of his family, was rumored to have become involved with a mature Xhosa girl from a powerful family and was given no choice but to leave or die. His own family had disowned him, so he left South Africa, penniless. He made his way to England, married, and then moved at the dawn of the twentieth century to the New World, to Canada, the place of my father's birth, to start anew and seek his own fortune.

∞

Of course, this story is so outlandish that when Ted Corday's younger brother, the highly respected cardiologist Eliot Corday, MD, was entrusted with a letter from their great-aunt Mary detailing the story, he one day sought the truth.

In 1988 Eliot was attending a medical convention in Paris and told one of his French associates, another cardiologist, about Aunt Mary's outrageous story of Kovna, the French army, and the treasure. His associate thought there might be a way to prove or refute such a claim, so they visited the Palais de Justice near Notre Dame Cathedral.

Early in the afternoon, Eliot found well-kept records of Napoleon's campaigns throughout Eastern Europe. And there, in an entry from 1812, read the following: Kovna, Lithuania: *Barils nombreux contenant pièces d'or* (translated to "numerous barrels containing gold coins").

Evidence! Provenance!

"We've found it...our very own pot of gold. Now, quick, let's hide it!"

The story of Rabbi Cohen's fortune turned out to be true. And as Ted and Betty would soon discover, fortune was something that ran in their family, although for them it was a fortune of talent and genius.

CHAPTER 2
THE NEW PIONEERS

David Cohen, broke, non-inheritor of the Cohen wealth, who arrived in Canada penniless at the turn of the twentieth century, must have had something more than luck to get through the next few difficult years. It must have been the intellect and resourcefulness buried deep within his genes, dating all the way back to Kovna and his Lithuanian ancestors. He had the uncanny ability to buy something from someone and immediately sell it for more to someone else.

He and his wife, Katy, finally settled in Winnipeg, Manitoba, which lies about three hundred miles above the border of Minnesota and Canada. David had wanted to settle east of there, but each time he pulled into a new town, he was greeted by the same kind of unwelcoming committee: in the daytime, a scowl and a number of anti-Semitic threats; at night, the large burning crosses that would sit high atop the nearest hill. Racists weren't only inhabitants of Alabama, Illinois, and Indiana… they had firm roots north of the Canadian border as well. So he went West to the new frontier.

David's business became selling all sorts of goods in small numbers after buying them in bulk. He opened a general store in Winnipeg, a town that was really more of a trading post in those days. His customers were not only the few permanent residents of this small tract but also the trappers and prospectors who lived in the great wild reaches of western Manitoba and Saskatchewan.

∞

Ted was David's eldest son. He was often left in charge of his three younger siblings by the age of twelve.

After Ted's father sold the general store and moved the family to Edmonton, Ted spent his teenage years building puppet shows for summer fairs. The puppets were actually marionettes that he and his younger brothers, Eliot and Hy, and sisters, Hazel and Jesse, crafted from wood and putty and strings. These beautiful puppets were, on average, one to two feet tall.

Ted and his brothers and sisters put on productions of fabled tales, such as *Aladdin*, *Hansel and Gretel*, and *Pinocchio*. His sisters designed and sewed the costumes; his brothers built and painted the sets, which Ted designed; and he wrote the scripts, set the lights, and then performed the whole show using his sibling crew.

They were successful, touring all the local summer fairs and town gatherings throughout central Canada. Ted would drive them from one city to the next, delighting children and parents as well. It was here that his love of entertainment became apparent. He would continue to return to do these shows every summer with his siblings even long after he had gone off to college.

At the University of Alberta he studied theater arts and was one of the forces behind the creation of the Banff School of Fine Arts, which still sits next to the beautiful Saskatchewan River. Today a plaque commemorating his vast contributions stands in front of the school.

By 1930, the Great Depression also had brought Canada to its knees. So, at the age of twenty-one, Ted moved to Chicago to pursue a law degree at Loyola University. He worked as a silversmith and also earned his way playing second violin in the Chicago Symphony Orchestra. All the years of his mother's forced lessons and endless practices, often ending with a whack on the head from his own violin, were now paying off. He played and paid his way through the university. After graduating he moved back to Canada.

He became an assistant district attorney at twenty-five. In his first trial experience, he witnessed a case brought against the prime minister of Canada on charges of adultery. After lots of scandalous testimony and a very long cross-examination, followed by pompous and erudite closing arguments from both sides, the judge found the prime minister not guilty.

Later, when the prosecutors and the defenders were summoned to the judge's chambers, the point was made very succinctly and clearly that although all the evidence showed no shadow of a doubt as to the prime minister's obvious guilt, it was just not right to oust such an important figure as the head of a nation over a little sexual dalliance.

His second trial was prosecuting a well-respected Chinese doctor who faced first-degree murder charges for allegedly killing his wife. The judge, jury, defense, and prosecution knew that the doctor was guilty. His crime had been front-page news in Canada. Yet the jury found him not guilty due to insufficient evidence, and the doctor got off scot-free.

This young attorney had seen enough. The next day, Ted handed in his license to practice Canadian law and moved south to the United States. He would never play second fiddle again.

Great moments are made from great opportunities. Leaving Canada was the blessing in disguise that would make Ted as much a pioneer as his father and his forefathers had been hundreds of years before in Kovna and South Africa and, later, Canada. He left his family in Edmonton, and other than returning for a year to run the family business and, most importantly, to help enable his younger brother Eliot get through medical school, Ted never had the slightest inclination or need to look back and wonder or regret. Something far greater than he could ever imagine awaited him a thousand miles away. His destiny lay before him in 1934, the year he turned twenty-six...and Broadway called to him.

∞

"Talent does what it can; genius does what it must."

Ted Cohen's genius did what it had to when he took the huge risk of leaving Canada in the 1930s for a life in the theater in New York City. He was a visionary. He took the plunge, jumping across the abyss from Canadian law to the law of the concrete jungle in Manhattan during the Great Depression.

And he made another huge step by changing his name to Ted Corday.

In 1935, as a new citizen of the United States and a new inhabitant of New York City, he decided to start his new life with a new name...a clean slate in the Empire State. He found his new last name while passing a poster for the famous Corday perfumes. He decided to blend in and give himself completely to his adopted country. A new Yankee Doodle Dandy.

There, in New York City, he stayed and flourished. First he worked as a stagehand, pulling ropes, cables, and curtains; then as a stage manager, pulling rank on crew and cast; and then as an assistant director; and finally, by the late 1930s, as a full-fledged Broadway director.

He loved the emerging black theater movement that had started with George Gershwin's *Porgy and Bess*, and he was close friends with its great singers and actors, including Paul Robeson and Josh White. He was connected to the Harlem scene, which was the hip thing to do in that decade. Billie Holiday was a friend, and he would later warn his soon-to-be wife, Betty, to stay away from Ms. Lady Day's Harlem parties... not a great place for a proper Boston girl. He also was enamored with the new popularity of radio, especially NBC's two national stations, NBC Blue and NBC Red.

He had always loved radio. As a child he had his own crystal radio receiver and was the envy of his brothers and sisters. Once he even cajoled his younger sister, Hazel, into trading her dog for the chance to listen to his radio. Such was the allure of this new tool of mass communication.

So great was radio's widespread appeal in the late 1930s that, following Franklin Roosevelt's fireside chats, Ted left Broadway shortly after directing his last two hit shows to become a full-time radio director for NBC. His list of credits was remarkable for a man only six or seven years in show business. The weekly broadcasts he directed of national dramas such as *Gangbusters* and *Counterspy* were the reason entire families would gather around the living-room radio during the evenings to be thrilled by the voices and sounds of this new age dawning. It was a time of joy and creativity. Then, in a moment, the world changed.

Ted was directing a Sunday-morning religious program and also doing the Betty Crocker commercials between segments. While the announcer was in the midst of describing how to cook and carve the family Christmas turkey, a young page from the newsroom handed Ted a telegram that was to be read immediately by his announcer. The time was about 2:00 p.m., and the date was December 7, 1941—the day that would live in infamy. Ted read the telegram to himself and then handed it off and listened firsthand to what millions of Americans would hear throughout the day: "We interrupt this program to inform you that the Imperial Japanese Naval Forces in the Pacific have just bombed the U.S. Naval Base in Pearl Harbor, Hawaii."

CHAPTER 3

FAT CANS AND
SUPERBOMBS

Ted Corday was drafted and inducted into the army in April 1942. Betty did not see him for the next three months, as he went through basic training at Fort Dix, New Jersey. He returned home a very different man. She was shocked and hardly recognized him when she met him at Grand Central Station. His hair was cut military short, his moustache was trimmed to the size of a pencil marking, and he had gained stature while losing weight.

At five feet, nine inches and 150 pounds, Private Corday was eager to go to war. All he strived for was to go to Europe and fight Hitler and his fascist, anti-Semitic forces. But Uncle Sam had other plans for him. Due to his age, thirty-four, and his experience in radio, he was seen as a far better prospect for Officer Candidate School and, later, placement as an officer in the Signal Corps, with the sole purpose of teaching radio communication and photojournalism to the units that went into combat.

By early 1943 Ted had entered and graduated from Officer Candidate School as a first lieutenant. He was assigned to the Army Signal Corps' training facility at Fort Monmouth, New Jersey, where he taught radio communication and photojournalism to thousands of young soldiers. The Army Signal Corps then was the equivalent to today's Army Reconnaissance Division, and during World War II civilian journalists were not allowed in any war zone on the European or Japanese fronts. The Army Signal Corps was solely responsible for gathering information, both photographic and radio transmissions.

To do so, a Signal Corps unit was attached to every division. They were the guys who took the pictures, both moving and still, of any invasion. They were involved with reporting all landings, and during the Second World War they sustained the highest percentage of casualties of any of the army's various units, second only to the U.S. Navy's Marine Corps.

They were always so few, the intelligence gatherers, in the midst of so many infantry, and they would continue to shoot away with their cameras in the face of the oncoming enemy instead of reaching for their guns. But they were the army's intel, its eyes and ears, and their first responsibility was to record the events on film and report them on radio before returning fire. Many were killed or wounded with their cameras or walkie-talkies still in hand, and many of those were Ted's trainees.

∞

Betty was working as an advertising liaison to any radio show sponsored by the products her agency, Benton and Bowles, sold. She was the conduit between production and advertisers such as Procter & Gamble. She was responsible for reporting each radio show's content to the sponsor and for carrying back any message to those shows' writers and producers. She didn't know it at the time, but this job in radio would be the start of her long and innovative career in broadcasting.

During the war, one such sponsor, Maxwell House, urged all housewives to save their empty coffee cans and later fill them with any excess fat used in cooking bacon or other fatty meats. Fat was used to make the grease or glycerin for munitions molds for bullets and other larger shells.

Commercials for Maxwell House and all other large canned-goods makers urged housewives to patriotically use these cans to save cooking fat and then return the fat-filled cans to their closest butcher, who, in turn, would furnish the armed forces with this much-needed product. The wonderful irony lay in the signs taped up in the windows of most butcher shops: "Ladies, bring your fat cans in here." No pun intended, just every woman doing her very best for the war effort. My mom always got a kick out of things like that...the humor in the midst of such serious times.

∽

Ted and Betty's war and radio worlds collided in an unusual way in 1944.

Ted rose to the rank of captain by early 1944 as the tide of war grew in favor of the Allied Forces in Europe and the Pacific. Being on the inside of intelligence, he was aware that the United States was in a race with the Russians and the Nazis to produce an atomic bomb—a superbomb that could annihilate an entire field division, or even a city, and thus would be the weapon to win the war.

The armed forces' project to build such a bomb at Los Alamos, New Mexico, was a heavily guarded secret. Even if the enemy knew the United States was trying to build the bomb, it didn't know how or where. Being an officer, Ted was only aware of the fact that the race was on and that whether it was the United States, Germany, or Russia, the first with the ability to drop the bomb would swiftly win the Second World War.

In 1944 Betty was working on a nighttime drama called *The Shadow*, and she had read one of the upcoming weekly episodes that revolved around the Shadow's heroic efforts to find out whether the enemy— always an unnamed, villainous face of evil—was capable of building a superbomb to destroy countless lives at one time. Ted was home on a weekend furlough when Betty told him one night of the wild idea the show's writers and producers had for this episode about a secret super-bomb. This was art imitating life in a very dangerous way.

Even when fictitiously depicted, the information, the way the script left unclear who had the bomb, could have endangered our national security. So Ted told Betty very casually that he thought the story was ridiculous and should be scrapped. But her excitement was apparently unwavering, and her conviction to let the show air this mysterious episode bordered on stubbornness.

Ted was in a pickle. He could tell her no and have to explain why, but that would be a breach of national security. He couldn't pull rank on his civilian wife. What to do? Then he remembered that Betty's uncle, Kirk Laughton, was a colonel in the air force stationed in Colorado. So he gave Uncle Kirk a call that evening. The call was pleasantly social until he got around to chatting about Betty's crazy story line for the national radio show. Colonel Laughton then asked Ted to put his niece on the phone.

He said, "Betty, Ted told me about the idea your writers have for *The Shadow*'s upcoming episode…"

"Yes," she said, "and…?"

"Well," Colonel Laughton explained, "I can't tell you why, and you can't tell anyone why, but you not only *can't* do that story, but as your uncle, and as a colonel in the United States Air Force, I'm ordering you *not* to do that story. You just find a way to kill it tomorrow and say the sponsor doesn't like it or some other decent reason…Got it?"

"Yes, Uncle Kirk," she meekly answered. By then she knew she was dealing with something important and immediate and highly confidential. The episode was never produced. Less than one year later, in August 1945, a U. S. Air Force B-29 bomber, the *Enola Gay*, dropped an atomic bomb on Hiroshima, Japan, and then another bomber hit Nagasaki three days later, bringing about the end of the Second World War.

Dust was settling across a shattered world. The clouds were dispersing.

CHAPTER 4

BETTY

Betty Corday was smart and a wonderful judge of character. Having never attended college, her formal education came from living in Manhattan after she graduated high school in Waltham, Massachusetts. She was a student of the school of hard knocks. Coming of age in the 1930s in New York City during the Great Depression was exciting for a starry-eyed, would-be actress, and, at the same time, horribly depressing in its ability to present rejection and all the other brutal aspects of big-city life. But Betty was a survivor, much as her father, Jack Shay, had been.

"Able to leap tall buildings in a single bound" was not just Superman's credo, but also that of those who lived through a time in our country when 25 percent of the workforce was unemployed, and many were so impoverished that the soup kitchens could not quench their endless hunger or feed their children. Those unable to work or to stand in line waiting had no chance. Few were successful. Many were overcome.

Betty was blessed. She was lucky to find work as a secretary in the typing pool of a large advertising agency, Benton and Bowles. Within years, she rose from being a typist to finding secretarial work and finally to an occupation that few women in the 1930s ever landed. She became an advertising agency representative assigned to monitoring agency clients' commercials on radio, a bourgeoning medium that was enthralling all of America during its most difficult and trying times. Radio became America's most popular form of entertainment during the '30s and '40s, and Betty was a part of it.

By 1940 Betty was marketing and monitoring advertising for Benton and Bowles and its client Procter & Gamble, as these huge advertising giants funneled more and more money into sponsoring radio shows and their commercials nationwide. Betty's power as a woman in her late twenties was not only new to her, but also somewhat astonishing to the male-dominated marketers whom she so effectively dealt with every day in every radio studio that she monitored.

Always the beautiful, blue-eyed, black-haired Irish Bostonian, she would coax and cajole her clients to find the most suitable spot in the broadcasts for her agency's commercials and then would beguilingly plead for the announcer who had the most mellifluous voice, to get the point of the ad over the airwaves with the most impact.

Even in those days Betty knew that women respond far more to the voice of a man selling Betty Crocker recipes than to the higher-pitched voice of a woman. The radio audience, especially in daytime, where she was assigned, was comprised totally of housewives. These women responded to the baritone of a man's voice in a more conditioned way than they ever would to a well-versed lady connoisseur. Who cared if the announcer had no idea that the soap he was selling really caressed and softened your skin? It was just magnificent to hear a man say those words, and Betty knew that was the secret.

So Betty succeeded and moved up in a business world run by men but whose product was bought by women. She was a very good judge of character and female desire. Give 'em what they want, but make them want more than just what they are buying.

When Betty met my father, Ted Corday, she was twenty-nine years old. In those days one might be considered an "old maid" at twenty-nine, but she seemed to know my father had been worth waiting for. They married in April 1942, when my father went to war and she went back to work. Her stature grew as she became the liaison for large advertisers, not only in daytime, but also in prime time.

With the male workforce depleted by the war, Betty was doing a job that only men who had been in the industry for many years had done before, and she was, of course, outstanding. She worked on the big national shows every evening, including *The Shadow*, *Gangbusters*, and many variety and news programs. She placed advertisers' commercials in the most advantageous parts of these shows and always with an eye and an ear on what the results were: What was the listener's initial response? What was the effect on market sales of these products? Should the announcer be a man or a woman, and how was she going to outdo herself next?

Three years later, when the war ended, soldiers came home and took back their previously guaranteed jobs in the workforce. Veterans were real heroes then. No soldier was overlooked. So Betty had to take a backseat to the men who'd been away at war. She had to learn to retrench and to slowly and sensitively reveal to her almost all-male constituency what the secret to her success had been.

It was simple really. When selling women's products, use a male announcer with a softly convincing, provocative voice. When selling men's products, use the opposite—a strong male announcer with an authoritarian, almost military command of his Gillette razor or Ford vehicle's capacity. And when selling products that cross the gender line, like toys and government bonds, use both a man and a woman, and even sometimes a child, to get the point across in a very comfortable, familiar way. Hit them where they live. Betty understood the radio medium so well that she was able to move from being an advertising liaison to becoming a producer on some of the most popular radio soap operas of the late 1940s, including *Young Doctor Malone* and *Pepper Young's Family*.

By 1950 Betty had become the mother of two boys and left the workforce to raise us. She would not return to the entertainment industry for more than fifteen years, although she would always be vicariously involved in her husband's achievements and, more importantly, the shows that he worked on, nurtured, and developed for the new medium of television: *The Guiding Light*, *As the World Turns*, and finally, *Days of our Lives*.

CHAPTER 5
MY BACK PAGES

The yellow taxicab pulled to a sudden halt at the curb of Central Park West and Ninety-first Street. The cabbie had looked casually in his rearview mirror after he was flagged and seen a very pregnant lady waddling and wobbling in the direction of his cab. Yes, he was free for the moment, but he certainly didn't want this fare and what he knew surely was about to happen.

Betty Corday got in at curbside and breathlessly directed him to Doctors Hospital. He turned and looked over his right shoulder at her and, in his own inimitable New York City accent, simply told her, "Not in my cab, lady!"

It was 8:30 a.m. on a sunny June day in 1950, and Ted Corday had gone to work one hour earlier, having no idea of the suddenness of this upcoming birth. Their three-year-old son was with the housekeeper, an ebullient resident of Harlem named Valeska. This child, Betty's second, was not due for another two weeks, and so she had not counted on this. There was only one choice. Hail a cab…now! And then get to the hospital. This baby was certainly getting ready to see for himself or herself what the outside world really looked like. And he or she wasn't waiting for anyone.

The ride across the park was harrowing but mercifully quick. This was long before the park was full of joggers, skaters, and parents running with their stroller-laden offspring in front of them, so the cabbie made it in record time.

At 8:49 a.m. the cab arrived at Doctors Hospital, this time coming to a screeching halt. The cabbie turned around to tell his passenger the fare, but all he saw was a woman balled up, groaning and moaning in the throes of intense labor. She was now lying on the floor of his cab.

A nurse and doctor, getting ready to go on shift, noticed the commotion in front of them as the cabbie opened the back door and ordered his passenger once again, "Not in my cab, lady!"

The doctor immediately intervened and helped Betty make her way slowly and carefully up the steps toward the hospital's maternity ward. Her ob-gyn, Norman Pleshette, MD, the father of actress Suzanne Pleshette, had received the call at eight that morning that she was on her way to the hospital. But now things were certainly moving faster than expected. He, too, was on his way but hadn't yet arrived. The friendly nurse and doctor threw a few dollars at the taxi driver and helped Betty into the hospital. He watched as she walked away and then, as any true New York cab driver would, checked the backseat of his cab.

Betty's water broke on the stairs going up to the hospital, and if any of the passersby took note, it would have been a New York abnormality. They were all too busy going to work at that hour or just enjoying a leisurely June morning in Manhattan. However, there was nothing leisurely about this delivery; it was right here and right now.

Betty was administered enough anesthesia to put her out in seconds, and a baby boy was delivered, as all babies were in those days, with great dispatch and very little sentimentality. And so I was born…and she slept.

∞

While they were building their careers, my parents also had two growing boys to handle. After my very sudden premature birth, things settled down. My first years were spent dealing with what at first seemed to be the typical symptoms of colic in preemies. But after a year of bloating and intense stomach problems, the doctor thought that I had a complete intolerance to all dairy products. My diet had all milk, cream, butter, cheese, and ice cream ruled out. No fun!

Today it is known that the condition I had was sprue, or celiac disease, which is a direct result of gluten intolerance related to any and all products made from wheat, such as bread, cakes, cookies, pasta, and most cereals. But not so in the 1950s. I never tasted butter, milk, ice cream (except for sherbet), or cheese (except for goat's cheese) until much later in my childhood. Even very acidic foods like bananas and grapefruit were eliminated.

The bloating and cramping continued until years later when I was sleeping over at a friend's and got fed up with the entire thing. I ventured out into the world of forbidden foods and found myself not only without reaction, but also feeling healthier, smarter, and stronger.

The only serious challenge to my health occurred in 1956, when I was six years old and entering first grade. Jonas Salk, MD, had just invented the first vaccine for polio, and it was hurriedly shipped to eastern U.S. cities from Salk's lab in Florida. Unfortunately, some of the refrigerated railway cars carrying the vaccine were not cold enough to keep the live virus in the vaccine at a low enough temperature, and an occasional batch became "hot," or dangerously virulent. Such was my luck that as I entered first grade I was given one of the first vaccinations to reach New York City and awoke the next day unable to move any part of my body from the neck down.

After my panicked parents called the doctor to our apartment, I was diagnosed with "infantile paralysis" from the polio vaccine being a bit *too* virulent. The prognosis was bed rest and "wait and see." The chances that I would develop full-blown polio were fifty-fifty. The first few days passed without any movement or response from different stimulations to my seemingly paralyzed body, especially my legs.

However, miraculously, after a week I slowly began to be able to move my feet and hands, and then later my legs and arms. After another week, I was able to rise from my bed and start walking…slowly at first and always with a pronounced limp in my left leg. Back to first grade I went in early November, and I always remember having to take the many flights of marble staircases at Trinity School step by step, one step at a time, right foot always leading, left foot doing the catching up. Our doctor encouraged me to not favor my left, but even more so, to run to each and every new destination, always trying to strengthen my legs. It worked.

As I reached second grade, I relished running to school, running up the staircases, and pushing harder than any of my classmates in all activities in the gym. An early-day Forrest Gump I wasn't, but my perseverance helped me develop stronger legs and lower body, and they have remained strong and trustworthy.

❧

I had two very close friends. One, Richie Epstein, lived in the apartment above us and was the son of a dentist, and most importantly, had a beautiful older sister, Barbara, who looked exactly like her mother. Their mother, Miriam, was tall, blonde, and extremely talented, to say nothing of being strikingly beautiful.

She had come from Germany, where she was a dancer and had appeared with her ballet company before Hitler in the 1930s. That was before "the purge" of all who weren't Nazis. Being a blonde, blue-eyed Jew, she was able to fly under their radar and escape with her life and family to America.

For me, listening to her play her Steinway grand piano through the

walls of our apartments was thrilling, inspiring, and most likely the beginning of my musical education, along with chapel every morning at
Trinity School. My father had long since stopped playing the violin, but
music was somewhere deeply embedded in his genes and also in mine.
He always had classical music playing on the phonograph, and I would
sit in front of it, playing on the floor.

Richie, however, was not as musical. He was very smart, loved science, and went on to become a doctor who now lives in New Haven,
Connecticut. Our afternoons were filled with making inventions out
of his father's dental supplies while listening to his mother play Bach,
Mozart, and Brahms.

Occasionally, when a big hurricane would blow its wild, windy rem-
nants up the East Coast, we would glue together three tongue depres-
sors to make a wooden helicopter and fly it miles across Central Park
from our sixth-floor window. On breezy spring days we would fill large
balloons with helium, attach a self-addressed, stamped envelope, and let
them fly from the top of the building, hoping for a return answer from
some faraway place in Europe or Canada.

The only response we ever received was from a disgruntled sanita-
tion worker in southern New Jersey. But life was good for me as a child
in its day-to-day simplicity. Evening meals were always with the family
and always preceded by a warm bath and then a half hour of the newly
created television show *The Mickey Mouse Club*. Those were such wonderful days because they were so perfectly simple.

I never thought of myself as much of a pianist. I had been the un-
witting and innocent recipient of an upright spinet piano my parents
had rented and put in the bedroom for my older brother, Chris. My
brother had long, slender fingers and was always told by his teachers
that he could make a fine pianist due to his beautiful hands. My brother

also had sung in the school glee club since third grade and seemed to have great pitch, a good ear for music—all the right ingredients, which inspired my parents to rent him a piano.

But Chris quit playing the piano after only a few visits from Mrs. Oxley, the piano teacher. She liked to use a ruler as a teaching device on her students' hands instead of instructing them how to rule the keyboard on their own. My brother's knuckles would always be red after his lesson, which wasn't due to overexertion or too many arduous scales.

Mrs. Oxley tried to make her students learn to play with correct hand position by balancing a pencil on top of each of their hands. Not only was this cumbersome, but it also was impossible to do and ended up in a clatter of falling pencils, piano keys marked with lead, and the subsequent smack of her ruler on the guilty hand or hands of the poor, shaken student.

Thus, it ended after a few weeks at twelve dollars a lesson. But alas, the piano had been rented for an entire year at a discount of two hundred dollars, a little more than fifteen dollars a month…a big expense for 1959. What a waste!

I would stare at it from my bed from time to time. Although it wasn't imposing, it was not a typical piece of furniture, and it allured me for some unknown reason. It had the mystical quality of being far more than it appeared to be. Enormously more. A key to an undiscovered universe with a new magical language understood by all but "spoken" by very few. The sweet language of music, all eighty-eight keys from low, low A to infinitely high C. What an intangible spectrum of color, mood, and thought. What a wonderful gift to be able to put those intangibles into air and have them land in an ear, near or far, with an expected or unexpected reaction and response.

As soon as I started playing, I knew I was home, like falling backward into a warm swimming pool. I was only in third grade. I would play and play many long, improvised discourses. I could have filled the text of more than a sonata or two if that little piano had known how to write down and transcribe all that my hands poured forth. I loved to hear all the sounds of that piano, and what was even better for me, nobody placed any expectations on my performance or even cared about what I was doing. I thought of music in mood or color. Happy, sad, angry, or scary. Yellow, blue, red, or shades of gray.

By the time I was in fourth grade, my parents started to take notice of my piano playing. My musical ability showed signs of promise, so they decided to ask me if I wanted any instruction. Not, of course, like Mrs. Oxley's, but more along the lines of going to music theory classes on Saturdays or maybe picking my own piano teacher.

I opted to try the first and was enrolled in a weekly beginning music theory class for children at the Juilliard School of Music on Manhattan's East Side. There I could meet all kinds of students and teachers and see for myself if I was interested in pursuing an education in music. But the classes were way over my head.

Learning the names of the notes and scales I had been so at home improvising seemed foreign and ungraspable. Music theory classes were two hours every Saturday morning and were set in classrooms like Trinity School, where the black chalkboards all had groups of five white parallel lines running horizontally across the boards to serve as musical staffs for instruction.

I was immersed in scales, arpeggios, the relationship of intervals between and among all notes, and finally counterpoint. What a bore! I could be playing in the snow in the winter or playing baseball in the spring or just home playing my piano instead of all this theoretical teaching. But I endured and tried to understand this new formality, if only by osmosis.

After three months I was falling behind and struggling to keep up with my new weekend classmates. My parents understood my quandary and talked to the school's instructors to help me find the right way to either deal with the problem or exit with dignity. That's when providence shined its light on me, in the likes of Tanamichi Sogito.

Mr. Sogito, from Japan, was on a one-year sabbatical at Juilliard, teaching the advanced and graduate students in piano performance. He was around thirty years old, extremely gifted, and small but powerful. He was somewhat world renowned and a master of the classics, especially Brahms, whose piano music is unquestionably difficult. However, to supplement his income and also quench his thirst for opening the "doors of perception" to beginning students, he took a few private pupils for one hour each on Saturdays.

One Saturday morning he visited our beginning theory class at Julliard. Mr. Sogito watched and listened as the students were asked to play something original they had composed or perform a piece from the beginning classical repertoire. Most played a bit of Bach or Mozart. The few who had yet to grasp those simple pieces but still loved to play the piano were allowed to play something they had composed themselves without writing their ideas in manuscript.

So I played a happy little piece I had written on all the black notes. When I was finished performing, the class was silent. No applause, no chuckles, no nothing. I sat for a moment at the piano, pushed the bench back, and reseated myself at my desk amid this imponderable silence. Our teacher thanked me. Mr. Sogito thanked the teacher, complimented the entire class, and took his leave to go home and tutor his young Saturday students.

The call came late that afternoon. Mr. Sogito was impressed enough with me that he asked my parents if they would like me to take a series of lessons with him over the next few months of Saturdays. The answer, gratefully, was yes—primarily because I had become disinterested in Juilliard's theory class. So began the beginning of the blessing that was to serve me for the rest of my life—the blessing of feeling and seeing music and sound instead of thinking and reading it.

Mr. Sogito met with me on Saturdays, usually in the early afternoon, from March until June. His wife was very pregnant and due in July. They would hopefully make it back to Japan, after June graduation and his recital at Carnegie Hall, in time for the birth of their first child.

I remember so clearly everything about those visits. The small one-bedroom apartment on Sutton Place near the Lower East Side was totally consumed by the Steinway grand piano in the living room. Mr. Sogito's wife would usually be napping at that time of day, and when the weather got warm and humid in May and June, Mr. Sogito would have to open the windows to keep the breeze coming in off the East River.

How beautiful the sounds of his playing were, and how fortunate for his neighbors! He never let his pupils play loudly or boisterously when the windows were open, but I'm sure he himself never held back or disregarded any dynamic markings when he practiced his vast repertoire of the classics.

He was not just technically brilliant; he was, more than anything, a master of interpretation. He understood the deep feelings and meaning behind the notes, especially with the post-Romantic impressionists like Debussy, Ravel, and Rachmaninoff. His method was in sharp contrast to the current rage in Japan, the Suzuki method, which stressed technical expertise first and overall.

I learned what feelings were in music before ever knowing the difference between an A or a B-flat. I learned how to play "Mary Had a Little Lamb" in ways that sounded happy or sad or scary or angry or combinations of all those emotions. I would play, and Mr. Sogito would listen and comment. Then Mr. Sogito would play, and I would listen and comment.

Thus, a common language of feeling was established. Mood before method…Passion before precision. Feel it before seeing it. Don't look at the piano keys; close your eyes, and let your heart and soul guide your fingers. And they did.

This beautiful and basic approach to music appreciation and application, both in performance and composition, would end up serving this young musician, which I now believed myself to be, for decades to come. It served me very well, indeed, but in ways I never expected.

∞

Summers were spent with my other friend, the country boy Danny Doherr, who lived with his large extended family at the far east end of Long Island on Little Peconic Bay. Danny was the opposite of Richie. A blond and blue-eyed descendant of a proud German American lineage, he was the consummate nature boy. If it floated, it traveled the waters as a boat. If it rolled, it was a steadfast vehicle. And if it in any way burned, it was a "super weapon."

The Fourth of July at Cedar Crest, the fifty-acre haven of woodlands where we summered, complete with little animals and great natural beauty, was always the most fun day of the year for us and the worst for the animals and trees. The greatest example of Danny's bold and fearless behavior occurred shortly after this holiday when his mother got a call from the North Sea Fire Department asking her to hurry home because the apple orchard was on fire. Upon arriving, she saw that more than half of the trees were burning from the bottom up and being doused by two engine companies.

When all was extinguished, she asked the fire chief, "How could this have happened?" It had been a dry July, but not that dry.

The fire chief explained that they had found a tampon under the roots of each apple tree. Danny had gone through his mother's bureau drawers and found a box of tampons. Being a budding pyromaniac, he assumed they were dynamite, judging from their long string "fuses." He then went through the apple orchard, placing one underneath each tree, and then went back to the first and lit each of these "fuses" as he scrambled through the rows of trees.

Upon reaching the top of the orchard, he looked back and waited for the explosions to commence. But, of course, nothing happened...only the slow burn of each string and then the ensuing combustion that slowly set half the orchard ablaze. The best intentions of mites and men...

Cedar Crest was always a magical place for me to spend summers, learning the great difference between the city and the country. Here was a natural, beautiful country paradise near the water.

My passage through adolescence moved through a very slow and perfectly straight inland channel. I approached the age of fourteen and high school, which was ninth grade, the upper school at Trinity, without any difficulty. The only complications—or, more truly, trials and tribulations—were played out by the other three members of my family. My brother became more and more of a problem and started on a hell-bent warp, tormenting not only me physically, but also my worried and confused parents emotionally.

Chris was sent off to boarding school in the ninth grade—Nyack Boys School in Nyack, New York, near the Hudson River and across from Washington Irving's famous hometown of Tarrytown. There he failed again, not for lack of trying and achieving good grades, but because of his delinquency in all things non-classroom related. Flushing lit cherry bombs down the toilets of his dormitory was the final straw, and the next day Chris Corday was sent home to Manhattan, a ninth-grade dropout.

Chris became content to torture his family by angering either my parents or me and then running away for a day or two. He would live on the New York subways while not at home, but only after stealing a bottle of scotch from our father's liquor cabinet. He would return one or two days later, drawn, haggard, hungover, and haunted by God knows what had happened to him and his already bruised and warped psyche while living under the city on its tracks in purgatory. He was like a literal Holden Caulfield from J. D. Salinger's novel *The Catcher in the Rye*. He then was enrolled at Riverdale School, also Upper Hudson River country, and again proceeded to wreak havoc on everything he touched.

I was exposed to my second taste of anti-Semitism when our family went to visit that school in the spring of 1962. I was eleven at the time and spent the afternoon swinging on the largest swings I had ever seen. They stood near the banks of the Hudson, looking east, just below the campus, and as I contentedly swung away, two upperclassmen came up to me and asked me if I was a "kike," too.

Having never heard this racial slur, I responded, "No, I'm not a kite!"

The older boys snickered and then left. Later when I relayed this strange question to my parents, they realized that this school was no place for their elder son. So again my brother was taken out of school.

But there was much more to his delinquency than just teenage rebellion. Chris had always been very difficult, temperamental, headstrong, and self-absorbed to the point of seeming to be very spoiled, which he wasn't. No, the basis for all this misbehavior and psychological drama lay not in the trauma of watching someone commit suicide, as he had years before, but may have been linked to a "fit," or more aptly put, a seizure that he had when he was two.

He was sitting on the toilet when, overcome and falling onto the bathroom floor in spasms, he lost consciousness for a minute or two. During this time his brain may have been deprived of enough oxygen to be damaged, perhaps permanently. Convinced he had just fainted, my parents never had him checked by a pediatrician.

No one wanted to believe his deep psychological problems were genetic, though the unthinkable diagnosis of paranoid schizophrenia surfaced repeatedly as he grew older. His life and behavior became more and more dangerous and destructive, to say nothing of self-destructive. So he plagued our parents, tortured me, and set up a karmic wake that would cost him dearly thirty years later. But for now, the pain my parents endured was far worse than mine.

Betty was a wonderful mother, never overly doting on us, yet making sure most of our needs and wants and dreams were fulfilled. She was the soft parent, probably because she was raised with only a sister in a household without testosterone. She had not grown up with boys, so we were a constant lesson. We were a labor of love as we defined our distinctive individual ability to be more physically different than anything a woman like Betty could imagine. Yet she toiled her entire life after we were born to be a good mother, not a perfect one. Yes, she did smoke a pack of L&M cigarettes every day, fed us things like tongue and always fish on Friday, and she worried too much about everything…but she persevered and loved both of us and was loved by both of us and our father, as the only woman in any family should be. She was respected, not revered. She was admired, not patronized. She was the most important part of all three of our lives.

My father was the light and lighthouse in our family, much as my mother was the safe port in any storm. Our father had what is now called a Type-A personality, but without all the ego and manic behavior. He was an extremely soft-spoken man—a man of few words, driven, but always intelligently succinct and well spoken. From radio dramas, he had migrated to television in the 1950s, directing *The Guiding Light*, as well as directing *As the World Turns* since its 1956 premiere.

Canadian lawyers never lose their British approach to the English language, and my father's command of so much vocabulary was always refreshing to hear. But even more, it was always brilliantly constructed in one long, flowing thought or two, and he made you want to listen.

Perhaps because he was the oldest son in the family, even though his sister, Jesse, had been born before him, he had always been the one who set the example for his younger brothers and sister. Ted's siblings looked up to him more than they did to their ne'er-do-well father. Their mother had always taken care of the family's general store in Winnipeg, so Ted was left home to look after his younger sibs.

Later in life this would help him in raising his own family, or at least trying his best against what became the steadily mounting odds against him in dealing with my brother. My father was a fearlessly brilliant director in radio and television during the '40s and '50s, the pioneering days of both media, and spent every day of the week in the studio.

When he came home at night, I would always be waiting to meet him at the door to our apartment. He would wrap me under his big, long, woolen houndstooth coat and hug me. It always felt good to be engulfed in the darkness under that coat—so much love would warm me and lighten any fear of darkness.

He loved to joke with our mother about her Bostonian accent, which she never lost even after living in Manhattan for thirty years. He would ask her to pronounce words that he would spell out for her, like "glasses" or "sawhorse," and we would always howl when she said "glahwses" or "sahhaws."

For about ten years after my birth, Ted and Betty were happy. So was our entire family. But the storm in our future was starting to quietly brew and loom larger on the horizon.

We had been riding high, if that were really possible for middle-class West Siders, without any real money to speak of. The 1950s brought the success of both *The Guiding Light*, as it went from radio to television in 1952, and later the creation and meteoric popularity of Irna Phillips's second soap opera, *As the World Turns* in 1956. Ted Corday directed fifteen-minute episodes, first on *The Guiding Light*, then thirty-minute episodes on *As the World Turns*, for ten years. An astonishing feat. But the advent of the '60s brought change to everything.

In 1963 the West Side had become more and more rundown as

it filled with a huge influx of Puerto Rican and Cuban immigrants. The old brownstone walk-down apartments that fronted all side streets from 70th Street to 101st Street became dilapidated tenements ruined by poverty and its evil sibling, crime. The streets were now filled with gangs, where they once had been filled by kids playing stickball. By 1964 it was time to move, time to get out.

Our father had always wanted to live in Beverly Hills, near his extremely successful younger brother, Dr. Eliot Corday. He had become "the cardiologist to the stars" in Los Angeles and was on the cutting edge in a rapidly advancing field of medicine. Heart medicine, as it came to be known, was starting to understand the nature of heart disease, then the greatest killer of all.

Eliot was a very important part of the department of cardiology at Cedars of Lebanon Hospital in downtown Los Angeles, and his practice in Beverly Hills had afforded him the ability to take up residence there in the 1950s.

But to Ted the concept of moving his family from his beloved Manhattan seemed at times impossible…more a fantasy than a dream. But again the grace and light of providence shone on this man, this modern-day pioneer, and our family, so we did move, but the reason we were able to was something Ted didn't expect and would change my parents' life and work. "California, here I come!"

CHAPTER 6
THE MOVE

It was my parents' mind-set to make the move west. Now to find a way to actually do it.

Moving is considered one of the seven most stressful events in life, preceded by death, ill health, poverty, marriage, raising children, and finding work. Moving for the sake of change, without the prospect of a new job or home, is doubly stressful. But in 1963 Ted Corday decided it was time to do both…move to the West Coast. Why? Because he heard his "muse" calling once again. Like his ancestors before him, he threw caution to the wind and dauntlessly rode the currents of change into a new world and a new life.

There were other practical reasons as well. At age fifty-five, he had already had two heart attacks in four years, the result of directing live daytime drama for more than fifteen years, as well as smoking two packs of Chesterfields a day. He often said he didn't direct *As the World Turns*, Chesterfields did. Now he walked to and from work every day…from Ninety-first Street to Fifty-fifth Street, CBS Television Studios.

The doctor's orders of daily exercise were becoming more and more risky. Ted was mugged one night on his way home by three thugs who took his money and left him with a couple of broken ribs. The city had changed so much since he had moved from Canada thirty years before, and though he always thought of it as his city, it was no longer home.

The final straw came when Procter & Gamble, which owned *As the World Turns*, told him it was time for him to stop directing and take a position as producer. In the early 1960s the producer of a soap opera was the "money man." He was asked to become like the shop foreman, who worked solely for the owner-sponsor and thus had very little creative input. For a man who was used to being the captain of his ship, the notion of becoming first mate was not first rate. But opportunities can be found in adversity.

Two of Ted's longtime friends were actors Jackie Cooper and Dick Powell. Cooper had recently become the president of Columbia Screen Gems Television, which had launched a few major nighttime hit shows—*Bewitched*, *Hazel*, and *The Monkees*—in the '60s. These shows established Columbia Television as a success, so when Powell, who was the head of Four Star Studios, suggested that Ted go to Los Angeles and talk to Cooper about getting a job directing one of these new shows, it seemed like a good idea. However, Ted had never directed comedy or variety shows. He was an ardent dramatist and couldn't imagine directing a half hour a week of laughs or music…and for only twenty weeks out of the year.

So Ted talked with Irna Phillips, the head writer and creator of his beloved *The Guiding Light* and *As the World Turns*. Theirs was a truly mutual admiration. Irna suggested to her loyal and brilliantly talented director that he might try to create a new soap opera on his own, and, of course, she would help him.

She came to New York early in 1964 for her semiannual dog-and-pony show…meeting with "the suits" from Cincinnati, her not so loving name for the advertisers from Procter & Gamble. But her real reason for coming was to meet with her dear friend Ted and help him make an important decision and take the step that would end up not only changing his life, but also those of countless others.

One afternoon they sat on the porch of our Southampton summer rental home with my mother and chatted about the current state of the medium. Irna raged against what she called the dying of the light that was being brought on by corporate and network creative control. She called them "temporary people making permanent decisions, who didn't know what they didn't know!"

She feared all soaps had become homogeneous, similar in their urban structure. She knew all too well that each and every one seemed to take place in a big-city environment and might as well have been set in the same generic high-rise, from penthouse to basement, one big, boring building...lots of big, boring soaps!

Why not have a new show that would be set in rural America...anywhere U.S.A., say in a small town called, for instance, Salem? The central figures could be the town doctor, his wife, and their four children. It would be more about small-town secrets and illicit Middle American romances than about hospitals, boardrooms, or courtrooms. *And it would be the first soap televised in color!*

Ted believed in never sawing the rungs off a ladder on the way up, for fear of falling through on the way down. He loved Virgil's credo "Fortune sides with he who dares." So he dared. He took the plunge, quitting his job at *As the World Turns* to go west in search of gold...much as his father, David, had in the early 1900s...and yet Ted never sawed one rung behind him.

He never distanced himself professionally from CBS or Procter & Gamble. This move, he knew, was the decision of a lifetime. It meant more to him, and to us, than anything that had come before. He would make the leap, go with his and Irna's idea, and while throwing caution to the wind, he believed his talent would get him through. He would go west! He would have to try to sell his and Irna's new show as an independent, family-owned soap opera. He would have to change his career and our lifestyle, completely unsure of what lay in wait. Success or failure, all riding "on-the-come." And most of all, he would give up all the intricacies he knew about producing daytime drama in New York City for CBS Television and move to Los Angeles and a very uncertain future in a very new and different culture, working for NBC for the first time since his radio days twenty years earlier. Launching any new soap opera is an extremely onerous and arduous task. Launching one in a completely new and almost foreign land was scary, both for him and our family. So much to give up and sacrifice, such a sweeping sea change in life…all based on his belief in one new, very unique show to be produced over two thousand miles from what was then home.

The thing about Ted, the thing most who knew him really understood, was how loved he was by everyone he touched, whether close to him or merely an acquaintance. He loved to touch people—an arm around a shoulder, the squeeze of a hand. My mother adored him. He was her true love, the only man for her, and their love was perfect in its mutuality. He adored her as much as she adored him. And their marriage, even though challenged by financial constraints and family religious intolerance, was never anything but gold. We, his sons, loved him, each with a heroic model of our own.

To my older brother, he was as smart as any father and able to inspire as well as teach. Being the firstborn, Chris had had great expectations placed upon him and had always proved he had the mind for it. But being the oldest means learning the ropes first, and that would prove to be an inordinate source of pressure, and in later years, a huge source of disappointment to our father.

Yet they loved each other and delighted in the kind of things fathers and firstborn sons share in the most special way—the first time they built a model airplane together, the first time they caught a fish together, the first time they went to a Brooklyn Dodgers game together, and so on…setting precedents for me where the bar was extremely high.

Our father became scoutmaster to Chris's first Boy Scout troop and thrived on taking all those New York City youngsters camping in the Vermont winters of six degrees, much the same as the winters he had lived with growing up in Winnipeg. My brother always excelled at winning our father's pride and adoration, even though he failed in school and was expelled or suspended many times. He was the firstborn, he was an Eagle Scout, and he was an absolute genius with our father's 35mm Nikon. He was, to my dad, "the once and future king," much as Arthur had been to Merlin.

I didn't get nearly the same amount of attention, but I didn't need it. I was more self-assured and self-reliant than my older brother and never felt the pressure or the responsibility of being the firstborn. In fact, I would watch and learn from my brother's many mistakes and know not to repeat them—a distinct advantage.

I got my father's real attention for the first time when once, while sitting at the family dinner table, the discussion came around to my brother's adjustment to first grade at Trinity School. Being only four, I wasn't really in school. There were no preschools in the 1950s. But as the conversation became more and more about my brother's every challenge as a seven-year-old first-grader in one of Manhattan's toughest private schools, I chimed in that I went to school every day, too!

"And what school is that?" asked my dad, somewhat taken aback.

"The *Ding Dong School*," said I. This first-of-its-kind show was on television every morning following *Captain Kangaroo* and taught by the irrepressible "Ding Dong Lady," Miss Frances, an earlier version of a scholastic Julia Child. Soon my father realized he had two equally bright sons. I could be as smart as my brother, and I could learn from him.

But Ted was still an enigma, not just to his family, but to all who knew him. He was a man for all people, deeply respected, appreciated, and reverently loved by his friends, coworkers, and most of all, his family. But his internal drive was a thing of mystery. It fascinated his friends and inspired us.

His dream was, and always had been, very basic: to live near his younger brother Eliot in California someday and watch our families grow up together in the safe, warm, sunny climate of Beverly Hills. But most of all, he had always dreamed of creating his own soap opera. After ten years in the theater, ten years in radio, and ten years in television, he had acquired the knowledge and refined his talent to the point that he knew he could do his own show. He would make a "better wheel" and not only add to the daytime drama medium but put his signature on it as well.

∞

So in 1964 Ted went to Los Angeles and met with Jackie Cooper of Columbia and the programmers at NBC. He had a well-known past as a director with this network as well as CBS, and his reputation as the man who pioneered soap operas from radio to television preceded him. But he had never created his own show. That was always left up to Irna Phillips or the advertisers, such as Procter & Gamble or Lever Brothers. Now he was teamed with Irna as a creator. Their visionary concept of a new daytime drama set in rural "any small town" U.S.A. was clearly unique. As was its title, derived from part of the 23rd Psalms' second-to-last line…"Days of our Lives."

NBC wasn't producing any daytime dramas at its West Coast studios in Burbank…only *The Tonight Show* and a few game shows. It was, however, looking for something to fill a new studio, Studio 9.

At that time there were no soaps on any network broadcast in color. Thanks to parent company RCA, NBC had been first to broadcast any shows in color—*Bonanza* and *Walt Disney's Wonderful World of Color*, both on Sunday night—and NBC was looking to continue expanding that new color broadcast format simply because it meant people would have to buy new television sets—color television sets—made by RCA, of course. News and talk shows like the *Today* show with Dave Garroway and *The Tonight Show* hosted by Johnny Carson, were soon to be aired in color. Why not a new soap?

The deal was made, and *Days of our Lives* was scheduled to debut in fall 1965. November 8, to be exact. That would not only give Ted time to start up a new show, but also give him and our family nearly a year to find a home in Los Angeles to rent, then pack up years of living in Manhattan, and move to the West Coast. A place where a million dreams had been made or broken.

⧜

So move we did, in the summer of 1964.

The upside to a cross-country move was iffy and very speculative at best. *Days of our Lives* and Ted were given a two-year contract at NBC, cancelable after the first year. Not much for which to uproot an entire family, change lifestyles, and move thousands of miles away to a life and culture that were altogether different and fraught with uncertainty. Then again the smile of providence shined its rays of sunshine on Ted Corday.

Before we were finished packing, Ted received amazing news: NBC had suddenly decided to launch not one, but *two* new half-hour soap operas to fill an entire hour of programming time. This bold move would readily appeal to sponsors' interest in providing larger blocks, or spots, of commercial time…close to fifteen minutes, or thirty commercials, available in both soaps. So Ted would be responsible for creating two new shows: *Days of our Lives*, due in November 1965, and a second, to be named, in March 1965. This meant that my father suddenly had to create a new show—and it was due in nine months.

Ted, whose roots ran back to the black theater movement in New York City, had always had the idea for an all-black daytime radio drama named *Westwind*. When he heard NBC was looking for another new soap opera, he pitched the idea to John Mitchell at Columbia Television, who took it to the network. However, NBC did not want to go into a potentially racially charged situation when setting out for the first time with West Coast soaps. Even so, having one production company, Corday Productions, working in one studio doing two shows would be easier to maintain than dividing the responsibility between two different production entities.

So Ted reshaped *Westwind* by changing the characters to racially white. But it still had the ethnic underpinnings of the original, only this incarnation was about poor Italians, Irish, and other immigrants living in a new, potentially richer, urban environment. It was to be called *Morning Star*, the last star to be seen before dawn and an image followed by many coming to the land of opportunity. It was also given the green light for a two-year contract, cancelable after one year. *Morning Star* was scheduled to debut seven months before *Days of our Lives*, on March 21, 1965, my mother's birthday.

No matter how fortunate or lucky one thinks he or she is, no matter how in control of life one seems to be, there is a higher power always at work for good and for bad. There is good in this world, and there is also bad.

As our family packed up boxes of books and pictures, all our best furniture, and the items of importance we would need for a new home in Los Angeles, it dawned on us that this would be the first time we all had ever lived full-time in a house. Maybe we would rent a house that had a swimming pool. Maybe someday, if my father's new shows were successful, we would even have our own home. What a dream! And dreams have the uncanny ability to drive people to do things and make sacrifices way beyond anything they have ever tried or thought of trying.

So try and strive and sacrifice we did. We gave away many of our material belongings—toys, games, old clothes, and more—to the Trinity School Church. Our parents gave away much unneeded stuff…that's what it had become, just stuff.

But the most difficult sacrifice was saying good-bye to so many old friends, teachers, fellow students, and coworkers. Thirty-plus years of relationships that all would now become long distance…a postcard from far away…an autographed holiday. For me, losing my two closest childhood friends—the city boy, Richie, and the country boy, Danny— was the hardest thing to endure. Such friends can be counted on one hand in a lifetime.

So pack and pack we did. We also had to say good-bye to our cherished summer rental home, Cedar Crest, on Peconic Bay, Long Island. This meant one last trip out to the end of the island to take care of leaving things in the same order they had been more than twelve years before when we first summered there.

Cedar Crest was a magical place. It had four beautiful, old Connecticut-style farmhouses that belonged to the same family, the Doherrs, and these houses seemed to be an organic part of a larger landscape—wooded, bluffed, creeked, sand-duned, and beached. In the summer the Gulf Stream pushed its way into Peconic Bay, over which Cedar Crest looked, and with its warm ocean currents brought a new harvest of sea life to the end of the island after a long, cold winter. The bay was always filled in summer with fish, clams, crab, and various members of their extended families. We had the best clambake every summer.

Those three months passed more quickly and with far more joy than any summer camp could. After a dozen summers there it was more difficult to say good-bye to the country than it was to the city. That pristine piece of eastern Long Island had shown our family, especially us boys, how beautiful life could be living with nature, clean air, and the sounds of the water and the woods.

Far away from Manhattan, even before the Long Island Expressway was built and the drive became a parking lot, Cedar Crest had instilled in our family a love of the land and a peacefulness in even the most stressed-out New Yorkers…which we inevitably had become by June 1 every year.

All of a sudden we had to close up the house in Southampton in the late spring of 1964. In so doing, we had to pull the old sixteen-foot Boston Whaler, the *Cobro*, out of its slip in the creek and trailer it down to the boatyard at the Shinnecock Canal. While cleaning the boat for the last time, in preparation for its impending dry dock, my father slipped and fell off the port side, badly scraping the inside of his upper left arm all the way up to his armpit.

The superficial abrasions covered a large area of what used to be skin. His inner arm was raw from the elbow all the way up and badly irritated by the effect of the boat's old paint and worn fiberglass. So he covered his arm with an antibacterial cream, loose gauze, and adhesive tape.

Later that afternoon, we trailered the Whaler and drove the six miles down North Sea Road to the dealer where the boat had been purchased and now would be resold. My father seemed to have bounced back from his fall by then, but the effects of this incident would have consequences no one could see at the moment.

We drove home that Sunday evening to Manhattan, having left Cedar Crest, Southampton, our idyllic summer retreat, for the last time.

∞

The Mayflower moving van was curbside at Ninety-first Street the next morning. Another sparkling, sunny Monday in early June. By that evening, the van was packed to the top, and as the movers closed its back doors, my parents, my brother, and I watched what was left of our life in New York City slowly move away down Central Park West into the sunset, headed for a destination nearly three thousand miles to the west. A destination as different as any could be from the one we knew, living with the rapture and stress that accompanies the millions upon millions of people in a city the size of Manhattan. Future culture shock was only a five-and-a-half-hour plane ride away...the next day.

CHAPTER 7

HOW THE WEST WAS ONE

One month later, after flying on an American Airlines 707 and then staying with our Southern California relatives, my Uncle Eliot and Aunt Marian, we moved into a nearby rental house in none other than Beverly Hills, famous then for *The Beverly Hillbillies*, not its zip code of 90210. For decades it had been a suburban haven for Hollywood celebrities, the elite, and L.A.'s nouveau riche. All flash and cash, no old-school culture to speak of, except for the entertainment industry. Even in those early days, the price of housing, whether sales or rentals, was much higher than anything on the East Coast—shocking to a newly transplanted Easterner.

But most shocking of all was the difference in people. New Yorkers and Angelenos are as different as apples and oranges. Our family had lived in Manhattan, where what was important was what you *knew*, what you *did*, and *how* you did it. Life in Los Angeles, Beverly Hills in particular, was about *who* you knew, what you *had*, and how you *got it*.

Culture shock set in. My brother and I had a very tough time making friends that first summer. Instead of living in the country comfort of Cedar Crest, Long Island, we were enrolled in summer school. We attended the most boring summer camp of all—Beverly Hills High School—home of a rich, famous, and extremely good-looking student body, many of whom drove Camaros, GTOs, and Corvettes. The legal driving age in New York in 1965 was eighteen, but in California it was sixteen.

So here comes the generic blonde bombshell, Barbie, in her convertible, wearing nothing but a bikini, on her way to Santa Monica Beach, and we two city boys from Manhattan, ages fourteen and seventeen, would stare speechless as she drove by, her hair blowing like golden fire behind her head and her white Vette purring through custom mufflers. Erotic and frustrating…the very things that create fantasy and the hormonal will to act upon it.

That summer passed by slowly, and the odd dullness of this wealthy suburban community, compared to Manhattan, started settling in heavily on our family as the days in Los Angeles got warmer and warmer.

As our family got used to the comfort of living in a three-bedroom rental at 624 North Roxbury Drive (at fifteen hundred dollars a month, an unheard of sum for us New Yorkers at the time), my brother and I looked for new friends. Chris didn't take long to find the unseemly element, even in a town so privileged. Some of those high school juniors, mostly sixteen to seventeen, were still exponents of the '50s with leather jackets, white T-shirts with cigarette packs, and wannabe bikers, most of whom were driving around in old '56 Dodges. So he joined a car club and got his license two years before he would have in New York. But this wasn't a normal Pleasantville, U.S.A., car club.

They enjoyed the traditional late-night habit of cruising, going to drive-in restaurants with roller-skating carhops, and smoking and drinking. Most of all, they enjoyed the nontraditional habit of stealing car parts from cars parked in garages or at darkened curbsides. It started with hubcaps and hood ornaments, easy and quick, and then escalated into far more larcenous behavior, culminating with breaking in, hot wiring, and grand theft auto.

This activity kept Chris and his auto parts theft gang busy for six months, over the course of that summer and his first semester as a junior at Beverly High. They got drunk, burglarized, and stole and stored thousands of dollars of car parts, stripped from the neighborhood's finest cars, in a small room above one of the affluent delinquent's parents' garage. They didn't do it for the money; they did it for the thrill of breaking the law.

When they were eventually busted, having been finked on by a rival Santa Monica club, all twelve of them were expelled from Beverly High. Being under age—and having turned over all the stolen parts to the Beverly Hills Police department and pleading guilty—they were given summary probation instead of facing felony charges. Now they were all dropouts.

It was 1965, and there were newer things to try instead of gangs and garage thefts. For the first time, drugs were easily available to the suburban middle and upper classes, namely marijuana and LSD. So Chris and his older friends turned on, tuned in, and dropped out to many places previously unknown and unheard of in Northern California and Arizona.

Chris was sent packing for boarding school in Scottsdale, Arizona: the Judson School. It was a kind of cowboy boarding school for affluent boys, even though our parents weren't affluent and had to borrow the money from our Uncle Eliot. But for Chris the Judson School was just another place to learn to party, without the onerous responsibility of meeting California's more rigid high school graduation requirements. In other words, it was a place for our parents to buy him an expensive diploma while he avoided getting arrested by Scottsdale's small-town constabulary.

Having Chris go off to boarding school was a much needed relief from the daily stress that came from the arguments, shouting matches, and eventual pushing and shoving between he and our father. Fisticuffs couldn't have been too far off when number-one son was ignominiously removed from his criminally idyllic life in Beverly Hills.

What had begun as the perfect father-and-son relationship had deteriorated over the past five years as Chris was first expelled from Trinity School; then sent to boarding school for the eighth, ninth, and tenth grades; and finally expelled from Beverly High. Now there was more than a brewing misunderstanding and acerbic resentment between father and son. At sixteen, Chris was already six feet, two inches, and close to two hundred pounds, and our father, at five feet, nine inches, and 160 pounds was no match physically for Chris. Their differences had never been reconciled since those long-ago episodes of running away from home to the scary solace of the New York City subway system.

Coincidentally, this was also a good time to remove Chris, a source of daily trouble, from the family dynamic. My father was busy preparing *Morning Star* to air on NBC in March and also dealing with what had become a nagging and persistent physical problem, his still healing arm that he had injured on the boat.

In 1965 Ted Corday took giant strides toward starting both new soap operas. He soon realized he would have two new "children" in these shows, something that would demand most, if not all, of his time, times two. He had raised two sons but now was faced with the daunting task of having two new mouths to feed in these two new daytime television dramas, born almost close enough to be twins.

But as he strode toward the future, he didn't look back. My father didn't know that fate was tiptoeing up behind him. He had no inkling of the fate that awaited him in 1965.

Tragically, it began long before he realized it. His scrape with the boat in the creek at Cedar Crest had never healed properly, and his arm was still raw and inflamed two months later in late July, after we had moved. He didn't give it much notice other than applying antibiotic ointment and an occasional bandage. Yet when his wound was still a problem by August, he saw a doctor. He was told it was an allergic reaction to the paint or fiberglass he had picked up through contact with the boat. He was given more cream and an oral antibiotic, and then Ted Corday went ahead with prepping a new cast, crew, and production staff for their debut on *Morning Star* in Studio 9, NBC's latest state-of-the-art television studio.

Preparing both shows for production proved to be a challenging task. *Morning Star* received most of his attention, because it was due to debut in March 1965. So he cast actors and found writers he had known in the many years that he had produced and directed soaps in New York.

These writers had come to California, the promised land, not only to get out of the East Coast cold, but also because the future of the entertainment business had rightfully taken its place in warm Los Angeles, starting with the movie industry before and after the Second World War and then with the advent of television production associated with the major movie studios like Columbia, Paramount, and Disney.

Desilu Productions' *I Love Lucy* had rewritten television comedy in a live three-camera format, and much of television was following in step. *Father Knows Best*, *Make Room for Daddy*, and *The Dick Van Dyke Show* were all part of the major studios' push to bring television to the West Coast. Add to that the new westerns like *Bonanza*, *Laramie*, and *The Big Valley*, and Hollywood saw an unprecedented boom in both production and newly transplanted talent in the decades following the '50s.

But *Morning Star* was fraught with all the problems an older child besets upon his parents. Breaking in a first West Coast soap meant setting up a videotape production company—in this case, Corday Productions—and breaking ground at NBC West Coast operations. So many bugs to work out, and so little "shake-down" time. Originally set up as a small New York corporation, Corday Productions was soon to be doing big business in Burbank, California, and learning as it grew. Only the networks or the giant advertisers like Procter & Gamble and Lever Brothers owned and produced their own soaps in 1965. Now a new, small, family-owned company was going to try to compete? Tall order.

Added to that, my father's health was not improving. He hid it from my brother and me and tried to hide it from our mother, but something was not right. His arm had never healed, the antibiotics hadn't done the job, and now he was weak and starting to lose weight. His brother Eliot was his closest friend in the world and loved him more than anyone else, but Eliot was almost in denial that his older brother could have gotten ill so soon after moving to the West Coast.

More tests were needed, but Ted just did not have the time to visit another doctor's office and then run through a battery of tests at some hospital in either distant downtown L.A. or Westwood. But as 1965 arrived and approached early spring, and *Morning Star* was due to start production, he was given no choice, by his own admission, other than to seek an answer to the nagging pain and swelling, not only in his left arm but now in both of his armpits and throat.

So in March an appointment was made for Ted to undergo a full series of blood tests and x-rays, the best tools medicine had at the time to diagnose the inconclusive symptoms he had experienced since falling off the boat in Southampton nine months before. Still the show must go on…and Ted worked tirelessly through the early part of the year to launch *Morning Star*.

On March 20, the day before my mother's fifty-third birthday, she and my father went to UCLA Hospital to have these tests done and try to take care of this nagging condition once and for all. Eliot was there for Ted and, as a cardiologist, had the knowledge to monitor the battery of tests that my father had to undergo.

Why was it that after forty years of wandering in the desert, when Moses delivered the children of Israel to the River Jordan, he himself was denied entry to the Promised Land of Israel? It just seemed to be God's will.

Ted had reached his own River Jordan. The news came later that evening before he was discharged from UCLA. Uncle Eliot stepped into the room where my father and my mother were waiting. Dr. Corday's face was normally the typical doctor's face of resolve and optimism in the face of even the worst prognosis, but this time his eyes gave it all away. He stoically tried to present the news in a positive light. But there was nothing at all positive about this diagnosis and prognosis.

My father had Hodgkin's disease, cancer of the lymph glands. In 1965, some years before the development of chemotherapy treatment, it was incurable. Even with cobalt radiation therapy, which was more devastating as a treatment than the actual illness, the chances for survival were almost nonexistent. Usually patients were given a little more than a year to survive.

After spending a lifetime trying to get to California and finally becoming reunited with his beloved brother Eliot, and then launching not one, but two of his own soaps, Ted was now suddenly denied all hope for the future. He could only take comfort that his spirit would live on in the memories of his loved ones and his amazing, yet-to-be-realized legacy.

My mother went to get the car from the garage at UCLA as Ted stayed to talk with Eliot and the specialists, all of whom were dismayed that they hadn't diagnosed the disease sooner. The news was impossible to fully comprehend. As my mother drove my father's car out of the hospital's garage, she was in such shock that she didn't notice she was driving the wrong way and impaled all four tires on my father's new 1965 blue Mustang convertible on the steel teeth of the wrong-way exit.

Even more anxious was the day one month later, shortly after *Morning Star* had gone on the air, when my mother went for the first time to put the key in the front door of our new house. It was a new home that my father had purchased by procuring a loan through the G.I. Bill and another loan from his younger brother.

As she started to open the front door, the afternoon sky, heavy with an impending spring storm, lit up with lightning, and a sudden crack of thunder directly overhead shook the house before she could get the front door open. Another dark and awful sign amid such horrible and tragic news. What had befallen our family, and why at such a magical time of so many new opportunities that now seemed to be vanishing?

When someone knows that their death is imminent and there is very little hope or time left, one of two things can happen. Many people give up, get their house in order, and wait for the end. Others fight on as if it is just another thing to be taken in stride and, even more so, accomplish their greatest achievements as their very last. So it was with my father.

He never gave in or gave up. He continued to work as always, with inspiring enthusiasm and a tirelessness that flew in the face of his dreaded disease. He never let on to anyone other than my mother and his brother that he was dying of Hodgkin's disease. His coworkers thought that he was tired-looking because he was overwhelmed and overworked with keeping *Morning Star* going in its first year while preparing *Days of our Lives* for debut in November 1965. But he also knew he could not beat the clock forever, or for more than another year. So he gave his final lap that amazing kick that only the very best of distance runners can find within themselves.

Chris, thankfully, was doing well in his senior year at Judson School. He not only was aware of, but he also seemed to inherently sense our father's failing health, so he behaved and achieved good grades. He never told me the reality of it all until a few months before our father died. Instead, in one magnificent gesture of loving fraternal understanding, he gave me a snare drum—a blue, metal-flake, Ludwig snare drum—for Christmas in 1965.

By February 1966 I was proficient enough to take lessons and convince my father that I no longer needed to practice in the soundproof confines of my bedroom closet. In fact, my father's sixteenth birthday present to me, sadly his last, was to take me to the pawnshops in downtown L.A., accompanied by my father's friend, Eddie Foy, Jr., the third of the famous Dancing Foys. Eddie knew the lay of the land in this seedy part of town. We found a matching set of blue metal-flake Ludwig drums with two cymbals and a high-hat for the well-adjusted cost of $150. Now I was ready to join the first of many wonderful bands over the next fifteen years. Music was back in my life, and it came at a time when such a distraction was needed most.

My father was very busy and very ill. He didn't have time left to read anything but scripts and budgets and floor plans. He would no longer be able to read to me the great pieces of literature that we had always shared at night before bed, especially *The Legend of King Arthur*, his favorite book and poem.

My father pushed harder into the fall of 1965, readying *Days of our Lives* for its beginning. This time, with *Days of our Lives*, he had the help of Irna Phillips, who reigned supreme in daytime drama with her own shows, *The Guiding Light* and *As the World Turns* at CBS and the newly created *Another World* at NBC. Irna also knew my father's health was rapidly failing and completely gave herself to the beginnings of this new daytime drama. She would dictate scripts to her secretary, Pat Falken Smith, over the telephone from Chicago to our home in Los Angeles.

All the while, my father cast the show and hired another entire production staff. This time he called on his dear friend MacDonald Carey, a star on Broadway in the '30s and later the star of many Hollywood action films. He also hired Frances Reid, whom he admired as one of the finest Shakespearean actresses in the legitimate New York theater. Her Ophelia in Shakespeare's *Hamlet* at the Columbus Circle Theatre was legendary on Broadway. He also hired one of his favorite directors, H. Wesley Kenney—Wes, as all called him—to produce this show. He hired Jack Herzberg to co-produce. Jack, my father's army buddy, had been a private adjutant for my dad during his days as a Signal Corps captain at Fort Monmouth, and Ted knew he could be trusted.

Providence brought them all together to start *Days of our Lives*. Now they were all of one company again, only this time in the company of NBC's Burbank soundstage, Studio 9. The West was not really lost for my father; it was now unified…a new company, a new family, one for all and all for one. The West could be won, and the West would be one.

CHAPTER 8

THE BEGINNING AND THE END

*D*ays of our Lives debuted on Monday, November 8, 1965, with the melodious opening lines made famous by lead actor MacDonald Carey: "Like sands through the hourglass, so are the days of our lives."

What a metaphor for a timepiece with thousands of moving parts. Originally the opening lines went on and on after this famous couplet for most of the thirty-second opening sequence. But Betty Corday, being her usual, intuitive self, pointed out that it was too verbose and self-absorbed and suggested that Mac instead introduce the show with only that couplet and then say, "This is MacDonald Carey, and these are the days of our lives."

Ted and Irna Phillips balked at first but then acquiesced, realizing Betty's past knack for naming hit shows. In the previous years the first episode of *The Edge of Night* was to have been "The Edge of Darkness." The first script for *As the World Turns* was originally titled "As the Earth Turns." And the yet unborn *The Young & the Restless* was first thought of by Bill Bell Sr., as "The Young & the Impatient."

All three titles were successfully changed at the last minute by Betty.

She was the woman behind a show produced and programmed mostly by men, not yet realizing her innate talent was far ahead of the curve, especially when it came to titling a new daytime drama. Betty was best at this, but she was soon to become the best in the industry at a far more formidable task.

By the time *Days of our Lives* went on the air in November 1965, it was not only the first soap broadcast in living color, but it was also learning, as do most second born, from the mistakes of its older sibling, *Morning Star.*

Morning Star aired nationally at 11:30 a.m. following *The Doctors* and preceding *Another World*. *Days of our Lives* would be given the noon time slot, following *Morning Star* and preceding *Another World*. While *Morning Star*'s time slot was fine, the 12:00 position in the lineup was then known as the "sweetheart time slot" in all of daytime. Why? Because the show came on the air at lunchtime nationwide.

The eight bells played by the celeste in the opening theme of *Days of our Lives* became the unmistakable theme introducing the show, but more importantly, it became the cue to viewers that it was lunchtime. Time to eat lunch and "watch my show!". And so America's love affair with the show started with these eight bells, heard every day in the opening theme…very subtle, very effective.

By November 1965 *Morning Star* was still not finding an audience after six months on the air. Not a great sign, even in the slow-moving ratings game that is daytime television. The show had no famous "stars," was still in black-and-white, and Ted's idea of morphing *Westwind*, originally an all–African American drama, into one that was homogenized, white, urban, and traditional was just not working.

More tragically, neither was the treatment for Ted's now faster-spreading Hodgkin's disease. In the later part of 1965 and into the first months of 1966, Ted endured eight cobalt radiation treatments on his cancerous lymph glands at UCLA. The treatments in and of themselves were not long, but the exposure to such intense levels of radiation was so high in risk that not only were all technicians moved behind two leaded doors, but Ted's body was wrapped in ice packs before, during, and after these treatments to keep his fever down and his body temperature below 103 degrees. It was very barbaric medicine compared to today's treatment.

Ted was so weakened from the radiation that he would have to rest for a few days after going home from the hospital, and he was never able to keep any food down for the first twenty-four hours. Ted went from 160 pounds in November 1965 to 130 pounds by March 1966. If anyone noticed at the studio, they all had the respect and compassion to never mention it to him or to each other.

Then the ax fell. *Morning Star* was abruptly and unceremoniously canceled in March 1966 after only one year. The elder child had not made it.

Then, as always, NBC held all the cards, and *Days of our Lives*, only five months old, appeared to be next on the chopping block, but my mother was extremely brave and supportive of my father. How does one save a show and a husband when both seem to be, above all odds, terminal? Had Betty and Ted toiled all of those years, uprooted their family, and traveled so many miles for naught? How do you hold it together and carry on when you're faced with the sudden possibility of losing much of what you hold dear and you have no control whatsoever over its fate? This was Betty's challenge.

∾

While the challenge was great, *Days of our Lives* had a distinct advantage over *Morning Star*—it had one of the best casts on the air. MacDonald Carey played Dr. Tom Horton; Frances Reid played his wife, matriarch Alice Horton; and they were surrounded by extremely talented actors who played their grown children and grandchildren.

John Clarke played eldest brother, Mickey; Ed Mallory played younger brother, Bill; Pat Barry played eldest sister, Addie; Charla Doherty, who originally played Addie's "bad girl" daughter, Julie Olson; and Marie Cheatham played Addie's younger sister, Marie.

John Lupton appeared on the show a few months after the first episode as Addie's twin brother, Tommy, and Denise Alexander played Susan Martin, wife of David Martin and foil to the jealous and impetuous Julie. Later that year, Susan Flannery was cast as Dr. Laura Spencer, the woman who came between Mickey and Bill.

The stories were simple, direct, and easily identifiable…and they had a '60s modernism unlike the other soaps. Julie was arrested for shoplifting in the first show, and Mickey fell in love with Laura Spencer without realizing his brother, Bill, held the most special place in her heart.

Addie's twin brother, Tommy, returned from the Korean War scarred beyond recognition and with such a bad case of amnesia that he fell in love with his sister, Marie Horton. Susan Martin was accused of doing all kinds of heinous acts by the very jealous Julie.

After all, *Days of our Lives* had the best writer in all of Soapdom, Irna Phillips, who was establishing her signature on another unique and fresh daytime drama. Wes Kenney was not just a fine director and producer, but he had that special ability, as did Ted, of getting the very best performances out of this cast—as only someone who understands the fine subtleties of acting and finding the subtext beneath the written word can. In other words, *Days of our Lives* was born under a good sign and was dealt some really good cards in its opening hands.

Then an unexpected card was dealt. In June 1966, only weeks before my sixteenth birthday, my father asked my mother to come into their bedroom, where he was resting after having one of his many weekly blood transfusions. His blood, type A negative, was kept in a few quart jars in our family refrigerator and served as a constant reminder of how terminal his illness had become.

Betty entered their bedroom and looked at Ted, the only man she had ever loved, and knew that his time was drawing near. But she refused to accept it or lay blame. There was always hope for a miracle. Her Roman Catholic upbringing had ingrained this into her beliefs, and damned if she was ever going to quit on the good Lord's everlasting gift of grace and miracles.

Ted asked Betty to grab a pad of paper and sit down. He then looked at her through the most hollow, yet loving eyes she had ever seen and said to her, "Would you mind taking a letter, Miss Shay?" (That was a reminder of her secretarial days when he had met her and they had fallen deeply in love.) She, of course, said yes, grabbed paper and pen, and waited.

What transpired next remains for reasons of propriety a bit clouded and unclear. But my mother later told me the gist of it went like this: He asked her to understand that he was not going to be there for her in a very short time and that he would eternally miss her, yet he believed they would be together someday in the far-distant future in heaven. He then asked her to understand that besides her role as a wife and mother of two sons, he was giving her the responsibility of caring for the only legacy he had left besides their children. He asked her to take over where he would leave off and save the only show of his that still lived and endured. He asked her to be the guardian and executive producer of *Days of our Lives*.

She, of course, balked at first and asked him how she could accomplish such a formidable task. He reminded her of all her days in radio and advertising at Benton and Bowles in New York and how she had been the producer for early radio soaps like *Young Doctor Malone* and *Pepper Young's Family*. That experience, plus her innate sense of what the difference was between drama and meaningless dialogue, would be enough to get her through. So of course she said, "Yes, Ted. Anything for you, my darling."

∾

Ted stopped going to work at NBC after July 4, 1966, choosing to work from home and use Betty and Irna as conduits to the cast, crew, and network. My brother and mother and I, as well as my Uncle Eliot and Aunt Marian, and their lovely daughter, my oldest cousin, Joann, hovered near our home all that summer. Knowing there was really nothing we could do other than be there for him, we quietly held vigil downstairs. He now was too weak to leave his bedroom, so we would visit him in groups or one at a time.

His illness was never mentioned. He was never asked how he felt. He never sought an ounce of pity. He was a rock in the face of the onslaught of his crushing disease. He was, beneath it all, accepting and not sullen about his fate. He did not want to be a burden. He did not want Betty and his two sons to remember him like this.

So after he dictated his final letter to my mother, Miss Shay, that was it, period. No denial or martyrdom. Just strength and bravery, and an unflagging desire to keep on working on *Days of our Lives*, reading every script and watching every day, and calling Irna every afternoon...as if all were normal and he believed the footsteps of fate he heard behind him weren't worth an iota of attention. But still he knew.

On the morning of July 17, a Monday, Ted's health had deteriorated to such an extent that he had to be hospitalized. Uncle Eliot came over early that morning with two ambulance attendants. Because my father was now so weak, and a stretcher couldn't make it up the two short flights of stairs, the three of them carried him in a bedsheet from his room, through the house, and downstairs to the waiting ambulance. This was the last image we had of him at home, being taken from our lives—on a sheet.

Two days later he went into a coma at Cedars of Lebanon Hospital in downtown Los Angeles. There he hovered between life and death, unable to speak, hear, or respond to anyone at his bedside. Yet late in the night he would occasionally speak placidly and clearly to his departed mother, father, and sisters as if they were there in the room with him. The nurses were never shocked by this and chose to tell my mother only after this had gone on for three days. His family was calling for him, and he was telling them he was on his way.

Ted Corday died on July 23, 1966, at noon. Shortly beforehand, my mother, my brother, and I were brought in to say our final good-byes. My Uncle Eliot was the cardiologist in attendance, and it was the only time my mother and brother and I saw him break down and sob, standing in the corner of the room after Ted was pronounced dead.

Ted Corday was buried two days later, on Monday, July 25, at the Los Angeles National Cemetery. He was buried without a funeral and with only his immediate family and a military color guard in attendance. He loved flowers so much—he had never cut them in our garden—and thus the request for no flowers was also observed. Only the United States flag, ceremoniously folded and given by the guard to Betty, was left. Then the seven national guardsmen fired three rounds, and Ted Corday, Captain, United States Army Signal Corps, 1908–1966, was laid to rest.

No one cried at the graveside. That wouldn't come for some of us until many years later. There was just the silence, the silence of grief overcome by reverence for a great man. Only my mother, my brother, and I, and our immediate Corday family, were there to say good-bye. There was no epitaph on his headstone. All it said in its traditional military way was:

Theodore Corday
Captain U.S. Army
May 8, 1908   July 23, 1966

Our Ted, our beloved husband, father, and brother, Teddy, was gone.

∞

Ted Corday's favorite song was "The Impossible Dream" from the Broadway musical *Man of La Mancha*. Its words said it all about his goal in life, which in the years following his death would prove greatly ironic. But his favorite tune, the one he always whistled or hummed, was "Strange Meadow Lark," written in 1960 by Dave Brubeck. It is the song just before "Take Five" on the Dave Brubeck's Quartet's first hit album, *Time Out*. It is a beautiful, lilting instrumental, with shades of great pianistic classicism coupled with a soft, swinging saxophone groove. Yet it is, above all else, poignant.

It sets two themes, one poignant and plaintive and the other happy and bright, next to one another as if to question why the meadowlark's song is so profoundly beautiful and yet strange. To this day it remains profound, yet instantly catchy and worthy of a thousand listens. It is as if in one long piece of music, Ted heard his innermost song. The song of the meadowlark. The refrains of "Strange Meadow Lark" were silently heard by all of us, his family, then and for all time. He never saw the first anniversary of *Days of our Lives*.

The loss that never goes away. Such was the man. A hero to his family and a pioneer to his industry...the serious dramatist, the devoted husband and father.

However, there is always a side of anyone's personality that escapes the headlines and stays hidden, a secret from all but his closest friends. He was known as being serious, but Ted had a subtle sense of ironic wit and social humor that few really knew except for his wife and kids and sister and brother. He was an intellectual joker! He loved life and laughter, seen through his serious-looking brown eyes...and he saw a lot of both in his short fifty-eight years.

∞

After that horrible July weekend, *Days of our Lives* never missed a beat. Even if the shock at Ted's passing was on everyone's mind at the set, no one stopped believing in the show. More so, in his memory, the cast and crew strived more to take a sad song and make it better.

Betty had little time to grieve. The show was now without an executive producer. NBC called her in for a meeting to discuss its future. They were very shocked yet saddened by the news of her husband's death, but more than anything they were concerned about the future of the show. Who would run it? Who would be the conduit from Irna, writing in Chicago, to NBC and production in Burbank? Betty said she would.

The network said they were very respectful of her husband's wishes, but they were not the executors of his last will and testament. They were, and would always be, the potential executioners of *Days of our Lives*. A harsh reality of the show's life.

They kindly asked Betty what made her feel she was qualified to do the job. She had never produced a television soap opera, and even though she had been at Ted and Irna's side all the way from the beginnings of *Days of our Lives* in 1964, she had no other qualifications. And she was a woman—a newly widowed one with two teenage sons and a highly mortgaged house to run. How could she even think of taking on a job like this? It was just too big a risk.

Her answer was, in the typical succinct fashion that exemplifies class, very truthful and direct. She explained to the higher powers at NBC that running this show—keeping it on budget and growing more productive—was not much different from running a successful household, which she had done for the past twenty-five years. She stated matter-of-factly that if she was given one hundred dollars a week to run her household and could save ten dollars a week every week for three months, then she would have saved enough to either splurge on a "big party," buy a new refrigerator, or save it all to buy Christmas presents at the end of the year. Quote…unquote.

They were, of course, shocked at what they thought was her naiveté, or just the stubbornness of a mother. But in the end, Larry White, head of NBC daytime programming, capitulated and agreed…on one condition. They would put Betty under contract for a three-month trial period, followed by another optional three-month trial period, and then make a final decision. It seemed to be a diplomatic way to keep Irna's interest in *Days of our Lives* and, at the same time, gave them three months to look for a really experienced executive producer to run the show. Having little faith that she would succeed, they passed Betty a baton with rubber bands attached.

Many, many years later, in the late 1970s, when *Days of our Lives* had survived to grow into a national success under Betty's wise and mothering hand, Wes Kenney's production wisdom, and Bill Bell's brilliant pen, Betty bumped into Larry White in an elevator at NBC. The elevator was filled with executives and programmers, who gushed to her about the success of *Days of our Lives* in NBC's daytime lineup. She looked at him, smiled, and asked him if she was still on thirteen-week options.

Such was her wit and disarming charm, such was the guiding hand and wise mother who would raise an infant show into a full-grown show-business legacy. But the road she faced would be filled with not only unimaginable success, but unbelievable drama, obstacles, and odds in pursuit of her husband's dream.

CHAPTER 9

HE SPEAKS IN RIDDLES, METAPHORS, AND CLICHÉS

One month later, life for us had started to settle down and get back to normal—if there's anything normal about life after losing a husband at the age of fifty-four, after twenty-two years of marriage, and a father to two teenage sons. So Betty decided to take ten days off, at the network's suggestion, and get out of Los Angeles for the first time since moving from New York City two years before.

She took us to Hawaii, a place our father had always dreamed of vacationing. She slept and read and rested and tried to forget the pain, while we swam and fished and lived near the beach, much as we had every summer of our lives in Southampton.

Upon returning home on Labor Day, Chris went off to the University of Arizona, and I went back to Beverly Hills High as a junior. Chris was trying to do the right thing by our father in getting a college education. Our mother was putting all of herself into *Days of our Lives*, to nurture the fledgling show.

My voice had changed in the months following my father's death, and at sixteen I seemed to have gone from being a gawky five-foot sophomore to a five-foot-nine junior in little more than a year. At Christmas, calls came from long-unseen friends from the East, most of whom had heard of my father's untimely passing but had not made direct contact with Betty since July. When I answered the phone to those long-unheard-from friends, there was always a shocked silence following my "Hello?" The next thing I heard was the disbelieving tone in their voices as they would whisper…"Ted?"

"No, Ken…"

"Oh, you sounded exactly like your father, sorry," they apologized.

"That's okay…let me get my mom."

Then one night just before Christmas and my brother's return from the University of Arizona, I came home late and was walking up the driveway to our house wearing a new pair of Bass Weejuns penny loafers that click-clacked as I strolled to the front door. I knocked quietly a few times. I didn't want to ring the bell and wake my mother if she was sleeping. There was always the hide-a-key on the back porch, but at this hour, she might still be up. She was.

The door immediately opened, and my mother stood silhouetted by the inside light. Still I could see all of her color was gone and she was shocked, if not a bit frightened.

"Oh, my God…I thought it was your father…your footsteps…they sounded so much like his…I'm sorry…"

But I was not sorry. For it seemed I had changed so much since July, and now I began to realize my role in the family was also beginning to change. Instead of being the younger, quieter son, I had become my mother's closest friend, ally, and sounding board at dinner. Every night, she would share with me all the challenges of her new life as a widowed executive producer in a man's business. My predicament of being a fatherless junior in high school, and her widowhood, never came up. It was about getting on with life. I was becoming more of a friend and partner to my mother and less of a son.

Then once again my brother found himself in trouble. He was

flunking out, this time from the University of Arizona in his first semester. Not wanting to cause our mother any concern, he would instead call me every week and ask for help, money usually, or maybe just to have someone to dump his problems on.

I had gone from being a younger brother to being more of a father to my older brother. I had gone from being a son to being a partner for my mother. In the course of less than two years, my life went from the fairy-tale life of a happy kid in New York to the newly found harsh reality of being a young man in Los Angeles.

I started speaking in clichés and metaphors and didn't know why. I started using the same language that my father had used and started giving my friends fatherly advice...none of which I understood.

One night, I spent more than three hours in our front yard talking one of my best friends down from a bad acid trip, yet I had no idea where this newfound knowledge of things I had never understood before was coming from. I had all the right psychological things to say to keep my friend from totally wigging out, yet I didn't know why. I had never taken LSD and really had no idea of the hallucinatory state of my very mixed-up friend.

But at the end of the night, my friend was back down to earth and able to drive himself the few blocks home to his now worried parents. Before he left, he asked, "How did you get to be so smart? Where did you learn to cope with my kind of drugged-out craziness? How did you know all the answers?"

I explained to my loopy friend that I was not as smart as he thought, but growing up with a difficult older brother had proven to be an invaluable lesson in dealing with insanity of sorts. I also knew that I was not quite telling the truth, because I had never given my older brother any really important advice. More so, I honestly had been the fortunate recipient of living with a bad example and learning how to improve by doing the opposite of all of my older brother's bad behavior.

❦

As profound as my life experiences had become, my performance in the last two years of high school was deteriorating. Not from a lack of intelligence, but mostly from lost incentive and the resulting complacency that comes with the loss of a father who was as much a mentor and teacher to me as a loving parent.

So I played my drums for hours every day after school and eventually joined a newly formed rock band at Beverly Hills High School. We were called Our Gang, and the band included four other juniors who, like me, were just starting to become hip to the new L.A. rock scene in 1966. We played the big, popular high school dances, primarily because there was no other competition in the school in insular, yet privileged Beverly Hills. We also had the cutest boy in the junior class as our piano-playing lead singer. And all the girls loved us…especially him.

Through these difficult later teenage years, I, the drummer, just hung out with the band and skated through my last two years of high school with a C average. I only applied to college because of the Vietnam War, which was raging by June 1968. By enrolling in any college, I had the possibility of staying out of the draft with a student deferment. By 1968 not many at Beverly Hills High School really wanted to go into the army through draft induction, and those, like me, who didn't have the affluence to move abroad, had to try for college acceptance and what was known as a 2-S deferment.

Of course, there were a few who couldn't wait to enlist and go to Vietnam. They were patriots, too. Sadly, our country was torn in half in 1968. Such a difference from my father's view of military obligation twenty-five years before! Ted Corday never flinched in his devotion to his country and the overall global and moral cause of World War II. But neither of his sons or our mother wanted anything to do with a "conflict" that was ten thousand miles away and wasn't even declared a "war." *Days of our Lives* had dealt with the story of Tommy Horton's return from the Vietnam War, but to avoid controversy, NBC insisted the writers say he was returning from the Korean War! Absurd times.

I finished Beverly High in June 1968, graduating on a brutally hot day, two days before my eighteenth birthday. The only people from my family that attended were my mother, my Aunt Marian, and my first cousin, Joann. My brother was in Arizona, and my other first cousin, Steve, was at Stanford finishing his sophomore year. My Uncle Eliot was extremely busy traveling the world for the State Department.

A month after graduation, my mother decided to reward me with our first trip to Europe. We went to London, Paris, Rome, Copenhagen, and Lucerne, Switzerland, on a two-week tour. Then it was home to wait until August for late acceptance to any university in California to which I had applied previously.

Thankfully, by late August 1968 I was accepted to California Western University, a private college in San Diego. Cal Western was more like a prestigious junior college that also fed the bigger state universities in California after a two-year program.

Meanwhile, *Days of our Lives* was thriving. William J. Bell had taken over for Irna Phillips and brought a new edginess and cultural identity to *Days of our Lives* as its new head writer. He brought in the character of Doug Williams, played by Bill Hayes. Hayes was a flimflam man, a con artist who shared a jail cell with Dr. Bill Horton and found all the knowledge he needed to scam Salem and, most of all, Bill's beautiful sister Addie Horton. Bill Bell created and wrote the triangle of Bill and Mickey Horton and their beloved Dr. Laura Spencer and brought it to fruition through the birth of Mike Horton Jr. Mike was believed by all to be the son of the not-so-happily-married Mickey and Laura but was actually conceived in the backseat of Bill Horton's convertible the night before Mickey's wedding to Laura. Plus, Mickey didn't know he was sterile. Only his father, Dr. Tom Horton, and Laura knew the truth.

The network programmer at NBC insisted the true identity of Mike's father be revealed to all within a few months. Bill Bell said he would reveal it when the time was right for both the story and the characters. The irony is that the "reveal" didn't come until eight years later in 1976, when Mike, then a teenager in soap opera time, had an accident and needed a blood transfusion. At that time, Mike found that his uncle, Dr. Bill Horton, was the only suitable match.

The magic of soap opera is knowing how to play a story out to its most magnificent, dramatic effect. Perhaps not in three months, but in ten years. That was the genius of Bill Bell, who had been trained by Irna Phillips. He was a gifted and wonderfully talented storyteller. My mother often said that had it not been for Bill Bell's writing, *Days of our Lives* might never have reached its fourth anniversary.

Days of our Lives had become a hit by its fourth anniversary…it was on a roll. And for me, it was out the door to college. To see the world, if San Diego could be considered worldly.

CHAPTER 10
COMING OF AGE

Sometimes, according to Greek mythology, the gods love to play out their idea of "drama" on the young, innocent, and unsuspecting. Whatever glee they find from such folly absolutely eludes these unsuspecting targets. Especially young adults between the ages of eighteen and twenty-one. I can only imagine their glee as they steered my course from ivy halls to island huts to farms during these years.

∞

The Quonset Hut lay hidden low in the nearby sand dunes off the white, shiny beach at Chun's Reef, on Oahu's North Shore. The structure was a leftover relic of the Second World War, built for the enlistees and volunteers who were barracked there in the early 1940s. Many, if not all, were the nights that a surveillance vigil proved inconsequential for these men, the inhabitants of this most distant outpost, over forty miles from Honolulu, on the complete other side of the island. The North Shore was dark and quiet at night, save for the blessing of a full moon. So the islanders would "talk story" with one another.

Even though there were only a few houses within miles of each other, this ancient island was not a lonely place. Oahu and the other four Hawaiian Islands are the most beautiful of the world's tropical island chains, and so are its people. "The jewel of the Pacific," the ultimate and even superior counterpart to Hawaii's sister island that vanished ten thousand years before and was the jewel of the Atlantic, "Atlantis." It was to this idyllic piece of island life that my next journey, an adventure in paradise, would propel me.

∾

My first year of college was my first year away from home and my first year of learning to be self-sufficient. I took lots of different courses and wondered what I was going to do in life, like most freshmen do. I stumbled through my sophomore year in 1970, more to avoid the draft than to learn, or more importantly, to choose a major for my college degree. At that age very few know what their path in life will be, so I grazed on the academic grasses. And I preoccupied myself with playing in a newly formed rock band.

Lucky Mud was a rock 'n' roll band formed by a senior at Cal Western and his wife, both from Northern California, and we sounded much like those bands from San Francisco who started the rock 'n' roll revolution on the West Coast. The "Haight Ashbury" had spawned famed artists like Santana, the Jefferson Airplane, Credence Clearwater Revival, and Janis Joplin's Big Brother and the Holding Company. Although we wrote all original songs, Lucky Mud sounded very much like those well-known bands of the Fillmore and Avalon ballrooms.

In many parts of the country at this time, the hippie movement was becoming troubled, especially with the infamous Rolling Stones concert at Altamont that summer. The dream was turning into a nightmare. But in San Diego things were different, more serene. Except for student protests, peace marches, and a few sit-ins to speak out against the war in Vietnam, nothing seemed of much importance in this quiet California city except the U.S. Naval Base, which was the most important one in the Eastern Pacific, thirty miles from Tijuana and the Mexican border.

Our band gained local celebrity playing clubs and campuses from Point Loma to Mission Bay and La Jolla. In 1970 San Diego was a great place to live and go to college. Then the draft laws were changed, and as of January 1970, induction into the army became based on 365 birthdate-related lottery numbers for all men between the ages of eighteen and twenty-nine. No more student or marital deferments. If your number was under 100, the chances were very good that you would be inducted and sent to war in Vietnam within a year, unless you were physically unfit for military service.

Many of my friends and roommates had birthdates that coincided with a low lottery number, and if they didn't want to go to war, they had to think of ridiculous ways to dodge the draft or choose the alternative, fleeing to Canada. Passing your physical was a given unless you were an invalid. Even the mentally ill were passed into the ranks to fill the need for five hundred thousand new recruits.

Lucky Mud played on into the spring of 1970, but everyone was marching to a different drummer. Our guitarist, Angelo Rossi, had number 27 in the lottery and knew he was a goner. Being a major naval town, San Diego had serious marine recruiting on campus and a draft board that didn't care who you were or what was wrong or what your parents had. If you could walk, hear, talk, and eat, you were fit and good to go.

Fortunately for Angelo, but unfortunately for my mother and me, my brother, Chris, had flunked out of college in Arizona by 1968 and fled to a hippie commune known as the Banana Patch in Hana, Maui. He had disappeared from civilization and our family and, within a year, looked the part of a veg-fed, long-haired, stoned-out, island beach bum. But he said he was happy living in the jungle. He had also learned the ropes of hiding out from the draft, and even more so, how to elude it if placed in the induction line.

Chris left the Banana Patch for a week's visit to San Diego that spring of 1970 and came to see me and hear Lucky Mud at Cal Western University. We all thought he was so cool, with his long Frank Zappa hair and black felt Borsalino hat. He wore only torn blue jeans and a T-shirt, no matter what the weather or the occasion was.

One day Chris told Angelo that instead of facing draft induction in San Diego, he should move with Chris back to Hawaii, change his place of residence and, more importantly, the location of his draft board. Why this would help keep Angelo out of harm's way was still a mystery to the rest of us in the band, but Chris was a very persuasive twenty-two-year-old. So within a week Angelo dropped out of college and moved to Hawaii under my brother's wing.

We were left with no lead guitarist and the nagging question of what was behind it all. There would be no replacement for Angelo, but the answer to our question would come soon enough and would bring us all to Hawaii and the Quonset Hut on Rocky Point for the summer of 1970.

❧

I'm the one that's gonna have to die
when it's time for me to die,
so let me live my life the way I want to.
Sing on, brother.
Play on, drummer.

None of us knew in March 1970 how poignant those lyrics from "If 6 Was 9" by Jimi Hendrix were, not just for the '60s revolution and anti-establishment movement, but for our band. They foreshadowed what was to transpire in the next six months.

On April 1 we heard that Angelo had visited the Honolulu draft board for his preinduction physical. He had been extremely well coached by my brother in becoming an artful draft dodger.

You see, the territory of Hawaii became the last of the fifty United States when it was granted statehood in 1958, and its people were proud of their new status. Many Hawaiians were of Japanese, Chinese, or Filipino descent. They had worked side by side with the native Hawaiian population over the previous hundred years, as a result of the advance in ocean transportation and the need in the islands for cheap labor for the cane fields and pineapple and coffee plantations. Now, some generations later, these Asian Americans had indeed become a large part of the population of Hawaii.

Whether from Japan, China, the Philippines, or the South Pacific islands of Samoa, Tonga, or Fiji, they were now Hawaiians, *kama'aina*, or locals. With that came all the pride and privilege that goes with rising from the depths of almost slave-class poverty to being venerable sons and daughters, landowners, and deserving of the same respect as descendants of the nearly gone, native Hawaiian people.

By 1970, twelve years after the islands were granted statehood, Hawaiians were among the proudest Americans and more than ready to serve their country in the Vietnam War. It was not only a duty, but an honor and privilege for a young Hawaiian man to enlist in the army or marines, whereas fewer than thirty years before, it had been impossible for any Asian American to serve in the U.S. Military in the Pacific during the Second World War. The few who did enlist at that time were only allowed to fight in Europe. The Hawaiian people, being from many Asian-Pacific backgrounds, had faced a very grim time in the years following the Japanese attack on Pearl Harbor. Thus, Vietnam became more than a faraway war. It became an opportunity for Hawaiians to prove how proud they were of their American patriotism and how ready they were to fight any foe.

Angelo appeared at his physical dressed in tight white jeans that had been dyed pink by my brother, a matching violet shirt, and a pink chiffon scarf. His long hair was coiffed in the most flamboyant of styles, and he looked every bit the part of a homosexual Californian rather than a proud native son of Hawaii.

When the induction sergeant asked him if he had any reason to not want to serve his country, he softly and coyly lisped that he was a homosexual, and although he would not mind taking a shower with all the other recruits, he could never take a shot at another man with a gun. He would not kill even a fly, let alone one of the North Vietnamese. And he was also a strict vegetarian. The sergeant, without blinking, immediately grabbed the stamp from the farthest right ink pad and imprinted "4-F" on Angelo's draft papers! "Physical impairment and disability." Never to be drafted into the U.S. Army.

But what was Angelo to do now that he had moved to Oahu, dropped out of college, and had no more cool band with which to rock? Simple. He just called the rest of us in Lucky Mud and told us all to follow him to paradise, where we didn't need school, could live cheap, and could get a lot more work doing big concerts.

∞

Days of our Lives, in the meantime, had reached its fifth birthday. It had gone from being a toddling new soap opera to a completely original, groundbreaking force that was overtaking its competition and making a name for itself as the new daytime hit of the early '70s.

It was Doug-and-Julie time. It was Bill Bell hitting his full stride as both a risk taker and a traditional storyteller in the purest of episodic, day-to-day, "must-see" television, long before NBC even knew what that meant. Every Friday's show was a cliff-hanger.

For the first time since my father's death, my mother was starting to feel not only at peace, but also proud of accomplishing the task he had so boldly set out to do and had given to her before dying. The future was beginning to look bright, and the glass was more than half full…it was soon to be overflowing. *Days of our Lives* had graduated with honors.

But what was becoming of her now grown boys? Where were they, and what were they going to do with their lives? Like most parents then, she feared for our safety if we were sent to war. She feared for us more than she did for herself or her country…and rightfully so. We had become college dropouts living more than two thousand miles from home. While my mother was starting to earn really decent money for the first time in her life, we, her sons, were trying to learn how to live "without," as new rock 'n' roll, hippie pilgrims in the Hawaiian Islands.

∽

The band members of Lucky Mud all dropped out of Cal Western and moved, without any foresight, to join Angelo and my brother in Honolulu in June 1970. One week later, all ten of us, including two wives and a soundman, were living on the streets of Waikiki Beach, Honolulu. We stored our band equipment in an old garage in a back alley off Ali'i Boulevard. We spent what little money we had living in cheap motels near Waikiki Beach.

However, Angelo and my brother had met a bigger-than-life hippie guru who lived on the North Shore, some thirty miles from the city. Krishna Sai Baba, originally Chris Butler, had a following of twenty or thirty devotees who lived with him in the aforementioned Quonset Hut at Chun's Reef. He graciously said we could all move there until we got work, but only if we joined in with his communal lifestyle and were willing to sleep on the floor with twenty other young hippies and runaways, many from out of state or out of the country. And we had to become vegetarians, practice Hinduism, and chant the Hare Krishna mantra day and night.

This temporary refuge lasted only a month until we rented two cheap, run-down surf shacks next to each other at Rocky Point, three miles north of the Quonset Hut. But the lessons we learned in the weeks we lived in the "Hut" were life-changing.

We lived on rice, beans, yogurt, fruit, and vegetables, most of which we could grow or find on trees in our garden on the North Shore. Twenty people, plus our ten, all had to share one bathroom, and there was no smoking (of anything) or drinking. It was roughing it in paradise for pennies a day.

The indelible experience of living with Sai's devotees for a month in the Quonset Hut influenced my thinking for the rest of my life. I realized there was much more to God than what my basic Judeo-Christian upbringing had taught me. I was turned on and intrigued by the tales of Krishna's acts of service and meditation, and also by living under one roof with so many people focused on the same acts of kindness.

Learning the Maha Mantra and Sai's teachings of Krishna's life made us all more loving and kind, because our lives were so simple and without any material encumbrances. It was as if Henry David Thoreau's Walden Pond existed on a higher spiritual plane there at the Quonset Hut in Hawaii and its surrounding tropical acreage. It was also the only time someone actually saved my life.

It happened in the most ordinary of circumstances, when the "gods" were having a go at one of their unsuspecting earthly victims... namely me.

I had been working all morning in the vegetable garden behind the Quonset Hut. I was joined by a young Japanese-Hawaiian man named Alan. He couldn't have been eighteen yet, but he had been blessed with a real Hawaiian green thumb. On those mornings I was assigned garden duty, he taught me how to plant chard and spinach, how to build a squash mound, how to train tomatoes, and much more.

This morning was typically hot for June. I had turned twenty the week before, and that birthday had passed without any special recognition, let alone cake. The devotees living in the Hut only cared about Krishna's birthday or Sai's, which we knew was coming in late July.

By eleven that morning, I was hot, pouring sweat, and working in the sun without a hat as Alan quietly went about doing all of his tasks without even a word or complaint. He was blissfully happy to be tending Krishna's garden for all the hungry devotees and Sai. I asked Alan if it would be okay for me to take a quick swim in the nearby ocean to cool off. He nodded, and I took off through the jungle for the blue Pacific, one hundred yards away. Strangely enough, this was the first time I had gone swimming since arriving in Hawaii a few weeks before. Not being much of an open-water swimmer, I was a virgin in tropical waters.

I jumped in, paying no attention to the surfers offshore. I just lay floating on my back and cooling off for the next twenty minutes. I was almost falling asleep as I floated in this beautiful, deep blue, 82-degree water. After I decided to tread water instead of floating on my back, I realized that in the previous twenty minutes I had been carried out to sea by a very fast rip current.

I also had not realized the size and power of the surf on Oahu's North Shore. The waves were breaking at ten to twelve feet in the shallow waters outside the coral of Chun's Reef, and I was being pulled steadily into their path and harm's way. Not having ever surfed in California and not being an experienced swimmer, especially in the ocean, I kept trying to extricate myself from this predicament by stupidly swimming straight toward the distant beach and, unknowingly, directly against the force of the riptide.

After another ten or fifteen minutes, I realized I was not only getting farther from shore, but I was also being sucked right into the shallow coral reef on which these giant waves were breaking. Even the surfers had stopped riding these waves, because they were getting so big, they were "closing out."

I panicked, which is the worst thing you can do. I was going to be caught up in one of these waves and dashed upon the sharp coral of the shallow reef, and that would be very bloody and bad, to say the least. I knew only sheer terror and started waving my arms for help. But none of the surfers sitting on the sand seemed to see me, or if they did, they didn't care about another "hippie geek."

Time froze. Minutes passed like an eternity. I was exhausted and started to cramp up in my legs. Then I started screaming, "Help!" as my feet felt the rapidly approaching coral reef. The reef was sharp and jagged and only a few feet below the surface. Still no one on the beach moved. They must have seen this act before…to their great local amusement.

Suddenly I saw Alan bolting for the water from the Hut. He had a surfboard under one arm and was in the water within seconds. He reached me just as I was about to get cut up on the reef or drown from the exhaustion of fighting the rip. He put me sideways on his ten-foot-long surfboard and paddled alongside the reef, parallel to shore and out of the rip.

Ten minutes later we were up current and headed for the beach. When my feet touched the sand, I collapsed at the edge of the Pacific and looked at Alan's smiling, yet unemotional countenance. I said without even thinking, "Thanks, man…how did you know?"

He said that he noticed I had taken too long a break, and when he went to find me, he saw all the surfers chuckling as they made light of my quandary out there, over my head in the giant waves off Chun's Reef.

I probably would have died that morning had it not been for Alan. I will always remember him and know that I owe him my life. Most of all, had I not been living with a bunch of loving followers of Sai and Krishna, I might not be here to tell my story. They were all happy to be God's children. I was just happy to be alive.

∞

The two married players, Mike Mitchell and Jan Garfinkle, and their wives were the first to leave the "Hare Krishna Hut" within a few weeks and rent their own little surf shack two miles up the road at Rocky Point. We moved our equipment into their garage, set up, and practiced whenever we could.

A concert promoter who lived on the North Shore heard us one night and booked us as an opening act at the University of Hawaii for the touring Buddy Miles Band. We played a weekend of concerts there on July 4 and July 5. Lucky Mud suddenly got hot. We were reborn in Hawaii that summer and began making money and a good living.

A few days later we played with Buddy Miles again at a party on a huge yacht in Waikiki Bay. There he introduced us to his friend Jimi Hendrix.

On August 1, 1970, we were the opening act for Jimi's last concert appearance, in front of ten thousand very high and happy rock 'n' roll fans at the Honolulu International Center. We played a short forty-five-minute set, and then Hendrix went on and played for two hours.

He was like watching a ball of fire move across the stage, leaving blazing trails and even more blazing images in our minds. No one I had ever seen before, or since—Beatles, Stones, James Brown, Led Zeppelin, the Who—no one had what Jimi Hendrix had. He burned with a white-hot fire. He was like watching a comet move across the sky…a short life, but the most brilliant light in the heavens. He was so great that, being a lefty, he could play a right-handed guitar upside down and sound better than Eric Clapton or Pete Townshend.

On September 18, Jimi Hendrix was found dead of an apparent drug overdose in a London flat. With his death, as well as those of Janis Joplin and Jim Morrison within the same year, the enchantment of rock 'n' roll had lost its luster.

We were scheduled to open for Led Zeppelin on Labor Day, but by this time the wives of our singer and guitarist had developed a horrible case of "island fever" and were ready to go home to California. If they went, their husbands would go, too, so we all packed it in, skipped out on the Led Zeppelin show, and moved back to California.

We didn't go back to San Diego to continue college. We moved instead to the beautiful town of Santa Cruz, on the north end of Monterey Bay, and took up residence on a two-hundred-acre farm, where we paid four hundred dollars a month rent and had to care for the horses and farm animals and upkeep of everything. We set up the band equipment in the vacated old barn and, for a brief time, became part of the new "Bay Area" scene. From that point, and during the next three years, we all faded into obscurity and gradually went our separate ways.

Thank goodness, *Days of our Lives* had survived and thrived through my hippie years as a rock 'n' roll drummer.

"The Farm" lay snuggled against the low-lying hills near the Santa Cruz Mountains…on Old San Jose Road, in Soquel, California. It was an old farm with a nineteenth-century Victorian house…four beautiful upstairs bedrooms and all the accompanying headaches of crappy plumbing and electrical malfunctions. But it became home to us hippie vagabond band guys for the subsequent three years.

They were three very long years spent in the oblivion of working an occasional bar or small rock concert, all for cheap money. We were four very wayward youths. On my twenty-first birthday, on June 16, 1971, I spent the day alone with the farm horses and my dog, Rudy. But the old upright piano in the living room proved to be all the comfort I would need that night. No male or female companionship could compare with the beautiful sounds that emanated from that hundred-year-old instrument. For the second time in my life, I remembered without a doubt that my fingers, hands, and mind were nothing more than a conduit for some amazingly wonderful ethereal force that evidenced itself in the music that seemed to come effortlessly through me. That was the best twenty-first-birthday present I could have ever hoped for…to know that the "gods" were laughing with me, not at me.

∞

The period from 1970 to 1973 may have been a slow time in my life, but *Days of our Lives* had become more and more popular each passing year. Again, it was still the era of the Mickey, Bill, and Laura story…a long-term story in which Laura had Bill's baby, which had been conceived when a drunken Bill forced himself on her. It wasn't until years later that their secret came out, when Mickey and Laura's "son," Mike, needed a blood transfusion and his "Uncle Bill" was the only possible match. This famous, slowly told and beautifully constructed story line was just one of the early signs of Bill Bell's unlimited talent as a head writer.

At first NBC wanted to either kill the story or have Bill Bell bring it to an end within three months of Laura's violation. But as I have previously stressed, Bill, in his own inimitable way, told NBC he knew what was best and would bring the story to a fitting conclusion when it was the right time. And my mother backed him up on this. An executive producer and head writer working in synchronized precision is the best recipe for production success.

The right time came years later and was such a smashing climactic "reveal" that *Days of our Lives* achieved huge ratings during those weeks when it garnered a 30-plus share of the entire daytime audience. This rarified air, unheard of in those days for NBC daytime, still stands as a zenith in the show's long ratings history.

This has to be qualified, however, by the fact that there were only three options for quality viewing in television then—NBC, CBS, or ABC—so getting more than tens of millions of viewers to tune in seemed not only possible but realistic. Betty Corday and Bill Bell, and the three wonderful actors—Ed Mallory, John Clarke, and Susan Flannery—all worked in perfect synergy to create this incredible achievement.

This story also included Mickey Horton's slow fall into despairing insanity over Laura's betrayal and then his subsequent attempted murder of his brother, Bill. My mother was dealing with my brother's instability at that time and knew a thing or two about depression, both Chris's and her own. She drew from her pain and his disillusionment to help Bill Bell bring reality to writing the story of a lost soul, Mickey Horton.

Earlier Mickey had run away from the law, developed amnesia—something new to daytime—and had become Marty Hanson. He met and fell in love with Maggie Simmons, played to this day by the beautiful Suzanne Rogers, still not knowing who he was.

Later he was institutionalized. Then it became a story of mental illness (never a good way to make the audience feel warm and fuzzy). But more importantly, it was a launching pad for one of the show's most important new characters, introduced as Mickey's psychiatrist—none other than the enchantingly fresh and brilliant Dr. Marlena Evans, played by Deidre Hall.

It was also a time when the show took a stab at interracial romance with the alluring relationship between Julie's son, David Banning, and his first love, Dr. Valerie Grant. The story went as far as a kiss as a Friday cliff-hanger before the switchboard at NBC lit up like a burning cross with dissatisfied and hateful calls from many viewers. So NBC panicked and *demanded*, not *asked*, that my mother and the writers pull the story immediately off the air and rewrite the ten scripts, already written, that called for much more than a kiss between these two interracial lovers. And this time there was no negotiating. NBC got its way; the story simply "went away," and *Days of our Lives* faced its first real political and racial setback.

❧

Meanwhile, back at the Farm, three years passed with little event, except for the night we were robbed at gunpoint by three linemen who worked for the Pacific Gas and Electric Company. They wanted to harvest the pot plants that had been "mysteriously" growing on the back forty of the farm, and no one was going to get in the way. They were all very high on speed.

One of them sat us all down together on the couch, and while he held us at gunpoint, his two buddies went to the back pasture, pulled up fifty or so plants, then loaded them into their station wagon. When they came back inside, they all discussed what to do with the four of us.

This was after the multiple murders by Charles Manson, and Santa Cruz had become the capital of mass murders in the '70s. There had been three grisly incidents nearby in the past two years. We thought for a moment that we might become part of another such grisly scene, but the thieves decided to lock us all up in the barn. Then they noticed it was filled with our band equipment. After threatening that they might return to steal our drums and amps unless we stayed quiet and didn't report them to the police, they left. We opened the barn window and crawled out as fast as we could. They were long gone. We were all scared to death!

We called our friend and father figure, Jack Farmer, who worked for IBM in San Jose, and he arrived later that night with a truckload of chain-link fence, outdoor floodlights, and an arsenal of shotguns, along with his German shepherd. We didn't see those uninvited county workers until a year later.

I was walking down the main street, Pacific Avenue, in Santa Cruz when I passed the same guy who had held us at gunpoint. He looked at me, I looked at him, and both of us recognized and knew what the other was thinking. And we just walked on. He was high as a kite again and just as aerodynamically volatile. I don't think that he wanted to revisit his craziness, and I didn't want to remember it.

After three years, we lost the rental on the Farm when the owners sold it. We kept trying to make do on nothing. I rented a one-bedroom studio apartment that had been the office for a motel long since gone. It sat fifty feet from the railroad tracks of the Southern Pacific in Capitola. That big old freight train, sometimes fifty cars long, would rumble by every morning and every evening and shake my shack with resounding regularity. Within a year, I would grow to love that sound. It would signify "good morning" and "good evening."

In the spring of 1973 I came down with a terrible case of influenza. For many days I didn't get out of bed except to make a new pot of soup whenever I heard and felt the Southern Pacific Railroad. I only had Rudy to keep me company, and I learned then, for the first time, why people talk to their dogs: They always listen and are always there with their free love. By Friday, one week after coming down with that "Asian flu," the fever broke. Lucky Mud had a big concert that night at the University of California at Santa Cruz, but I was still feeling way too weak and out of it to play the drums.

Fortunately, my mother was in town as a judge, representing *Days of our Lives* at the Miss California beauty pageant held at the Santa Cruz Civic Auditorium. She called me to see how I was doing and was alarmed to learn how sick I had been, let alone how out of touch I was with her and her life in Los Angeles. She wisely invited me out to dinner that night. She insisted that I needed a good meal before playing the concert.

I agreed and met her and her good friend and traveling companion, the producer of *Days of our Lives*, Jack Herzberg, at the restaurant of the downtown Holiday Inn. I know she was a bit shocked at the way I looked. She hadn't seen me since Christmas. I had lost a lot of weight and looked pale and sickly, even dressed up in my best band duds, a green velvet jacket and a green polka-dot shirt. She ordered me prime rib, baked potatoes, vegetables, soup, and apple pie...the works. I ate it all in a heartbeat. Best meal I'd eaten in months, and I was ready to join the band for the gig.

Later that same night, after Lucky Mud had finished our second set for a wildly ecstatic, jumping dance hall at UCSC, I was packing up my drums and electric piano. I looked offstage at the now empty concert hall and saw my mother standing at the back. I knew then, as I do now, that even though I was twenty-three and trying to be independent and my own man, my mother was not only most special to me but also a very special human being. She had watched the entire dance concert without letting me know she was there. She then came out of the darkened hall and up onto the stage, much as I'm sure she had done so many times when my father was directing on Broadway.

She only needed to smile at me, and I knew that not only was she the best mother anyone could ever dream of, but I was one very lucky son. She said that my drumming was great, and that she had no idea I could play the piano in the band. That comment, coupled with the impression the University of California and its wild student body had made on me that night, forced me to want to be a better son and a better man. It made me want to go back to college and learn how to write and read and really understand music.

I reapplied to UCSC and was accepted as a junior in the fall of 1973. My life, once again, was about to be changed by Providence.

Returning to college in September 1973, I enrolled in the best-kept secret in all of the University of California's campuses. UCSC had a total student body at that time of a mere twenty-five hundred students, housed at four different "colleges" on the thousand-acre campus.

The mid-twenties can be the most important years for choosing a career or a path in life. I became a music major, specializing in jazz and ethnomusicology, the study of world music. I played the drums in one of the university's many jazz combos. The musicology studies, although important, had to take a backseat to taking piano lessons for the first time since Mr. Sogito taught me in New York.

Mozart, Bach, Beethoven, and Chopin are more difficult to learn when one starts late in life, so I built a small repertoire of five short and well-known piano works and then tried to explore some longer and more demanding works. I focused on studying and understanding famous piano compositions that were way beyond my playing capacity but still well within my ken, which is defined by Mr. Webster as "one's total scope of knowledge and understanding."

I completed my studies and received a bachelor of arts degree in music from UCSC in June 1975. And still the academic world called. That summer, I applied to graduate school at San Jose State University, partially because UCSC didn't have a graduate music department then, and SJSU's master in music program was as good as the ones at Stanford or the University of California at Berkeley.

I had started seriously dating and was really enjoying the affection of female companionship for the first time in my life. I had a new serious relationship almost every six months or so, yet I gave no thought to getting married and making the same mistake I had seen so many of my friends make in the late '60s and '70s. In those rebellious, free-love, and open-living times, their early marriages meant early kids, followed by early divorce. So marriage would have to wait…a long time.

During this time, I lived alone in a small log cabin–style home in the woods above La Selva Beach, ten miles south of Santa Cruz. La Selva Beach is a peaceful and quiet little beach community that sits on the bluffs overlooking Monterey Bay, just south of Aptos and halfway between Monterey and Santa Cruz.

My log cabin, as I called it, was two bedrooms with a huge A-framed living room and cost $250 a month to rent. It sat on a few acres filled with Monterey pines, about three hundred feet directly above the beach. The living room was dominated by an extraordinary stone fireplace so open that I could walk inside the hearth and look up at the sky through fifteen feet of Carmel stone chimney. It was the warmest fireplace imaginable. Great for cold, foggy nights, the right company, and a good bottle of Napa Cabernet, which was rapidly becoming famous. I lived alone with my small baby grand and now four dogs, so I had lots of mornings and evenings to study or play the piano.

In hindsight, those four learning years played an important part in my future. I was doing graduate studies, blessed by the good fortune of being the beneficiary of a college savings account started by my parents more than twenty years before, which now paid for my tuition and books. I could relax and really start weighing my priorities in life while completing my master's thesis.

The most important influence on me at the time came from my graduate school mentor. I was extremely fortunate to have Lou Harrison agree to be my mentor and sponsor. He was a famous composer, known worldwide for his introduction of Balinese gamelan music to the modern symphonic repertoire. Large orchestras were playing his works, and Lou's music evoked images of faraway Bali, Sumatra, and Thailand with its polyphonic and pentatonic melodies and rhythms.

Lou was also a very cool cat. He had long white hair and a white Fu Manchu mustache and goatee. He was portly and jolly in an erudite sort of way, and always wore flip-flops...even when we were having "one of the coldest winters one summer in the Monterey Bay area." At those frigid times, he'd just wear socks under his sandals...and still look cool.

Ironically, though, as influential as he was, someone would change my life more profoundly during a semester break visit to L.A. That is when I met the new music director for *Days of our Lives*, Linda Line.

∞

Linda was young, very cute, and very bright. She was also not happy with the old library of *Days* music cues that she had inherited with her new job. She wanted to update the music to create a new, more orchestrated sound—something more like film music.

At the time, the music for *Days of our Lives* was being recorded in Italy. It was budgeted to be recorded only once every two years, which seemed to be enough in those early days of worn-out, reissued soap opera music. But Linda wanted something new…not just piano, organ, or guitar. She wanted strings and woodwinds and even percussion.

She also knew I was a composer, or at least was working at becoming one. I think more as an attempt to impress my mother, she threw me a bone and asked me to write five or ten cues that she and her conductor could take to Milan and record within a few months. In turn, I asked her out to dinner. Good deal.

Sometimes opportunity knocks so hard you can't even get to the door before it comes off its hinges. Linda and I had one date, which turned out to be a lunch at NBC instead of a romantic sojourn. Nevertheless, I was smitten. Not with her, but with the entire process of watching the scoring of *Days of our Lives* go down, live in the studio. She actually spun vinyl recordings and "dropped the needle" at the appropriate dramatic moments.

As I watched and observed, I realized that not only was the music kind of corny and boring, but there was much more to writing music for a soap opera than meets the ear. All the other aspects of production—acting, directing, lighting, writing—were the actual canvas for which the music served as a frame. I had been bitten by the show-business bug and didn't even know it. I smelled the greasepaint, heard the roar of the directors and actors and producers, and was thoroughly intrigued and enchanted.

The cues I wrote came back from Italy poorly recorded and at completely different tempi (time signatures) than I had written. Yet they started getting more and more airplay as Linda became more familiar with each of them. I actually started making money in residuals from BMI royalties! For ten cues, about thirty minutes of music.

Before the *Days of our Lives* music, I had been playing drums in a duo in a little nightclub in Santa Cruz that was more of a dive and cover for the poker games in the back room than a real venue for entertainment. One night, Huey Newton, of the infamous Black Panthers in Oakland, came into the club, pulled out his .44 Magnum, and emptied it into the ceiling before Big Al, the owner, could get out of the card room, call the cops, and have Huey arrested for the umpteenth time. My dear friend and band mate, Gene Barnholt, always kept his Air Force–issued Colt .45 under the keyboard of his Hammond organ.

But after the residuals started coming in, these few cues threw off more "mailbox money" than I had ever dreamed of—more than the fifty dollars a night I was making playing my way through grad school four nights a week.

And I was starting to see that a career as a nightclub drummer had more than financial hazards. You could actually get punched out if you didn't play "Proud Mary" or "Satisfaction" every time they were requested, ten or fifteen times a night, complete with complimentary shots of Jack Daniels…to be consumed before playing the request.

The choice between a career as a drummer or one teaching as a postgraduate was becoming much easier for me to make. But that path was going to divert me into a completely different and much larger road. The road to fame and glory…with a price, of course.

∽

In the fall of 1977, just after my graduation from San Jose State with a Phi Kappa Phi, 4.0, top-of-the-class record, I received a job offer as an associate professor in music at San Jose State University. It had an annual salary of fourteen thousand dollars starting pay, plus income from private lessons. A master's degree would have its benefits.

At the same time, Linda Line quit her job at *Days of our Lives* to go to work for Procter & Gamble as a daytime executive. The new music director at *Days of our Lives*, Ken Heller, suggested that he and I write a an entirely new and different music library for the show.

This was, of course, met with raised eyebrows and an equally raised music budget. But Ken Heller prevailed upon Columbia Pictures Music to foot the bill for a large, two-day session in Wembley, England, in spring of 1978. It had happened…now it was time for me to make a move, so I decided to dump Santa Cruz for life in LaLa Land.

The door had been opened to a much greater profession. College had taught me some very valuable lessons. Namely, how to read, write, compose, and score music, whether for a small or large orchestra, and, more importantly, how to believe in myself, my talent, and my ability to communicate through the marvelous language of music, sweet music. Unfortunately, the life of one near and dear to me was sadly off-key.

CHAPTER 11

BROTHER EAGLE, SISTER SKY

While my mother and I and *Days of our Lives* were finding success, my brother Chris's life and mental health were deteriorating, falling into a whirlpool so deep that none of us knew its full and dangerous extent. It is said that "into every life some rain must fall," but this was a storm approaching, carrying a devastating threat to more than just our family.

In 1970, after all of us in Lucky Mud had left Hawaii, Chris had journeyed to Southeast Asia and had disappeared from all traces of his past and family. Ostensibly there as a "stringer," or freelance photojournalist, for *Life* magazine, he had sold all of his Nikon cameras for methadrine and became an addict, shooting up on the streets of Saigon, Vietnam, and later Bangkok, Thailand. He returned a few years later, via the State Department's insistence and enforcement, not only with serum hepatitis but also deeply scarred by what he had seen. By the time he came home in 1973, he was fifty pounds underweight and jaundiced.

Chris was also facing serious charges from the State of California for drug trafficking, and could only avoid doing time in a long-term prison by pleading not guilty by reason of insanity for all of his crimes. He had been, by this time, diagnosed as a paranoid-schizophrenic by more than one physician. Serving time in a state mental institution would prove to be further damaging…not the place to put a severely schizophrenic person. But he chose this over the long-term dangers of a state prison.

When I asked my brother shortly after his return why he had stopped taking pictures in Southeast Asia and sold his cameras, he simply said he could no longer look through a tiny box at something that was bigger than life—the war. It was all so painful for him. He needed something to kill the pain. The horror of the Vietnam War was seldom directly brought home to the American people by the press and foreign news correspondents of the time. Photographs weren't enough. What we saw on television news broadcasts wasn't the real story.

So Chris had to choose between serving a three-to-five-year sentence in prison or pleading insanity and being institutionalized in a state mental facility for at least a year or two. No one, especially if they were white, middle-class, ex-hippies, survived well in the Big House that was the state penitentiary. So he chose to serve time in the state mental institution in Camarillo, California.

Scenic Camarillo was just five miles from the Pacific Ocean, but Chris might as well have been back in the Southeast Asian jungle. Those who were sent to Camarillo State Mental Hospital lived in a zoo that reeked of desperate survival instead of helpful rehabilitation. And neither my mother nor I was ever fully aware of how awful his plight had become, and how the bomb that would bring about the end of his life had started inexorably ticking.

We didn't write Chris off. No, we loved him no matter what. He was my parents' firstborn. He was my only brother. So we trusted that the system would help him and straighten out his life, which seemed to have come off its tracks. But what transpired in the five years following his being sent to Camarillo became at first a growing concern for us and then later a never-ending nightmare of terminal proportions for my brother.

How things went for Chris at the men's mental ward at Camarillo we never fully knew. My mother was besieged and beleaguered by what had happened to him. She was completely unable to help him, due to the institutionally imposed separation of visitors from patients. She could not reach him. I couldn't reach him. We couldn't reach him. And he was starting to fade further away.

One of the few times I saw him there while visiting from Santa Cruz, he seemed more detached, distanced in a pharmaceutically imposed way. He was being drugged as a punishment for taking drugs. Even though he was very sedated, he would come out of it occasionally and show flashes of his old brilliance. But the luster was gone and he grew more tarnished by the florescent glare of the "system."

What had happened to my older brother? What had happened to my idol? Where was the guy who taught me how to fish, how to raise hell, how to cut classes, how to pick up girls…and how to be a man? Where was my older brother who knew to give me a drum to play at Christmas and then helped me beat out my frustrations when he knew he was the source of many of them? Where was the Eagle Scout? Where was the Robin Hood dead-ass shot? Where had he lost himself? Where had he left himself? Could he ever return to us? Would he, if he could?

After serving two years in Camarillo, Chris got out only to be rearrested within a year for selling pounds of pot in San Diego. And so again, after copping a plea of mental illness, back into the cuckoo's nest he went, only this time to the very modern private facility then called the Thalian's Unit of Cedars-Sinai Hospital, the psychiatric wing of one of the most highly regarded hospitals in the United States. The same hospital where our father had died on July 23, ten years before.

∞

"The whirlpool is spinning faster."

Chris told me this in so many words a few years later, and when I asked him how deep the vortex was, he only said that I didn't want to know. But I knew his descent into paranoid schizophrenia was accelerating—most likely due to the large doses of the drugs thorazine and stelazine that he was administered by the hospital, three times a day.

Now he was no longer a prisoner of the state or a hospital patient; he was a prisoner of his own mind and a patient with no patience. He would, on occasion, get phone privileges and call me. He would start the conversation in a cordial, seemingly rational way. But then out of nowhere, he would tell me that people were coming through the air-conditioning ducts in his room and stealing his underwear. The other patients and doctors were out to get him. What a sad thing to watch… his life was so wretched, no matter how hard he tried to change it. He always fell back into the whirlpool.

In the 1970s psychopharmacology had not advanced as far as it has today. There was no Prozac, Paxil, Ativan, Seroquel, or SSRIs. There was Lithium, a somewhat brutal and archaic antidepressant, and Phenobarbital to help cut the edge of anxiety and despair. Electroshock therapy was available, if all else failed. That was the most dreaded option. In large doses, as it was given then, it might destroy the person's brain.

How could the heavens, the fates, and even God have abandoned him? He who also appeared many years wiser than his age. He who couldn't shed a tear at his father's grave was now weeping with a fear that knew no limits. With a pain that, as Aeschylus said, "drips sorrow inexorably on the heart until we understand and grow from the horrible grace of God."

So we prayed to the heavens. My mother and I, and his few friends. We all prayed to the fates. Wouldn't they save him? Couldn't they save him? Please, couldn't God help him save himself? But the answer wouldn't come soon, and when it did, it would not be the answer we wanted.

CHAPTER 12

GONE TO AN HOUR

In 1975 *Days of our Lives*, ten years after it debuted, expanded to one hour. It was the second daytime drama to make the leap. By 1979 my mother was sixty-seven and, by that time, had been producing *Days of our Lives* every day since my father's death, about thirty-five hundred episodes.

She was starting to grow weary of all the bickering and jockeying for power that came with her job as the owner and the executive producer. She had never been in it for the politics or ego; she had never taken a screen credit as Betty Corday. She was always listed at the top of the credits, known as "the crawl," as "Executive Producer…Mrs. Ted Corday." *Days of our Lives* was always her anchor, her passion… almost like her third child.

Now the '80s approached, and with them, the rise of soap operas as not only a cool thing to watch for a voracious audience, but also a huge, money-making cash cow for the network, NBC. It was Luke-and-Laura time on *General Hospital*. It was Roman-and-Marlena and Bo-and-Hope time on *Days of our Lives*. It was breakout time for daytime drama.

It was the beginning of the golden age for *Days of our Lives* and the coming of age for me.

I decided to move back to Los Angeles and took up residence in the little pool house behind my mother's home in Beverly Hills. I still detested the city, its social class structure, and the grossly commercialistic projection of self-entitlement. At this juncture I was a somewhat successful composer and definitely a wannabe producer.

For me it was a life-defining collision of two lifestyles. I wasn't sure I wanted a career in television. I rationalized that during the week I would live behind my mother's house in a twelve-foot by sixteen-foot space—just big enough for a queen-size bed and one chest of drawers with a television on top. Then on the weekends I would commute to Santa Cruz to my cozy log-cabin home near the shore.

I had been in love with and living with the same wonderful woman for two years, but we never spoke of marriage. We, along with my trustworthy old dogs, lived together in the cabin in La Selva Beach. I was a weekend commuter, and it certainly had its perks. I was constantly meeting people the same age who were also weekend commuters, and I made a lot of new friends. It was the '80s, I was in my thirties, and life was good…very, very good. Disco was dying and dot-com was coming.

Then one day I knew I had to choose one or the other—an idyllic life in country comfort with a beautiful woman who had also been my best friend for three years, both living off low-paying jobs, or move to the big pond of Tinseltown and all of its completely baffling show biz and stress.

Thank the Lord I chose the latter, complete with the heaps of adjustment and crow eating that came with it. Because by the time my mother was in her late sixties, the inexorable weight of my brother's ill health, coupled with the fact that she was a woman working alone in a man's world, started to make her sick. She had had two heart operations for pericarditis—an inflammation of the sac surrounding her heart—and the doctors were suggesting that she should consider stepping back and maybe retiring, giving her heart a rest while retaining ownership of the show.

But she knew from experience that the executive producer made the show go in terms of casting, production, and story. She did not want to turn a family-run show, and her and Ted's legacy, over to a corporate Johnny-come-lately. She used to say what Irna Phillips had taught her, that temporary people, such as these, make permanent decisions...and they also didn't know what they didn't know. A dangerous combination.

Executive producers are subject to network approval, which usually means the network has its choice in who occupies that position, and that choice or priority might very well be watching out for the network, not necessarily what had become, after fifteen years, the "*Days* family." Corporate thinking and the concept of a family-run show are antithetical, creatively and economically.

So Betty Corday boldly suggested that I seriously consider learning all aspects of the show's production...maybe someday even run the business?

But who said I, Ken Corday, was cut out for this? I had no theater background, knew zip about acting—and even less about balancing a budget or ultimately taking on the battles with the feisty head writers and network executives. No way could I ever make this work.

I also had the stigma that was the most difficult: nepotism.

I retreated to my Santa Cruz log cabin in the redwoods. There, I seriously thought it over for a few weeks, and I realized that I had been bitten by the bug. I wanted to learn the ropes at *Days*, to see if I was cut out for it. Even more, I felt I owed it to my mother to try to give it a real go.

∞

That was one very trying year...1979.

I got busy and focused all of my energies on answering fan mail by the hundreds, getting coffee for the producers, and hanging around the studio a lot for the better part of a year. I was basically a gofer and survived on my music residuals.

Eventually I attempted to assume the role of assistant producer. I still wasn't completely qualified, but the time had come. I would have to find a way to make a place for myself.

Three men, all twice my age, with tons of experience and matching egos, were standing in line waiting for an opportunity to take control of the show, or more appropriately, circling like hungry sharks. They knew that my mother was growing weak. As in Homer's *Odyssey*, she was Penelope. I was Telemachus, but my father, Odysseus, was gone. His ship had sailed away forever, and now these false suitors were all drooling over the spoils of her domain.

One of the men was a lawyer. At his suggestion, my mother had given him an interest in the business in exchange for his expert legal and business advice in taking *Days of our Lives* to one hour from a half hour. A shrewd agreement! He made Betty Corday, and *Days of our Lives*, a good deal richer, and he got to share in the profits. He would continue to collect a healthy percentage of her earnings for the life of the show.

The second executive was the vice president of Columbia Pictures Television at that time. He loved to shout at my mother, both over the phone and in person, while trying to assert his ultimate authority over *Days of our Lives*…and its profits. I resented the fact that any man would have the nerve and the ill manners to raise his voice to my mother. My father had never, *ever* raised his voice to my mother, but now this big-time executive, the same age that my father would have been, was yelling at her in meetings and in front of other people. That had to stop!

My father, as the creator of *Days of our Lives*, and therefore, my mother in his stead, *owned the copyright* to *Days of our Lives*? Hmmm… let's see now…? That meant that Corday Productions and therefore the Corday family owned the show. It was dawning on me who it was that held the cards in this game…a realization that showed the savvy business decisions my parents had made designing or laying out the show.

There also was the co-executive producer who had been with *Days of our Lives* for years and thought, therefore, he had the right to assume command and control of the show after my mother stepped down. Who knew better how to handle the cast? Who knew better how to keep the network at bay? Who knew best how to wheel and deal? Why *he* did, of course. Except for one key detail: He had a contract that was due to expire in a few months.

So into this man-made fray, dominated by three over-fifty, testosterone-charged heavyweights, I would have to leap. A daunting task for someone like me, who seemed to be to everyone else, especially after only one year, just "the boss's son." A huge challenge, to manage these politics while still trying to prove myself.

It's difficult to comprehend the magnitude of a situation like this. If I eventually succeeded in defending my mother—her legacy, as it were, and thus the family's legacy of *Days of our Lives*—I would most likely bring about the end of at least two, if not three, careers on the show. I would also most likely gain the harsh rebuke and long-term ill will of three men whom I really didn't know. It was a tight spot, and I didn't want to hurt anyone. And I honestly didn't even know if I would eventually want the job of running the show. But when it came down to it, I cared about my mother, and thus I wanted to try.

My father was a superb chess player. He taught me a valuable lesson in the game: "The pressing pawn wins the game…because the pressing pawn, usually overlooked, can become the most powerful piece on the board." So I learned. I waited. And I pressed on.

CHAPTER 13

THE ONCE AND FUTURE KING

By late 1979 I was trying to find a place on *Days of our Lives* where I could be useful and productive, and protect my mother and her legacy, without feeling dismissed or under a microscope because I was Betty Corday's son.

Early on I got to know Ed Mallory, who played Bill Horton. Ed was a kind and very bright human being who loved to act and, to his final days, devoted himself to his craft and his talent. Ed taught television production at the University of Virginia after he left *Days of our Lives*, and he and I stayed in touch until he passed away in 2007.

But back in the day, Ed was what my mother endearingly referred to as "Peck's Bad Boy." Ed Mallory was all of that and more, much as his character, Bill Horton, was a rascal, a hotheaded doctor, and a philandering romantic.

Ed's performances were dramatically wonderful, yet he was very hit-and-miss in following the written word of the head writer, Bill Bell. No one dared change a word of Bill's writing. But Ed did…and Bill didn't like that.

One day I watched rehearsal of a scene in which Ed had an extremely long monologue as he was scrubbing up for surgery beside MacDonald Carey, who played his father, Dr. Tom Horton. Ed just could not remember his difficult medical dialogue in that scene, so he decided to write all of it down inside the pre-op sink. He figured he could read it as he was looking down, ostensibly washing his hands, during this routine preoperative procedure.

All went well during dress rehearsal. Ed made it through all the multisyllable medical terms for Dr. Bill Horton's upcoming brain surgery on his wife, Laura, who had a massive tumor. Of course, the director, the producer, and the crew knew what Ed had done.

When it came time to tape the scene for real, the stagehands turned the sink into what is known as a practical one, so sound effects would not have to create an onstage sound of water in a working sink. When Ed turned on the tap during the taping, he didn't expect the water to be flowing. He had written his lines in ink around the inside of the sink. The splashing water started making the ink run, and Ed, or rather Dr. Bill Horton, was at its mercy. He totally "went up." He forgot all of his lines, and after a very long pause in his monologue, the kind that had a gaping hole so large that you could drive a truck through it, he simply looked directly into the camera and exclaimed, "All my f---ing lines just went down the drain!"

Ed was funny and endearing and always kind and respectful to my mother and to me. One day we were chatting about nothing in particular at the coffee machine when he jokingly referred to me as "the once and future king," the literary name for the young King Arthur. Of course, at the time, this comment went completely over my head. I just laughed and sloughed it off.

Many years later, after his long successful run on the show came to an end, he sent me a small steel sculpture of the sword Excalibur and the stone from which it was pulled by young King Arthur. To this day it sits on my desk, right in front of me, as a reminder of Ed's gentle kindness and how fate and luck brought me to my real purpose in life. At the time he said the comment to me, I didn't understand what he meant. But *he* did. He seemed to know what the future had in store for me. The old psychic's predictions were coming true.

∞

As Don Corleone said to his young son Michael in *The Godfather*, "It was supposed to be easy for you, Michael." Yet it wasn't easy for young Don Corleone. And it wasn't easy for me either. No way was it easy.

Push finally came to shove in early 1980. Wes Kenney, our first producer, had left *Days of our Lives* and was replaced by our brilliant director, Al Rabin, who had never been a producer before. The show was being head-written by two new writers, Gary Tomlin and Michelle Poteet Lisanti, both of whom had recently taken over for the wonderful Elizabeth Harrower, who was also Susan Hayes's mother.

The show was not doing great in the ratings…nor had it been doing well for the past year. Thus the changes in staff had occurred, all with my mother's approval, with the goal of a better, improved show. But by the end of 1979 *Days of our Lives* was really slipping. Three days before New Year's Day 1980, my mother and the head writers were asked to come to New York the following week for a meeting with the president of NBC, Fred Silverman, and no one said no to Mr. Silverman.

Fred had a background in daytime with CBS and, after a very successful stint as president of ABC, had come to run NBC in 1978. He had made many sweeping changes to NBC's lineup. Yet NBC was still the number-three network in the ratings race, behind CBS and ABC. No wonder, with shows like *Hello, Larry* and *Supertrain*.

It was panic city at 30 Rockefeller Center, NYC. Again, lots of temporary people were making permanent decisions…and *Days of our Lives* was up for renewal in three months. Cancellation was suddenly a real and looming threat. This meeting had been demanded.

There was also a problem that would prevent Betty Corday from going to New York. My mother suffered her second cardiac episode, what we called a "mild" heart attack (as if any heart attack could be considered mild), at Thanksgiving in 1979. After surgery she had been released from the hospital and was home for Christmas. Like my father had done fifteen years before, she never let her fragile physical state be known to the world, outside of her doctor and brother-in-law, my uncle Eliot Corday, and me.

We were very concerned about the stresses on her health in dealing with a *Days of our Lives* that was, amazingly, so close to cancellation. A long trip to New York was out of the question…especially when it included confronting the volatile and often overbearing Fred Silverman. With brand-new writers and a brand-new producer, she and the show were exposed and at risk. What to do? Desperate times call for not only desperate measures, but also a good amount of prayer.

Thankfully my dear mother could boil a complex situation down to its essence. She knew she couldn't go, but she also knew the answer to her quandary.

We talked by phone on New Year's Eve, and she suggested that *I* go with the producer and writers. *I* would go as her representative and meet with her boss, Fred Silverman.

I questioned her thinking. I had not been back to Manhattan, my birthplace, since we moved west in 1964. I was excited at the prospect of seeing my old stomping grounds and dear friends who were still living there, but I felt like I would be the sacrificial lamb thrown to the network wolves. I was scared to step up. So I suggested that she think it over, have a nice glass of champagne, and then we'd talk on New Year's Day.

What I didn't know was what transpired immediately after we got off the phone. She telephoned her aforementioned shrewd legal-eagle adviser for his thoughts. He told her that sending me to New York in her place would be a fatal decision. He said that with the newly hired producer, the new head writers, and an unknown Corday, *Days of our Lives* would be ill-represented and vulnerable. He offered instead to go alone in her place and not be accompanied by any of the "talent" or "the boss's son." She thanked him for his advice and told him she'd take his words to heart.

As we counted down to New Year's that night, the question loomed in my mind: What would the new year bring? Cancellation, or a pick-up and a new two-year contract for *Days of our Lives*? There was so much at stake, and the decision that was hanging in the balance was the ultimate cliff-hanger to the end of my first year working on the show. Suddenly I was looking at carrying the responsibility for the livelihood of four hundred employees and the continuing viewership of six million people. It was quite the test, and I was still unsure if I was up to the challenge.

CHAPTER 14

DO OR DIE

The best moments in life can happen in a blink. So it was when I blinked on New Year's Day 1980.

My mother woke me at 9:00 a.m. The phone rang for a long time. I rolled out of bed and shook the champagne cobwebs loose. I was still accompanied that fine New Year's Day morning by a rapturously beautiful, five-foot-eleven goddess, lately of Beverly Hills and a former ballerina. Was I still dreaming? Nope, this was real.

I warmly greeted my mother in the most erudite, Upper East Coast fashion, but I couldn't disguise the morning fog still in my throat.

"Happy New Year, Mom. How are you? I hope this will be the best year ever, for both of us"…beat…silence.

Then she said, "Oh, I'm just fine…and from the sound of your voice, I can tell you are, too."

"So what are your New Year's resolutions?" I asked, skirting the embarrassment of my first hangover of the year. She could always tell.

"Oh, I don't know, really," she continued. "I guess I'd really like your brother to come home or at least call."

"I'd love that, too, Mom, but his doctors are watching him all the time, and it's better that he's in the hospital, where they can make sure he takes his medication."

Long pause…very long pause, then silence. Then she tacked to the right, hard.

She told me she had been thinking all night about the situation, about the meeting in Manhattan and the pick-up of the show. She said she had really strong feelings that it would be wise and prudent for me to go in her place and accompany our new producer and new head writers to New York City…the next day!

I was speechless…and quite excited. Could I, at the ripe young age of twenty-nine and "green" to the business, pull it off and help the cause, and maybe even save the bacon? Suddenly I was excited by the seriousness and importance of this moment. The acceptance of this challenge brought not only relief, but also closure to my decision. The time had come. Time to rescue my mother and the show. Time for me to grow up.

So the die was cast. I said, "Yes, I'll go."

On the night of January 2, we four relatively young and inexperienced representatives of *Days of our Lives* landed at JFK airport. It was so bitterly cold that I remember our producer, Al Rabin, who was never without a smart line, standing next to me at curbside as we waited for a cab and saying through his shivering, "I can't move!" I had forgotten how the wind off the water of the Atlantic Ocean cuts right through to the bone.

I felt like a returning prodigal son, wild and wind-blown…and that wind made me feel lost, scared, and certain that my fate was in someone else's hands.

On January 3 we reported at 9:00 a.m. to the command meeting at NBC that had been called by Fred Silverman…only Fred never showed.

Instead he sent two literary critics from the *New York Times* whom he had hired to watch *Days of our Lives* for the previous two weeks. They were supposed to tell us what was wrong with the show and how to fix it. Then they would report back to Fred.

It was astounding. They hadn't done their homework. They didn't know anything about *Days of our Lives*, especially the stories of the previous fifteen years! They didn't know that Bill and Susan Hayes were married in real life. They didn't even know Doug and Julie, their characters, were married on the show. They thought the Hortons were only on the show in the beginning, 1965, and they had no idea who Deidre Hall (Dr. Marlena Evans) was.

All of a sudden I felt a huge surge of relief and then giddiness. I knew for sure that our newly assigned critics were ill-prepared for their task and all we would have to be was smarter than them. I remembered my father's lesson: "Press the pawn across the chessboard, and you win."

So after picking our jaws up off the floor, Al Rabin, Michelle Lisanti, Gary Tomlin, and I taught them a thorough lesson in the story and history of *Days of our Lives* that lasted for two days of long meetings. It proved to be very embarrassing to the *New York Times* critics. But most of all, it was bewildering to Fred Silverman, who kept sending down questioning notes to find out what was going on and getting back very confusing messages. In the end, the critics backed off and decided to let us run the show (and probably told Uncle Freddie that *they* had fixed it all)!

Surprisingly, the folks at NBC never asked where my mother, the executive producer, was. Nor did they once question who I was or even my presence there as the guy from Corday Productions.

We went home two days later with an "approved" story line for the next year, which featured the reuniting of Doug and Julie and a major story for Marlena. We returned secure in the knowledge that we had pocketed a pick-up of the show for the next two years, a huge accomplishment.

In the end, it didn't matter who we were or what our titles were. We had saved the show because we knew the show. It was *our* show.

What a wonderful world it suddenly appeared to be on the morning we drove to JFK for our return to L.A. A morning fresh with new snow, a foot of it that had fallen all night long. I gazed out the window of the back of the cab on the way to JFK and longed to be home in Los Angeles. Yet even more so, I longed to stay in Manhattan, because I realized that this great city was forever going to have the most special place deep in my bones.

CHAPTER 15

NOT SO FAST,
YOU LUCKY DOG!

The underlying story line of many Greek dramas is:
"Take a sympathetic hero, put him up
against insurmountable odds in order to
achieve a very worthy goal…"
More succinctly:
"Get your hero up a tree, throw rocks at him,
then find a way to get him down…"

By 1980 my official title was assistant producer on *Days of our Lives*. But even after the NBC meeting I was not seen as a hero by those associated with the show, let alone a sympathetic hero. Personally, I did not feel anything like a hero; however, I was certainly up a tree. Pick-up or not, no one cared. And I was still kind of scared.

My quandary: How could I keep going and prove myself to myself and everyone else on the show as its leader when I had said from the start I was eventually leaving? I really knew nothing about daytime television production. I was a musician and a composer with a master's degree. I was supposed to be teaching at San Jose State University, not wondering about how to succeed in a new business. That, coupled with the reality that I was the son of the owner of the show, "the boss's son," made things doubly difficult.

After running the show since 1966, my mother had created a franchise, a glittering gold mine for NBC, and an enduring legacy for me. She was nearly seventy, and much as my father knew what her destiny would be before he died and asked her to take the helm, she must have also seen or known *my* destiny, even though I seemed to be in denial of it. But as I continued to struggle to find my place, I was having ongoing doubts about making a real commitment to a life in daytime television in LaLa Land.

∞

Meanwhile, my brother had been deinstitutionalized due to the passage of California Proposition 13, which effectively pulled money away from state-run mental institutions, such as Camarillo State Hospital.

People with mental illness were thrown out on the street. Someone must have trusted that mental patients undergoing treatment, sometimes for extended periods of time, could get by on their own, could take their own medications on their own, and could stay out of trouble living on their own in the outside world.

All of a sudden the percentage of mentally ill homeless people ballooned, and the streets of Los Angeles were far more unsafe than they had ever been before. This not only applied to the general population, but even more so to those newly discharged patients who had been lost to themselves and were now becoming lost to all of us.

The world can be a scary place to live when you are left without a rope to hold on to. Many were only given enough rope to hang themselves…and more than a few did so in the time immediately following the passage of Proposition 13.

The burden on my mother was growing. *Days of our Lives* was taking its toll on her…and my brother was becoming more of a dependent again, at the age of thirty-two. From 1980 on he was unable to work another day in his life. And he never got better.

∞

But despite all this, my mother was reluctant to push me into accepting a permanent position on *Days of our Lives* as the person who would end up running the show and relieve her of that awesome responsibility. She internalized the stress of dealing with a more and more competitive environment and sometimes a belligerent Columbia Pictures and NBC. She brought home all the gnawing problems of a show with a new co-executive producer and young head writers. She knew that the "old guard" was changing and that she was a part of it.

Wes Kenny had left. He had produced the show from day one. Associate producer Helen Hall, costume designer Joe Markham, director Frank Pacelli, casting director Trudy Soss, audio engineer Ernie DiLutri, and many more also had left. Those who had been young in 1965 were now much older. The times were changing. Television had become more and more about youth. Both in front of and behind the cameras, our originals were retiring or being let go to make room for the next generation.

Characters who had driven *Days of our Lives* since day one were becoming walking anachronisms. Mickey, Bill, and Laura were old hat, as were Doug and Julie and Don and Marlena. A younger character, and first of his antihero, James Dean kind, was Chris Kositcheck, played with new, blue-collar intensity by Josh Taylor.

But who would step up, both in front of and behind the camera, to take *Days of our Lives* into its next five or ten or twenty years? The show was overdue for a major change in many respects. It was time for me to climb the tree, no matter how high or scary it seemed. I knew in my heart that it was the right thing to do for my mother, but I was still in denial.

She knew better than to hit my guilt buttons. Up to now, she never, ever asked me to step in or take over. In fact, she had only asked me to go to New York that January to represent her and our family because she was ill.

But by the early '80s many things had changed. *Days of our Lives* had hired a new head writer, Pat Falken Smith, who had been Irna Phillips's secretary and one of Bill Bell's favorite script writers in the early years of the show. NBC had two young daytime programmers in Lucy Johnson and Michael Brockman; Grant Tinker had become the new president at NBC, taking over for Fred Silverman, and he would bring Bill Cosby's show to the network. All that started the pendulum swinging in the right direction, and Columbia Pictures, which was Corday Productions' partner and distributor, had been bought by Coca Cola...a big show-business acquisition at the time. They had hired Herman Rush, a very talented executive, to run the television division, and Herman was very good to the Cordays and *Days of our Lives*. Things were rapidly changing...for the better.

One late winter day, a rainy February Monday, I was hanging around the control room in the old Studio 9. Our producer at that time was Jack Herzberg, who had been my father's Signal Corps assistant in the army during World War II, a dear friend of our family, and the show's producer since day one.

Some weekends Jack loved to take my mother and me to Tijuana, Mexico, a two-and-a-half-hour drive from Burbank. We would eat like royalty, drink like fools, and go to the jai alai games and horse races and bet like crazy. Jack never made a pass at my mother or tried to act like a father to me. He respected us as friends, and we always had a ball on those trips.

Jack was the definition of "fun, fun, fun." He ended up judging the Miss California pageant after my mother gave it up (due to her honest, deep-set, feminist belief in equal rights), and Jack also relished judging the all-nude California beauty pageants. Jack loved the nudist colony life and must have been very comfortable with his ego and body, which at the time was fairly representative of the over-sixty crowd. Jack also loved to date the extras on *Days of our Lives*, especially the extremely buxom nurses, some of whom had, surprisingly, won the Miss Nude California title.

Jack and I would wake up early on Saturday to play golf, which neither of us was very good at, especially when super hungover from a long night of "El Tequila Fiesta" in Tijuana. On Sundays we would stop for a lunch on our way home from Mexico at converted coastal homes that were open on weekends for inexpensive meals of local lobster and homemade frijoles and tortillas. Those wonderful and remarkable meals usually cured our hangovers. My mother and I truly respected and loved Jack.

However, on that harsh winter day Jack was not his usual jovial self. Unfortunately, he had fallen asleep in his producer's chair in the control room. I don't remember who was directing that day, but they sure weren't worried about getting any notes or changes from production. There was a "Who gives a damn?" attitude throughout the stage.

Coincidentally, Lucy Johnson, the daytime director at NBC, and her close friend Fernando Rocca, an executive from Columbia Television, decided to make a surprise visit to the set that day. They peeked into the booth and saw Jack asleep behind his newspaper, which reflected the complacency apparent throughout the control room and the stage.

They were still standing unnoticed in the hall peering into the control room as I happened by. They turned to me with a dubious and slightly irked reaction on their faces. I returned their glance, but instead of trying to cover for Jack (which couldn't be done), I just shrugged my shoulders, turned my hands upward, and said *nothing* in a subtle and understanding manner. I couldn't cover for Jack, but I also couldn't sell him out.

They pulled me aside. I remember that moment as if it were moving frame by frame. Lucy was dressed in a full-length Burberry raincoat, and Fernando was, as always, impeccably dressed, head to toe, in Yves St. Laurent, complete with a cravat. The ensuing silence was thick. They were obviously upset.

Fernando spoke first. He explained that he (Columbia) and Lucy (NBC) had been talking and had come to the decision that it would be good for the show, the studio, and the network to "make a change." I held my breath. Here was the top brass, and they were telling *me* that the ax was going to fall. Why me...and on whom would it fall?

More silence. Then Lucy softly suggested that *I* should become coproducer with a yet-to-be-named hands-on acting coach as my counterpart.

I was dumbstruck! Were they kidding? "Why me?"...the words came out before I could get my foot back out of my mouth.

Then their mouths started moving, but I didn't hear a word they said. However, I do remember distinctly hearing, "You are young and full of new energy, and you went to New York last year and got the pick-up...and we know a wonderful casting director..." Then their words seemed to all start to run together.

I was excited at first. I then thought, my own mother knew nothing of this? I hadn't given it much thought. It was life-changing! Upon reflection, it was the decisive moment in my professional career.

So after about a nanosecond, which seemed to last an eternity, I said, "Yeah, sure...you bet...sounds great."

Good-bye, Santa Cruz's yellow brick road...Hello, L.A. But how to deal to with all the spiders, snakes, and vampire bats that resided in the forest I was about to enter? I knew that some very opportunistic wolves were still near, and they saw me as the very lucky dog who was a real threat to their ambitions. Simple. I would either kill them with kindness or learn to love them.

I had been tapped by the network, the studio, and then my mother. Sent into the fray with great expectations, but not entirely without questions. What about my home, life, and honey in Santa Cruz? Would I keep living in the pool house behind my mother's house? So many questions.

With this decision, made first for me by NBC and later approved by my mother, I would have to change my entire lifestyle. My father had taken far greater risks than this with his life and career more than fifteen years earlier. This also meant moving for me. A new home in a new city, lots of now-distant close friends, and more than anything, I would become a permanent part of the everyday decision making on *Days of our Lives*, a permanent resident of Los Angeles, and prominently responsible for much of the show's success or failure, especially the business of running Corday Productions.

This was, in retrospect, one of the key moments in my career on *Days of our Lives*, and there was a palpable inner uncertainty on my part that I was afraid I would never be able to hide. But that was okay. I still had much to learn, and everyone with whom I worked knew it, understood it, and supported me. But what about my very ill, needy, and potentially dangerous brother? Was my being so close to him putting myself in harm's way?

CHAPTER 16

THE GLORY YEARS

I remember walking through the San Francisco airport early one morning in early 1976. I had just gotten off the red-eye from Hawaii at 7:00 a.m., and as I glanced around with weary eyes, I saw a newsstand opening. I bought the morning paper.

As I waited for my change, I looked at the shelves and saw a new copy of *Time* magazine. On the cover was a full-page picture of Doug and Julie from *Days of our Lives*. The title of the issue was: "SOAP OPERAS—Sex and Suffering in the Afternoon," and the "m" in *Time* had its top two red points coming through the top of Susan Seaforth's head, like a pair of horns.

It hit me like a hammer that Ted and Betty Corday's little daytime television show had become part of a national craze, as had the whole soap opera genre. What used to be totally *uncool* for any young, hip, eighteen-to-thirty-four-year-old's television viewing was now *so* popular that college students were adjusting their class schedules so that they wouldn't have class between noon and 1:00 p.m.

They couldn't miss their favorite soap. They would hear the opening theme, listen to MacDonald Carey's voice, and sit down to have lunch with *Days of our Lives* every weekday. If they had class during that hour, some had their boyfriends or girlfriends watch and take notes. *Days of our Lives* had reached its tipping point. It had become a success story of national proportions.

The daytime drama craze grew even stronger. The advent of the '80s brought new life to *Days of our Lives*. Head writers Pat Falken Smith, Margaret DePriest, and Sheri Anderson helped put Salem squarely on the map. They literally gave a new geography to the show…from the Salem river front, to the lake district, to the mansions on the hill, to the creation of lots of new restaurants, pubs, and honky tonks…Salem became more physically real than ever before.

They collaborated to create the entire blue-collar Brady clan— Shawn; Caroline; their sons, Roman and Bo; and their daughters, Kimberly and Kayla. They also introduced a new upper-class and villainous family called the DiMeras—Stefano and his son, Tony, and daughters Renee, and later, Megan.

After Pat and Margaret moved on, Sheri brought wealthy Greek tycoon Victor Kiriakis to Salem. He was revealed to be the past lover of Caroline Brady and the biological father of his illegitimate young rebel son, Bo Brady.

The style of the show also improved dramatically. The ambitious production of *Days of our Lives* started using many exteriors, or location settings, to shoot the climactic scenes at the conclusions of their compelling stories. More comedy elements were also added.

Scenes were getting shorter. Instead of prolonged two- or three-minute dialogue between two characters over a cup of coffee, the scenes were tighter and faster paced, seamlessly blending from one to the next as three or four main stories played out each new day. And the characters performing them were new and fresh and, above all else, young.

Blue-collar bad boy Bo was star-crossed in love with upper-middle-class, white-picket-fence Hope, the daughter of Addie Horton and

Doug Williams. Bo's older brother, Detective Roman Brady, had saved Dr. Marlena Evans from the Salem Strangler after spending weeks on her apartment floor every night in a sleeping bag.

The superspy, "James Bondian" Shane Donovan was wooing Kimberly Brady off her feet. And probably the most au courant of all these new relationships was the unlikely but highly charged coupling of Kayla Brady, the youngest of the siblings, with antihero, bad-to-the-bone Patch Johnson.

After losing her hearing, Kayla taught Patch not only how to speak in sign language, but also how to cry and feel his heart and soul again. Under head writer Leah Laiman, she redeemed the one-eyed man and made him Salem's new hero. All of this was done in the '80s, around the time that *Days of our Lives* celebrated its twentieth anniversary. Many obstacles had been overcome. Much had been learned, and much had been changed for the better in Salem.

However, my mother, Betty, was not faring well at that time. She couldn't enjoy the glory years of *Days of our Lives* or her newfound wealth. She was becoming more and more ill from her recently diagnosed lupus disease...a result of a bad blood transfusion received following her second heart surgery. She had also started to experience serious bouts of depression, a depression she never shared with anyone. In addition, my mother was now in her seventies, living alone, and subject to a constant barrage of phone calls and visits from my schizophrenic brother.

At this point I had given up any notion of living the easy life in Santa Cruz. I put a down payment on a little house in the San Fernando Valley. It was a two-bedroom 1950s tract home on Burbank Boulevard near Sepulveda, fronting on lanes and lanes of traffic. But I didn't mind the noise. I owned my first home...in Los Angeles.

Chris had become so plagued by his paranoid delusions that often he would call me in the middle of the night with desperate cries for help. He would tell me that someone had stolen his belongings, and now he knew they were watching him from across the street…watching and watching. After I had calmed his fears, he would call back an hour later only to tell me that the thieves were now climbing through the air-conditioning vents and coming to get him. Whatever he had been exposed to years before in Southeast Asia had scarred him deeply. Or had he been tortured throughout his life by these living nightmares? The bomb was ticking louder…and faster.

It was then that my mother took to the bottle. She already believed I was covering for her, watching out for the state of the show as well as the family business, Corday Productions, and she was beat…totally exhausted. Her descent into drinking was rapid. She had never before been a drinker. But now, many were the Monday mornings that her beloved housekeeper, Carrie Mason, would call to tell me that she had found my mother passed out on the bathroom floor with an empty bottle of whiskey lying next to her. I would leave work in Burbank, race over to her home in Beverly Hills, and help Carrie pull her up off the floor and put her into bed.

My mother had become inconsolable. She was incapable of going to work at the office or the studio. She was gaining weight, and worst of all, she seemed to be giving in to her fear and guilt over my brother's incurable illness, as well as her own alcoholism and depression.

She had been a widow for a long time. She had loved only one man, and that man, my father, had been dead for more than eighteen years. She had had eighteen years without someone to hold her in the night and warm her bed. Eighteen years without a spouse's love or support. Eighteen years of loneliness. Eighteen years of grief over the loss of her husband, who, by all rights, should have been able to enjoy the fruits of his brilliant career, and now, she was living with a gnawing and growing grief over her oldest son's inability to get better. How could she be such a success, yet those things she held close and dear to her heart were so unreachable? My father was gone, my brother was going, and my mother couldn't enjoy life, even *Days of our Lives*, her pride and professional joy.

∞

Luckily for me, in 1983 my best "find" and my saving grace in her beautiful sisterhood entered my life: Shelley Curtis. I clearly remember the first time Shelley came to NBC to interview as a replacement for our coproducer, Lynne Osbourne. Shelley had on a very long raincoat, a red sweater, white shirt, and black slacks and was carrying a little pink umbrella. I walked with her through the rainy midway on the NBC lot and escorted her up to the third-floor executive offices to meet with NBC's daytime director, Lucy Johnson.

The interview was short, sweet, and extremely well timed. Shelley had worked for our toughest competitor, *General Hospital*, and had learned from brilliant executive producer Gloria Monty how to make the young stars of that show the focal point. Who can forget Luke and Laura's wedding? Shelley was the associate director who was instrumental in putting that special show together in the edit room at ABC.

She got the job in a heartbeat. She was now about to become a full-blown producer on *Days of our Lives*. NBC was as happy as I was, and the cast would soon be, and Shelley, teamed with Al Rabin, Pat Falken Smith, and Sheri Anderson, made for a formidable production team.

During the next few years, Shelley helped to make Bo and Hope, Patch and Kayla, and Shane and Kimberly the newly minted first super couples of *Days of our Lives*. She left the bulk of the supervising of production to Al Rabin. She left the business to me. She let the directors direct, but she really cared about the look of the show, which became much more stylized and "with it."

Most of all, she would work for hours with our young, new heroes and heroines to get the best performances possible. She coddled and babied and spent hours with them. She never settled for second best and spent many long days and nights in the studio with the cast to get the best take. And it was always worth the added time and expense.

Stephen Nichols (Patch), Mary Beth Evans (Kayla), Peter Reckell (Bo), and Kristian Alfonso (Hope) were her "pets," and she always made sure they left nothing on the floor. She made sure they gave everything they had, no matter how late we had to stay in the studio. Shelley Curtis made her mark and set the bar forever high for all the art directors, costume designers, and hair and makeup artists on the show for many years. She took the look of *Days of our Lives* from the '70s into the '90s in just a few years. She was as unique and individualistic as all the super couples she helped to become brilliant young daytime stars.

For all of my mother's deterioration and my brother's helpless and unstable mental state, *Days of our Lives* was thriving, much as any teenager approaching his or her prime would—and with the raging hormones to match. Thaao Penghlis, who played Count Tony DiMera, told me at the time that there were now so many "young studs" on *Days of our Lives*, the walls of the studio were dripping with testosterone.

Once my dear mother had phoned to tell me she had been called to an emergency meeting by the senior vice president of daytime programs at NBC. The year was 1976, shortly after *Days of our Lives* became a one-hour show. My mother and the producers were told that the show's ratings were sagging and that the network, especially the daytime programmer, thought she knew how to fix the problem immediately. The programmer demanded that they, NBC, wanted to see more *skin* on the show.

"Okay…We'll do it…that's easy," said my wise mother.

Two weeks later, when these newly enhanced shows began airing with massive amounts of exposed boobs, cleavage, and bikini bottoms in almost every scene, the phone rang again. This same network VP was so rattled by what she saw that another emergency meeting was called in her executive office. She went into a tirade, asking over and over why her wishes had not been addressed or even acknowledged.

My mother, Wes Kenny, and Jack Herzberg were astonished at this reaction and speechless. Hadn't they stripped almost every woman on the show of as much clothing as possible, with the exception of Alice Horton? What more did the network want…fully naked women? They were seeing lots of skin!

At this, Lynne Bolen, the NBC VP, stopped dead and looked at my mother and each producer with a look that could kill.

"No," she screamed, "not on the women…*on the men.*" Or rather off the men. She wanted to see each man who had any kind of good body with his shirt off and preferably in boxers or briefs. That's what she wanted, and that was what every woman watching *Days of our Lives* wanted.

After that the show moved forward ten years in the course of a few. The '80s became the time of the "beautiful people." Never before had society placed so much emphasis on the way we looked. People wanted to appear to be as perfect as possible.

Cigarette advertisements on television had been banned in 1971 by federal law, and the ad revenue void that law created was filled by the makers of new personal hygiene products. No longer was it acceptable for the man of the house to return home after a long day in the office reeking of cigarette breath and body odor. In television commercials, members of both sexes came home after a long day on the job smelling sweet and had breath that was always "minty fresh" to go with sparkling white teeth. Products were being created for odors that people didn't even know they had. Beauty was big business. Youth was the emphasis.

Prime time was filled with lusty shows, each in turn filled with amazingly beautiful people. Who knew that *Dallas*, *Dynasty*, and *Knots Landing* would become such huge hits? The formula was simple: copy soap operas, but at night!

With so many beautiful people on *Days of our Lives*, what else could they do but lust after one another? And lust they did. Kisses went from closed mouth to lots of lips and tongues. Then the camera would cut away to another scene in which two people were lying in bed, making out, one on top of the other, barely covered by a sheet, and always accompanied by sparse dialogue and lots of implied fooling around under those sheets. (And always to my music.)

We pushed the envelope on every show. Because of federal budget cuts, the networks had gotten rid of most of their employees in their standards and practices departments. The censors had been fired! Shows weren't allowed to use the seven forbidden words, but they could show as much sex and murder and mayhem after 9:00 p.m. as they wanted. *Days of our Lives* was no exception. Even at one in the afternoon. Of course, there was a limit, but every soap opera was pushing the envelope.

So now it was time for the men to show off their bodies. Nautilus equipment had been introduced. Men (and women) were changing their bodies in a big way for the better. Guys with six-pack abs, tight butts, and big pecs became the fashion.

So Bo or John or Roman would take off his shirt, and instead of swooning, his woman would touch him all over, all the while telling him how much she loved him and wanted to make love to him right there and then. The men showed skin whether they were in an empty pool hall or a hot shower, feeding their ladies strawberries and whipped cream, or riding together on a motorcycle.

"Go for it!" was the mantra. And we did. *Days of our Lives* became very steamy and hot and provocative and, of course, controversial in the '80s. But more than anything, the show became more passionately romantic than ever. What a time of change!

These were the glory years for *Days of our Lives*, chock-full of Soap

Opera Digest Awards, People's Choice Awards, and TV Guide Awards. Most rewarding of all, a new energy and life came to a twenty-year-old show that had reinvented itself—or more appropriately, its couples—and come up with an even hotter recipe for soap success.

∞

But I still needed a mentor who would be in the trenches every day. Thank goodness, Al Rabin, who was then supervising executive producer and had been running the production of the show since 1979, understood what my situation was and would become. He was with me in New York City when we both had our baptism under network fire, and he was there for me as a role model in the studio. He was solid as a rock for me and the cast and crew. *Days of our Lives* had recently been moved from the comfortable environs of Studio 9 on the NBC Burbank lot to the Sunset Gower Studios in Hollywood.

Gower Studios was converted from the old Columbia Pictures stages and offices of the 1950s. They had been sitting empty for more than a decade. Our studio at Gower was very large, a former recording stage for large orchestral scoring. It was also on the same lot where *General Hospital*, our fierce competitor at ABC, was taped. The studio was drafty, cold, and full of vermin and had none of the warm and homey security that we had felt at "mother" NBC Burbank. But it sure was large, much larger than Studio 9.

Gower had no commissary, and the parking was terrible. So in order to eat or just take a walk, one had to venture out into Hollywood. Gower Studios was three blocks east of the famous intersection of Sunset and Vine, and it was virtually impossible at that time to walk the streets, even for a quick sandwich, without being approached by a hooker, a drug dealer, a homeless person, or a pimp. And after dark… forget it. Hollywood was a magnet for crime central in the '80s. The LAPD Metro Division was getting a lot of screen time.

So in effect, *Days of our Lives* had been sent to Siberia. But Al and Shelley and a string of new head writers—a new one almost annually—kept the show running seamlessly in transition. All the while, Al Rabin stood by me and kept saying, "Ken…you're better than you think you are!" He was a coach and a rabbi, all in one. He was always sure of himself and sure of the outcome, which made me feel sure about myself. He taught me never to second guess myself.

He was more of a friend to me than he will ever know. Even his laugh, so honest and healthy, still rings in my ears. I'm reminded of him when I hear myself laugh in that same wonderful way.

Al was a very smart and cool cat. He put his signature on *Days of our Lives* in the early '80s when everyone was watching what we were doing. He produced some amazingly complex shows—full-blown rock concerts, weddings in Greece, and Civil War plantation reenactments filled with romance and allure. Adventures out-of-doors like never before. Whitewater rafting down the Kern River with John and Marlena. Using the sets on Universal's back-lot tour for Jack and Jennifer's wedding. And countless spy capers shot in the night, with fog and gunfire and all the trimmings of feature film productions, although we shot those scenes at some godforsaken off ramp at some small town truck stop or train station. Al was an important part of making *Days of our Lives* come of age. His contributions helped the show earn eight Daytime Emmy Award nominations for Outstanding Direction and Outstanding Drama Series.

Days of our Lives was born again and destined for a long run at NBC. My mother's influence waned, but two other strong women, head writer Pat Falken Smith and producer Shelley Curtis, had brought fertility and the age-old "rites of spring" to *Days of our Lives*. We had a new generation of beautiful people, and I was proud to be a part of it all, behind the camera and involved in everything.

But where were all the snakes, vampire bats, and rats that were supposed to have been waiting for me? They seemed to have been pushed aside, more by time and change and progress than by any act of mine. They had made a lasting impact on the show, but regardless, the show had moved on without them.

Days of our Lives was about to confront its next big challenge. A test that I had never really believed was coming, yet ultimately, one for which I was destined. It would be a time of joyful celebration and profound sorrow. A story of surviving and blossoming.

CHAPTER 17

THERE SHE GOES

I met my wife-to-be in 1984 at Columbia Television when we both won a quarter of the office pool for the Super Bowl. It took me three months to ask her out. After that it took about one minute to realize that not only was I smitten, but that this was the woman I was going to be lucky enough to marry.

Our wedding day arrived on May 3, 1986. Sherry Ann Williams was the most beautiful bride to grace a bright Beverly Hills morning as she drove up in her limousine. She looked like the cover of a bridal magazine. Absolutely stunning, a perfect image of bridal beauty. I pinched myself as I couldn't believe what a lucky guy I was to have won her heart.

We were married at 1:00 p.m. on the grounds of the famed Greystone Mansion overlooking Los Angeles. It was the best day of my life. She looked so absolutely radiant that I forgot all the words as I repeated my vows, but I didn't forget to kiss her.

Twenty of my good friends had given me a trophy at my bachelor party the night before. It was the size of a large statue. The inscription underneath the flexing Adonis read: "For the longest unmarried streak by a non-gay producer." I was no longer a bachelor at the age of thirty-five!

∽

My mother had made it to our wedding only with the help of a portable oxygen tank and the supportive arm of her dear friend, former *Days of our Lives* producer Jack Herzberg. The wonderful, bright, and deep intelligence she had once possessed had been struck down by a cluster of partially debilitating mini-strokes. She was also suffering from the rapid onset of emphysema caused by thirty years of smoking. So she was there, but not really there.

In her late years Betty began to read a new literary work every day, be it a lengthy novel or a terse real-life story. How painful it must have been for her to do this yet have no one to discuss it with…no one to share in her physical desperation nor in her final brilliant foray into places in literature that she had never ventured. It was as if she were trying to fill any gaps that had developed in her world of knowledge. So that when her time was up, she would have a more worldly understanding of life as recorded through the centuries, as well as seen through the looking glass.

She had suddenly and purposely stopped overeating and drinking alcohol at the age of seventy, without the help of anyone or any diet or any sort of twelve-step program. Whenever she was in pain, which she often was, she never complained. Why? What good would it do?

She was thankful and grateful for all of her talents and blessed accomplishments on *Days of our Lives*. She was also grateful that I had stepped in, much as she had twenty years before, to help keep the program running on the same family track.

"Keep it all in the family," she would say…and say again. "Protect the writers, producers, cast, and crew. Keep three square meals a day on everyone's table."

My mother was so resilient and courageous that when she was

hospitalized in September 1987, she asked that I be a witness to her final will and testament. She called all of her doctors into her hospital room one day, with me in attendance, and demanded that right then and there they write at the top of her hospital chart...in big, bold red letters..."D.N.R."...do not resuscitate. She wanted to go when her time came with no interference.

❦

Through her own sheer will and determination and with her indomitable courage and wonderful nature, my mother made it through her last year. She staggered often, but her mental stride was even. She knew what she had to do. She had to try to impart to me all that she had learned from my father. In the intervening twenty years she had never tried to assume his role of paternal mentor, but now she was not dismayed by this new challenge. She taught me much as Br'er Rabbit taught the fox.

Ol' Br'er Rabbit, as the fable goes, had been caught by Br'er Fox and Br'er Bear. While they argued between themselves about what his fate should be, Br'er Rabbit kept begging and pleading with them: "Please, don't throw me in the briar patch." Of course, after so much hysteria, he was thrown into the briar patch and, to his cunning delight, found himself home in a safe and comfortable place. No punishment: He just fooled them into thinking the wrong thing.

My mother had always approached me in the same manner, with reverse psychology. When I was growing up, and later in college, she would always profess that show business was the last place a guy like me or anyone else should end up having a career. It was no life. And I always subconsciously bought into it.

"She's right," I would say to myself. I should play piano and drums and teach music, write great songs and symphonies, and get my PhD in music.

But she knew better. She knew that if she never pushed me into it, I would come to it myself, of my own accord, playing my own song. And it worked. I had walked in backward through the front door of *Days of our Lives* and daytime television and said I was leaving. I was only there to visit. Not too long a stay. And not only did I think everyone believed me, but I had believed it, too.

But now I had finally come to own it. In 1986 my mother asked me to become co-executive producer, sharing her title, on the same day that I told her I was getting married. She and I both knew that the time had come, and I agreed.

To get all of her things in order, we had some planning to do. How would I take over Corday Productions? Who would control its stock? How would I learn the most important lessons in daytime television in such a short time? I had been working on *Days of our Lives* for only five or six years, and I was still "green." I had much to learn. And my mother didn't have much time.

She began my final tutorial less than a year before she died. Her lessons were simple, yet filled with subtext that belied her apparent Bostonian indifference to any platitude. I would learn by experience but most of all from just being in her presence. And she would give me an invaluable set of rules.

- Rule One: "Life is not a dress rehearsal." It may seem like a soap opera at times and it may seem boring at times, but never, ever leave anything "on the boards" when all is said and done. Give 'em your very best always, and don't cheat yourself out of anything, because you'll cheat the world as well.

- Rule Two: "Take care of your family…above all else…and take extra care of your brother." This lesson was the hardest—a stunning and challenging way she had of asking yet imparting wisdom at the same time.

"But most importantly, remember that only three things are worth a damn in making a great daytime drama":

- One: "Never forget, you're only as good as your last show." Don't wallow in last month's or last year's successes. They are long gone and forgotten.
- Two: "You've got to *love* the business you're in." Love making soap operas, more than 250 every year, year in and year out, and all they stand for. You've got to love and appreciate and understand the power of the genre.
- Three: "You've got to love the people you work with." For 260 days a year they are your friends and family, and if you support one another, you will succeed and endure for a long, long time.

I took her sage advice to heart. It has served me well.

∞

On the afternoon of November 17, 1987, Betty Corday died at Cedars-Sinai Hospital, the same hospital in which her husband, Ted Corday, had died twenty-one years earlier.

I had visited her in the ICU that morning, as I had every day during the week since she had been admitted to the hospital. She had been slowly slipping away. That afternoon, while I drove home over the Hollywood Hills to the Valley, I kept wanting to turn around and go back to Cedars. I got home, tried to call my brother, and then told my wife that I wanted to go back to the hospital. She got behind the wheel and said, "Let's go." My brother hadn't answered the phone.

We drove back to the hospital, arriving there by 5:00 p.m., and realized we had just a few moments left with my mother. I sat next to her bed and held her hand. She was coherent, but her breathing was so labored she couldn't speak. Yet her eyes were saying so much. She looked at me as only a mother does when leaving her child alone, even with a babysitter. She didn't want to go. She wasn't afraid; she just wanted another moment with me and my wife. We sat quietly for what seemed like forever. She couldn't speak, but I could tell she wanted an answer.

Instead of saying my usual, "You're going to be okay, Mom," I just said, "It's okay, Mom," so she would hear it from me and know I wanted her to let go—and go with God. She understood what I meant, and I understood her time was at hand.

The phone rang at the nurses' station. I was called out of her ICU in response to a call from her pulmonary specialist. The doctor also knew she was failing and asked me if he could try to make her time easier by putting her on a respirator. I stumbled for an answer. I knew what her wishes were, and yet I wanted to let the doctors do their best to make her comfortable. Then I looked up and noticed the ICU nurse standing at the glass door to my mother's cubicle.

She was gesturing to me, emphatically, to come right now. I put the phone down and sleepwalked back into my mother's cubicle for the last time. Again I sat next to her. She squeezed my hand once and gracefully crossed her legs, her final gesture of defiance. Her blood pressure began to drop rapidly, and when she drew her last breath, her eyes were closed and her face had a look of complete peace that made her seem half her age. Then she let go of my hand.

No one knows how special the moment of birth and the moment of death are unless they've been there and seen those moments for themselves. It was a great privilege to be there with my mother when that miraculous moment graced our lives.

The nurse and my wife and I stayed in that room for a long time after the resident in charge pronounced the time of death. There was calm and peace in that room. There was beauty and light in my mother's passing. She was with my father again. They were backstage in a place that holds all the energy of the past, waiting for the curtain to rise.

∞

Elizabeth Mary Carver Shay Corday was buried three days later, on the Friday following her death. The funeral was for immediate family only and with a closed casket. The eulogy was delivered by MacDonald Carey.

MacDonald Carey was not only Dr. Tom Horton on *Days of our Lives*, but he was also one of the highest-placed laymen in the parish of the Church of the Good Shepherd in Beverly Hills. This church had been the place of mass and holy obligation for my mother for twenty years. She was a faithful, yet somewhat removed parishioner. She was thrilled that President John F. Kennedy and his wife, Jacqueline, attended mass at Good Shepherd each time they had visited Los Angeles. It is a wonderful and blessedly sacred sanctuary. Never enough baptisms...always too many funerals...but some of the most notable Roman Catholics in the United States attend mass there with gratitude and appreciation of God's grace.

Mac's sermon was perfectly concise and extremely poetic, as only Mac could be. He loved my mother as a friend and fellow parishioner, but also as his employer and the wife of the man who had given him his best job.

The only other people in attendance were my wife and I; my brother; my mother's nurse, Pat Powell; her housekeeper, Carrie Mason; my Uncle Eliot and Aunt Marian; my cousins, Steven and Joann; and Joann's husband, Roger Kozburg.

After the mass started, my brother moved from the right side of the church, where we were all seated, and sat down on the left side, away from all of us. As a recently catechized Catholic, he knew every word of the mass and made each response in an overly loud voice, as if to let us "non-Catholics" know we were not on the inside of my mother's religion. I felt so sorry for him. Why was he separating himself from his family? Why was he so afraid? Why did he have so much anger?

The mass concluded. The funeral procession moved to the Los Angeles National Cemetery, where my mother would be laid to rest in the grave next to my father. It was a clear and very bright November day, in direct contrast to the day of her passing, when it had been dark until the skies had opened up with rain as day passed—and my mother had followed suit. This time there was no color guard, and no shots were fired. Only prayers.

My brother did not show up at the cemetery. I knew his pain and guilt were inexorable. The priest said the Our Father and the Glory Be over my mother's grave, and I wept for a long time on her casket before the time came to lower her to her resting place.

At this veterans cemetery, the second largest in the United States, my father and mother occupy the same hallowed ground...reserved for the heroes and the faithful and proud servants of the United States Armed Forces, all of whom were prepared to make the ultimate sacrifice for their country.

Their headstone reads as follows:

Theodore Corday

Captain U.S. Army

May 8, 1908   July 23, 1966

And

Elizabeth

His Wife

March 21, 1912   November 17, 1987

A Jew, a Catholic, and a legacy.

✼

On the night that my mother died, I had a very vivid dream. Too vivid and too real...but telling. It seemed to be happening long in the past, yet we were both looking our best. I felt like I was a child of nine or ten, even though I was seeing things through an adult's eyes.

My mother and I were walking down Madison Avenue near New York's Garment District. I had been there before with my mother, either to pick out new school blazers or to take a somewhat off-limits look at the furriers' outlets. She especially liked the mink coats. She had always dreamed of having the financial means to justify buying one, but no matter how much money she had later in life, my mother never felt she deserved one.

We were walking on the sunny side of Madison Avenue. We arrived at a large, nondescript building and entered. We walked through the marbled lobby, got on the elevator, and as the doors were about to close, a newsboy swiftly slipped in between them and deposited his large bundle of newspapers on the floor of the elevator.

I distinctly remember looking at the headline, but all I noticed was the day's date—November 17, 1987. It was that same day my mother, who was very much alive in my dream, had died. Not a word was said among us. The newsboy took his bundle and got off on a higher floor.

The doors closed, and my mother and I went to the top floor. It was the floor we visited whenever I had to get a new navy blazer and matching tie for Trinity School. But when the doors opened and we stepped outside, we were standing inside an interior stairwell, one that ascended in four sections of ten or so stairs at a time. We were still inside the building but deep within its back staircase, much the same as every large building in Manhattan has for safety and fire escape, or elevator failure. Only we had gotten off the elevator as if it had reached its limit, and now we were climbing these stairs, hand in hand, to floors above us that were unnumbered and unreachable by any other means. We climbed for what seemed like a long time, staircase after staircase, floor after uncharted floor.

Finally we reached the landing of the level just below the top floor. My mother spoke to me for the first and only time in the dream. She looked at me with great love in her eyes and said, "You have to stay here, and I have to go up there."

Then she let my hand go and climbed the remaining flight until she came to a door that I hadn't noticed before. She looked down at me, and just as she reached to open the door, I woke up with a start.

It's obvious that in this dream she was telling me that she was going up to heaven and that I still had to wait. But how symbolic the dream was! The back staircases of New York City buildings are filled with shadows and smells and spirits, yet through these strange yet familiar surroundings my farewell journey with my mother took place. The reality of it all...this recognizable part of Manhattan...the newsboy... the elevator...the stairs to the unknown floors...made it seem far more than a dream. It was palpably real. It was my mother's way of showing me that she had moved on to a better place and that I needed to let her go.

Three days later, on the day my mother was buried, I dreamt once again—and for the last time—of my mother. Only this time she was with me and my father. We were walking along the boardwalk in Atlantic City. Each of them was holding one of my hands. As they walked with me between them, joined by our hands, they were looking not at me, but straight ahead. They had a beautiful glow of happiness in their faces, but I could only see their profiles. They either couldn't or wouldn't look at me. Then suddenly they both let go of my hands at the same time. I stopped and stood transfixed by what I saw next.

As gently as they had let go of my hands, they reached at the same time for each other's hand and, after joining hands, continued to stroll down the boardwalk, leaving me behind.

Then I awoke.

I knew they were finally together again...after such a long time...in a place that I knew had been one of their favorite East Coast romantic getaways. And off they went. Together. Forever.

CHAPTER 18

THE HOURGLASS LADIES

*D*ays of our Lives has had many equally impressive heroes, and as most admirers of the show know, women always swoon at these sympathetic leading men. However, their feats of daring could never have been accomplished without the support and love and advice of the women in their lives, whether mothers or wives. Where would they be without their women?

So it is to these women, our wonderful female characters and "heroines," that this chapter is devoted. They were, are, and always will be the most important characters on *Days of our Lives*, because soap operas are a women's entertainment medium for the most part. Our heroines stand for all things wise and wonderful in Salem and in life, and their actions empower our female viewership.

Add up the number of years that their characters have been and still are on the air, and that total exceeds 250 years, a number that is still growing. Our heroines have survived because they are so beautiful, so intelligent, and so honest, both as characters and as actors…real ladies who live real lives.

The progress of stories about "love conquering all adversity" can easily be traced through the lives of these nine ladies…the Hourglass Ladies…named not only for their beautiful figures but also for their figurative beauty. They are all daytime goddesses.

∾

First and foremost of all the great Hourglass Ladies of *Days of our Lives* will always be the late Frances Reid, who portrayed Alice Horton. Regretfully, Frances passed away at the age of ninety-five. That was a very sad day, not only for me personally, but for the extended *Days of our Lives* family and the entire Hollywood community. From day one until she taped her last scene, Frances epitomized the past, present, and future of the show. She was truly one of a kind. Her class cannot be matched, and her shoes cannot be filled…she will be missed for all the rest of our days. Alice was the eternal matriarch of the show, having been on the air since the first episode, more than forty-four years ago. Alice *always* told the truth and *always* knew best.

She was the very first leading lady of *Days of our Lives* and yet seemed to be more than that. She constantly had the drop on her loving husband, Tom, played by MacDonald Carey. Yet she played all of her cards with a poker face that hid the secret beneath Frances Reid's beauty. She was and will always be our shining example of love, beauty, and talent combined. She is the diamond in the crown of *Days of our Lives*. She was like a second mother to all of us.

Frances's mind was like a steel trap, and she spoke like a soft cat-o'-nine-tails. My mother told me that way back in the early '70s Frances held a bridal shower at her backyard pool for one of our actresses, Brooke Bundy, who played Rebecca. Many of the ladies in the cast attended, and being in the early '70s, the advent of breast surgery and enhancement through silicone implants was in full display.

Many of the actresses had recently been "enhanced," and as the all-woman party at Frances's home grew more relaxed (aided by the effects of champagne), these lovely ladies started disrobing and showing off their new breasts. The idea seemed to catch on until all but my mother and dear Frances were topless or in the swimming pool, or both.

Both Frances and my mother were at or near their sixties at the time. Frances looked calmly at my mother and said that she wouldn't unless my mother did…Of course, neither of them did. They just watched and howled at all the happy young ladies and then enjoyed their champagne and afternoon in the sun.

As an actress, Frances portrayed Alice Horton in such a frankly heartwarming way that no one could help but love her and trust her. She was everyone's "talk to," on camera and off. Because Frances was so genuinely talented, with years of experience in lead roles on Broadway and in prime time before *Days of our Lives*, Frances Reid made Alice Horton sing with vibrancy, even in her nineties. She also gave her character that great and subtle quality of seeming to know everything that was going on in Salem or with any of her family or friends without ever being told. And she could always be trusted with the knowledge. Her advice to her fellow cast mates was simple, very simple: "Be on time and know your lines."

We will go on without Frances, much as we have done without MacDonald Carey, but her passing leaves an unfillable hole in the fabric of the show and in my heart. Superlative is the adjective that always best defined Frances as a person, an actress, and the matriarch of the Horton family and *Days of our Lives*. Tom and Alice's favorite song, "Always," speaks of the endurance of their love and that love conquers all.

∞

Next among our great Hourglass Ladies is Susan Seaforth Hayes, who plays the character of Julie Williams. She is married in real life to Bill Hayes, who plays Doug Williams. Julie was the first spitfire in Salem, a young, beautiful woman who had a serious attitude problem and was a true vixen. However, over time, both Julie and Susan have matured. They are now wonderful bright lights on and off camera. Yet they are still as entrancing as ever.

I have worked with "Susie" for more than thirty years, and I still have a bit of a crush on her, because she is so damn smart and outspoken, with her giant IQ, yet so vulnerable and totally open to others. Any conversation with Susan keeps you on your toes and either gives you a good feeling when it's over or makes you want to read the book or paper she's been reading to catch up. Despite her many levels of smarts, she is never condescending. You always want to hug Susan after talking with her.

For me, Susan is like having a sister who is just a bit older but far wiser, down deep, than I will ever be. To the viewers, she is a zesty beacon of strength who can always be trusted and counted on, even if she does some things in the somewhat caustic and often volatile way that only Julie can. There's only one "La Hayes," and we wouldn't and couldn't have it any other way.

When Susan was very early on in her run on *Days of our Lives*, her character, Julie, and Doug Williams (Bill Hayes) were falling in love. Their first kiss on camera started innocently, then Bill stood up and put on a phonograph record, their favorite song, "The Most Beautiful Girl in the World." They danced and went into a hot and heavy kiss, at which time the phonograph stopped working. In those days, there was no editing, and the scene had to be started over. The phonograph didn't work until the tenth take, but it certainly didn't seem to bother either Bill or Susan. It was the first time we or either actor knew of their mutual attraction.

Susan is beautiful yet volatile and should not be treated with anything but kid gloves. She is bright, shiny, smart, and voluptuously sharp! Razor sharp. Susan was on the cover of *Time* magazine, eyes pouring tears, cleavage popping out, and as alluring as Ava Gardner or Marilyn Monroe. But be careful if you are another character playing in the same scene as Susan. If you don't know your lines, hit your "marks," and rise to her level, you will definitely get an earful. Even if it's a few caustic comments or false praise before the next take.

Her looks are trumped only by her biting ability to take any scene and charge it with an energy born of brains and lots of time spent in front of the camera. She is an original, and that's because Susan is unique in her ability to be alluring, speak the best Queen's English, and bat the biggest eyelashes, all as she clips out the dialogue in any scene with jest, panache, and the strength that comes from the security that only years of great acting can bring. Susan Seaforth Hayes was our first superstar actress and still to this day shines as the emerald in our crown. And she is still "the most beautiful girl in the world" to her husband, Bill Hayes.

∞

Suzanne Rogers is another leading lady and veteran of thirty-plus years on the show. Suzanne is one of only four actresses from *Days of our Lives* to ever win an Emmy Award. She always embodied the sweetness and ravaging redheaded beauty that is as much a part of her character as it is that of the actress. Suzanne is a white light, and, as such, Maggie Horton has shined for more than thirty-five years with a brilliant luster that lights up all of her scenes and all of those she touches as a person.

She is our angel and the one I go to in times of need or struggle, because I know she will always impart wonderful advice. She comforts me and becomes even more of an example of what the "perfect sister" would have been like. If I were ever to have been blessed with one, I would have wanted her to be just like Suzanne Rogers.

As an actor, she is not only very good, but I can also say I have never heard her deliver a line that is not honest or spot-on. She gives herself and a lot of her life to *Days of our Lives*. We are all blessed to have her in the studio, always smiling, always tranquil, even though I know she can have an Irish temper like mine. She is also the perfect practicing Roman Catholic. Faithful to priest, parish, and parishioner.

But most of all, Suzanne understands what each of her friends possesses as his or her own special gift, and she can feed each of us her love in her own special way. She knows many of my deep, dark secrets, and I know they will always be safe in her heart, just as they would be in Maggie's safekeeping. Suzanne has also heroically dealt with, offscreen and now on-screen, the rare muscle disease, myasthenia gravis, diagnosed in 1984.

From her very early days as a Rockette at Radio City Music Hall in Manhattan to her *Days* as Maggie Simmons, a cripple with the red dancing shoes, to today as a restaurateur and class act, she has always been one of the very best of all of 'em. As an actress, she is the sweetest and also the softest of all, because that's who Suzanne Rogers is. Everybody loves Maggie, our perennial rose, ever blooming, ever bright and sweet smelling, and ever ready to add beauty and serenity to any place or anyone's heart that she inhabits. I will love her forever. She is our red, red ruby! She burns even brighter now as a widow, having lost her on-screen husband, Mickey, in 2010, after a wonderful long marriage. Today finds her character standing smack dab in the middle of many of our stories. She has inherited Alice's place as *Days'* matriarch Horton.

∞

Peggy McCay has played Caroline Brady since the early '80s when head writers Margaret DePriest, Pat Falken Smith, and Sheri Anderson established her as the matriarch of Salem's "other" family, the blue-collar, salt-of-the-earth Bradys. Her character is widow to Shawn; mother of Roman, Bo, Kimberly, and Kayla; and grandmother to Sami, Eric, Shawn D., Zack, Chelsea, and Will, and many more.

Peggy is a hoot as a person. She clearly belies her many years in a distinguished career in television by making Caroline Brady so fresh and so very much her own character, unlike any other woman on the show. Peggy, like Caroline, is always there at every turn, giving herself and her love to all of her *Days* children and friends behind the camera as well. She was and is our very best cheerleader, and she cares for and respects the show far more for what it has given her than what she gives to it.

She has always been fashionable and chic, even when the producers gave her notes asking her to keep the character more of a fishwife than a fashion plate. She always brings snap to any scene she graces. She is just *so* enthusiastic, and all the actors and crew love her. Her enthusiasm makes the Brady Pub center court in Salem.

But she isn't just a "talk to," as we say. She is not a sounding board for our main characters. She *is* a main character, with her own strong point of view. She loves being in a good story, and whether with Victor, Bo, Roman, or her grandchildren, when she is given the ball in any scene or story, she always gets the first down and sometimes the touchdown.

Ironically, she was the only person outside of our immediate family and MacDonald Carey to attend my mother's funeral at Good Shepherd Church in Beverly Hills. She was an altar woman at the church, but she was there, quietly, unbeknown to us, because she cared about my mother and has always been there for me and my children, just as Caroline Brady would have been for anyone grieving in Salem.

Peggy is a wonderful actress and everyone's idea of the perfect mother. We are blessed to have her among our magnificent nine Hourglass Ladies. My kids also adore her…and she remembers them at every holiday with lots of wonderful homespun gifts. Thank you, Peggy, for giving so much to us all. We are all the better for it. She is our den mother, and our beautiful white pearl.

∾

Kristian Alfonso was brought to my attention in 1982 by Brian Frons, the director of daytime at NBC. He told me about a fantastically beautiful girl who was a successful model with the Wilhelmina Agency and had graced the cover of thirty international magazines, including *Vogue* and *Harper's Bazaar*, by the age of fifteen. Though she was then a cover girl, NBC had high hopes we could bring her on the show and recast the character of Hope Williams many years after her childhood. It was time for a new generation of Hortons.

Kristian was then, and still is, a totally ravishing woman, classically beautiful in a Greco-Roman way. Athena and Juno would have been jealous of Kristian's perfect face. The camera literally cannot take a bad shot of that face, that "fancy face" as Bo so lovingly calls her. She has launched many big stories on *Days of our Lives* over the past thirty years, and Kristian and Hope grow more beautiful with every new day of our lives.

She has come such a long way from her initial innocence. Who can forget her riding away from her botched wedding to Larry Welch on the back of Bo's motorcycle in the '80s? And still she was just twenty years old at that time.

Kristian is breathtakingly beautiful, but what comes across even more is her inner beauty and warmth, whether on camera or live in person. A better face a show could never have; a better spokesperson for all modern women and mothers you will never find.

Her parents brought her up well in a Roman Catholic, Bostonian lifestyle, and their lessons are still the foundation for her wonderful life and career. She is a devoted wife and a mother to three sons and has a husband who matches her beauty with a similar strikingly handsome presence and style of character. What a gorgeous family they are!

Kristian was always the show's "baby" grown up so well, embodying the wisdom and grace of her "Gran," Alice Horton. But she was also the first in the hot, new generation that came to Salem in the '80s. She and her star-crossed love interest, Bo, would light up *Days of our Lives* and become as phenomenally popular as any couple before or after.

She and her sweetheart of a costar, Peter Reckell, went through some tumultuous times when their characters and real lives were becoming adults. But they aged timelessly. Both Kristian and Hope were always smarter than anyone and would only get in trouble when sacrificing themselves for the men they loved. Kristian and her character of Hope are the purely sympathetic, root-for, leading ladies. That's been true from the time Kristian was just an ingénue through *so many* difficult stories to today, where her stature, as well as Hope's, is a shining example to all women of how to live a good and happy life.

My hat's off to her, and she will always have my heart. She is a very fine and funny woman and a blessing for *Days of our Lives*. She is, without a doubt, our shining sapphire, the one we can always depend on to handle the big story.

∞

Then there is Mary Beth Evans, who plays Caroline Brady's beautiful, Irish-eyed daughter Kayla. Mary Beth is a Southern California–born beauty, a real surfer girl now married to a well-known plastic surgeon. And she has three beautiful children, who are now young adults.

Kayla also never seems to age. She still is young looking and vibrant. And she is always busy trying to keep her man, Patch, out of trouble. She recently returned to *Days of our Lives* after a long absence, much to everyone's glee, and it seemed as if not a day had gone by since she left. She is still beautiful, still completely Kayla, and still a lot of guys' secret crush.

When she returned, Mary Beth didn't particularly want to see flashbacks of her and Stephen Nichols/Patch from times long gone. When she forced herself to look, she realized how good the character was then and how good she could make her again. And Kayla is *always* good—as good as her golden hair and heart.

Mary Beth once told me she was embarrassed in high school by her very full lips.

"Why?" I asked.

She told me her classmates used to make fun of her and call her "rubber lips." Well, today those lips have been the center of attention in many close-ups and kisses with Patch!

Mary Beth is a timeless beauty and always makes time beautiful for all of us at *Days of our Lives*. She's so sweet and so smart. Everyone loves M. B. She is our pretty pink sapphire! As an actress, when she cries, we cry. When she laughs, we laugh. And when she's passionate about something or ticked off...look out! Mary Beth is truly believable, both on and off camera. She is the perfect girl next door, with an old soul yet so young, a testimonial to the actress's ability to involve us, the viewers, in anything and all things that she does.

∽

Then making her usual breathtaking entrance is Deidre Hall, our daytime icon. Deidre, or Dee, as we know her, was the most important part of our first super couple, first with Roman Brady and later with John Black. Marlena Evans Black is one of the most recognizable characters and faces in all of daytime television.

Dee is a powerhouse, both as an actor and as a person. She is the mother hen as much as she is the mother hawk...able to function in a nurturing and yet predatory way, if need be. Deidre was born on Halloween and is always good for a treat. Just don't cross her, because she can play a mean trick as well.

Dee set the bar for all of the daytime divas to follow and deserves far more recognition and appreciation from her peers in the Daytime Television Academy. Yet she doesn't give a hoot about Emmys or what

Issac and Leah Cohen (late 1800s)

Ted Corday, University of Alberta (circa 1930)

Captain Ted and Betty
Corday, VE Day, 1945,
New York City

Betty Corday (circa 1930)

Ted Corday (second from right) directing *Gangbusters*, NBC Radio, 1946

Ted Corday (first from left) directing *The Guiding Light* radio program, 1951

Ted Corday (first
from left), Director,
The Guiding Light
production moment,
CBS Television, 1952

MacDonald Carey and Frances Reid, *Days of our Lives*
Episode #1, November 1965

Betty Corday and Cast, *Days of our Lives* first anniversary, November 8, 1966

John Clarke, Betty Corday, and Ed Mallory (top row from left to right); Suzanne Rogers, MacDonald Carey, Frances Reid, and Susan Flannery (bottom row from left to right), 1968

Ken Corday's graduation from San Jose State University, with Betty Corday (mother) and Christopher Corday (brother), 1977

Betty Corday holding the Soap Opera Digest Award for Favorite Soap Opera for *Days of our Lives*, 1979

Ken Corday
and John
Clarke (Mickey
Horton), 1977

Ken Corday, Producer Shelley Curtis, and Supervising
Producer Al Rabin, 1982

Ken Corday and his wife, Sherry, on their wedding day, May 3, 1986

Ken Corday and Frances Reid accepting his parents' Lifetime Achievement Award at the Daytime Emmy Awards, 1988

Ken Corday, Cast, and Crew celebrating Episode #8,000, 1997

Ken Corday with Lee and Bill Bell, 2002

Ken Corday and Cast backstage at the People's Choice Awards with Julia Roberts, 2002

Sheraton Kalouria (NBC), Ken Corday, and Jeff Zucker (NBC) (middle, from left to right) with the Cast, 2003

Ken Corday and
Suzanne Rogers, 2003

Ken Corday and Cast, People's Choice Awards, 2003

Ken Corday and Cast celebrating Episode #10,000, February 14, 2005

Ken Corday and Cast celebrating *Days of our Lives* fortieth anniversary, 2005

Alison Sweeney,
Ken Corday, and
Kristian Alfonso
(left to right), 2006

Ken Corday and Cast toasting *Days of our Lives* fortieth anniversary in front of NBC, 2005

Ken Corday (first row, middle), Cast, and NBC's Marc Graboff (first row, first from right), Ben Silverman (back row, middle), and Bruce Evans (first from left) celebrating Episode #11,000, 2009

Ken Corday (first row, middle), Cast, and Sony's Steve Mosko (first row, left of Ken Corday), celebrating thirteen Emmy nominations, 2009

everyone thinks of her. "That's their business," as she so aptly and often reminds us.

Deidre Hall cares about Marlena's story and her own two beautiful sons more than anything else in life. Dee has worked with wonderful leading men: Jed Allan (Don Craig), Wayne Northrop (the first Roman Brady), Drake Hogestyn (John Black), and Josh Taylor (the second Roman Brady). Deidre has brought out their best. She has helped them realize their full potential as actors and as daytime stars. She is a gifted actress who loves to sink her teeth into any great story line for Marlena, and she never leaves anything in the dressing room when she pours herself into her work onstage.

Deidre is fiercely protective of her character, her sons, and her close friends. Her twin sister, Andrea, who has been on *Days of our Lives* for short stints as both Samantha and the kooky Hattie, learned much about acting and life from Deidre. Andrea stayed home with her family in Florida and taught challenged children while Deidre jumped into the chaos of making a name for herself as a successful actress in Los Angeles.

Deidre has always placed love of her family and her zest for living a great life before her career. Yet few viewers would know that, judging by how perfectly consistent and joyously stable her portrayal of Marlena has been for more than thirty years. The fans are absolutely nuts about her, and, amazingly, she never seems to age.

Whether stalking people as a homicidal, hypnotized mass murderer or playing a demonic psychiatrist possessed by the devil, Deidre has always found a way to get under what the script calls for, find subtext closer to the truly heroic character she is, and always deliver the huge knockout punch that sends the character, and any story she is centered in, out of the ballpark. Marlena is, as one head writer nicknamed her, the "Goddess of Wisdom, Beauty, and Light." Deidre deserves the best because she is the best, our Katherine

Hepburn and Grace Kelly rolled into one. She is our yellow, and priceless, diamond.

✎

Renee Jones, who portrays beautiful Lexie Carver, chief of staff at University Hospital, is our next Hourglass Lady. Renee first came to the show in 1982 as Nikki Wade, a secretary at the Salem Police Department who was a spoiled rich girl. Her run on the show as Nikki was short-lived.

But to our infinite good fortune, Renee returned to *Days of our Lives* in 1993 as Lexie Carver, the wife of her former boss, Abe Carver. Lexie had the difficult struggle of overcoming her past, after finding out she was born out of wedlock to her gypsy psychic mother, Celeste, and her father, the evil Stefano DiMera. For the past seventeen years, she has been fighting the dark urges that accompany her DiMera blood and DNA.

At times she has failed and fallen from grace as one of our heroines, but in the end she has found love, honesty, and self-respect on her own and through her marriage to detective, police chief, commander, and now mayor Abe Carver. Lexie has pulled herself away from the dark side and now only works for good and just causes, as a wonderful doctor and good friend to Salem's most in need. The redemptive power of Abe's love helped her overcome her adultery, plotting, and general malevolence to reach her rightful place in the crown of *Days of our Lives* heroines.

Even though I've known Renee personally and professionally for almost seventeen years, I wish I knew her even better. Renee is quiet, extremely gentle, and reserved in a respectful yet alluring way. She and I have occasional quiet chats at the coffee machine or the water cooler, but still waters run deep.

Like her costar James Reynolds, she is a classy person with great humility. I know she has endured difficult physical challenges, yet they seem not to have affected her resilient beauty in any way. Her skin is just as soft and unlined as the day she first stepped onstage. I often kid her that she must have a portrait of herself in her attic (as the literary character Dorian Gray did), and that portrait must grow older every day, because Renee always retains her youthful look and never seems to age. She is kind to all of us and, as an actress, relishes any good story for Lexie.

Recently, head writer Dena Higley created an important story reflecting Dena's own experience dealing with an autistic son. She gave the story to Lexie and Abe, who discovered their son, Theo, to be autistic and had to come to grips with and accept their son's huge learning challenge. Renee delivered dramatically big-time as a mother who had to first deal with her husband's denial and then get through her own stages of guilt, remorse, and panic in finding ways to help Theo make himself a better place in life. Renee did her homework, researched all she could about autism, and not only convincingly portrayed Lexie but also gave of herself to Autism Speaks, a national autism society.

Her career exemplifies her talent and beauty. Renee was the first African American model to appear on the cover of *Teen* magazine. Her film and television credits are many: *Star Trek, In the Heat of the Night, 21 Jump Street, Highway to Heaven, Santa Barbara, Hardcastle and McCormick, Trapper John M.D.*, and as Diane Moses on *L.A. Law*. She was also on *The Jeffersons, Diff'rent Strokes, WKRP in Cincinnati, Night Court*, and in *Friday the 13th, Part VI*.

But her long, enduring run on *Days of our Lives* is what makes her stand out. She is a wonderful example to the rest of our cast as an actor and a person with great soul and gentility. I always look forward to her bright smile and gentle hug every time our paths cross in the studio. Our occasional one-on-one, face-to-face, sit-down discussions in my office have always been serious and accomplished great things for me, Renee, Lexie, and *Days of our Lives*.

There are only two kinds of actors, according to my mother. The first kind is like a lightbulb that exudes energy and brightens any scene in which he or she is placed. The other kind is like a vacuum cleaner that sucks the energy and light from the scene he or she is in. Renee is the first kind, a one-hundred-watt bulb.

Renee Jones is one of the nine brightest lights that are our Hourglass Ladies. In her shy, reserved way, she knows this to be true and is proud of it and her ability to light up Salem. She would find her rightful place in the crown of all these heroines as an alexandrite, a rarest gem that also contains her name, Alexandra.

∞

Finally, there's Samantha "Sami" Brady, a character portrayed with glorious conviction and tenacious ownership by Alison Sweeney. Sami has grown into a powerhouse of a woman before our eyes. She often transcends emotion and logic. She has stepped on her own toes, gotten in her own way, and often has done the wrong thing, especially in her fifteen-year love-hate relationship with Lucas (Bryan Dattilo).

Sami has always been her own worst enemy. Yet, what better way to learn to do the right thing than to live with your mistakes, some of which haunt Sami to this day. Over time, we have come to understand Sami and have watched her grow and mature as a woman and a mother to become who she is today, a heroine.

Sami has been involved in some important story lines and issues. Alison Sweeney received a lot of mail from girls who have suffered their own weight issues. She has published books about her days on *Days of our Lives* and her own personal struggles and successes. After a long journey dealing with this problem, Alison has overcome it. She is in fantastically healthy shape and, what's more, has become the host of NBC's *The Biggest Loser*. Alison is a powerhouse, and that's what makes Sami run.

Sami has run an amazing race on *Days of our Lives* since her debut in 1993. Alison was only sixteen at that time, and she threw herself into her work. Her character was a very troubled teenager. Troubled enough to be the victim of date rape and then shoot her rapist in his private parts! Troubled enough to go to any lengths to break up her sister, Carrie, and her beau, Austin Reed, with whom Sami was obsessed for many years.

Very early on, Sami even kidnapped Marlena and John's baby, Belle, because she hated her stepfather, John Black. Belle was returned unharmed on Christmas Eve, but Sami still has taken years to get past herself and her angst over anything that doesn't go her way. The list of her bad behavior went on and on.

Sami has lied, stolen, cheated, and been a complete bitch in *Days* gone by. But to her credit and that of the writers, Alison Sweeney was always convinced that Sami would grow up someday. She always emphasized this when she and I would discuss her character's future...and I agreed. Sami has just taken a long time to change. And in that slow transfiguration from poisonous caterpillar to incandescent butterfly, she has earned our trust and admiration.

Like any great Brady woman, Sami now has the sacrificing care for her family that we all strive for. She is a lioness still but also a good den mother to her four children (Will, Johnny, Allie, and Sydney) and loving mate to the man in her life, Rafe Hernandez (or is it really E. J. DiMera?).

However, when she gets going, when she loses her temper and her cool, and her face flushes and she growls in defiance, she is still our hotheaded, Irish beauty with the heart of gold and a mean left hook. Just ask E. J. or countless others of her male admirers. When Sami loves you, it's not mercurial; it's undying. When she doesn't like you, it's not just bad; it's horrible but justified. Like her grandmother, Caroline; her mother, Marlena; her father, Roman; and her aunts and uncle, Kayla, Kimberly, and Bo; Sami is a Brady through and through, and the Bradys *are* the heroes and heroines of *Days of our Lives*.

Alison is as driven in real life as Sami is in Salem life. She married the man of her dreams, with whom she fell in love at twenty, and now they live happily together with their little son and daughter. Alison is an all-American mom. She is patriotic and in touch with what today's woman wants, needs, and stands up for.

Alison is well on her way to a long career in television, both on *Days of our Lives* and in doing other projects, whether NBC's reality shows or new concepts of her own. Alison is driven, but anyone who really knows her knows she puts her family above all else. How does she find the energy and stamina to do two separate shows and always bring such peerless and powerful intensity to Sami's performances? The answer can only be that she is one of the Hourglass Ladies: a character, a woman, and a heroine for the ages.

If she were a jewel in the crown of these nine leading ladies, Alison would be a pink diamond. Hot, bright, shiny, and colorfully rare, filled with clarity, quality, and cut from the Brady mold.

$$\infty$$

So there they are…the magnificent nine, the Hourglass Ladies.

If *Days of our Lives* were to wear this bejeweled crown for real, Frances Reid (Alice) would be the diamond. Susan Hayes (Julie) would be the emerald; Suzanne Rogers (Maggie), the ruby; and Peggy McCay (Caroline), the pearl. Kristian Alfonso (Hope) would be the sapphire; Mary Beth Evans (Kayla), the pink sapphire; Deidre Hall (Marlena), the yellow diamond; and Renee Jones (Lexie Carver), the alexandrite. And Alison Sweeney (Sami Brady) would be the pink diamond. What a perfect crown for our show! And beyond value…priceless.

We are blessed to have been the recipients of these wonderful women's talents and love for the show. May they live on in daytime for many, many more of the days of our lives. For without their role models, none of our lady viewers would look forward to seeing what happens next…how the redemptive power of their love sets the Hourglass Ladies apart and is so alluring to all, especially their men, and most of all, our viewers.

CHAPTER 19

THERE HE GOES

Almost three years from the date of my mother's death, *Days of our Lives* reached its twenty-fifth anniversary on November 8, 1990. "The Big Silver" was a spectacular milestone for the show, even though it was sad that Betty Corday didn't get to be there. She must have known when she died that *Days of our Lives* would achieve this anniversary.

Brandon Tartikoff, NBC president, visionary, and friend, spoke at the anniversary party for *Days of our Lives* at the Beverly Hilton. He was very complimentary and said that any show associated with the number 25 was unique at NBC, in that few of the network programs at the time were achieving a 25 percent share in audience ratings, let alone twenty-five years on the air. *Days of our Lives* had done it…and done it with class! My father and mother's baby had grown into a fabulously talented and successful young and vibrant adult, and NBC was ecstatic…and exceedingly good to us.

But as November passed into December that year, things did not fare well for my brother, Chris.

∞

Chris was now forty-two years old and had recently developed adult-onset epilepsy. Even though he saw his therapist (meaning prescribing psychiatrist) three days a week, life for him was deteriorating at a very rapid pace. His fuse was very close to its end.

In early December, while getting into his car after a doctor's visit, Chris had a seizure. I did not find out until many days later. Thank the Lord he was not behind the wheel of his car at the time. Following this epileptic episode, Chris was taken back to his doctor's office. He realized where he was and his need for more of his preventive medicine, Librium, which was administered immediately. He was excused by said nameless physician and sent home, again driving his car!

Meanwhile, Chris had become enamored with the Los Angeles Police Department. He was spending a few hours a week doing volunteer work whenever he could at menial chores at the police academy or the LAPD Metro Division. Cleaning, mailing, easy stuff. Except that for Chris there was something else to this charity—an agenda.

By age forty-two he had collected forty-three handguns. He had in his possession one gun for each of his years…plus one. He had slowly and carefully accumulated them over the previous three years, using any savings he could muster from his trust fund.

Why would anyone want to have that many firearms? He was neither a gun nut nor a collector of authentic pieces. He never, ever used the guns. He never went to the shooting range to practice. Why such an attachment for the first time ever, and by a convicted drug felon, to the police department and to so many dangerous weapons?

Why? Because the authorities could teach him. He could study cases or, at best, learn vicariously about the heinous acts of violence perpetrated in the streets and in the homes of Los Angeles by its residents—on themselves, as well as their victims. How he slipped under police radar, even as a volunteer, has always astounded me.

I'll never know what his plans were. Who knows what psychotics are truly thinking? They don't just dream of castles in the sky; they build them in their minds and then move in. But I was deeply concerned. Too many deadly weapons and ammunition in one place, in one seriously ill man's hands.

***

When December arrived in 1990, two startling and telling events took place. Chris called me, and for the first time since my daughter had been born in September 1988, he acknowledged that she existed and that he was, in fact, her uncle. Until this time he had denied her existence, her birth, her name, her age, and her sex, as if she had never been born. He couldn't deal with having a niece or having his only brother and remaining family member dedicated to a daughter, as well as a wife. So I was startled when he called and told me he wanted to see his niece.

One afternoon he stopped by to see her, bringing her a sweet, blue swing in the shape of a horse. He and I set it up in the big tree in our backyard, and my wife and I watched as our two-year-old played and swung. We also watched Chris as he enjoyed the moment. We had no feeling of any threat or fear, either for her or for ourselves.

Then he quietly took me aside and asked for a few words in private. I still can see it today, those next few moments, frame by frame. We went into the living room and sat down face-to-face. After a very long silence, I thanked him for being there for the first time for his niece. She apparently was taken with him, as most people had always been…at first.

He smiled, and in that smile he seemed to recognize her beauty and brightness, as well as her being the first of the next generation of our family. But his mind was elsewhere.

I gently asked him how he was doing, and he said he wasn't doing well. I asked him if things were getting worse, and he said yes.

I asked him if I could do anything to help, and he paused. He looked at me as if all the years of prolonged psychological trauma had never been there, standing between him and me and our family.

"Little brother, I'm stuck in a whirlpool," he stated clearly. I asked if anyone could do anything to help him or save him, and he just looked through me and said, "You have no idea how deep it is." In hindsight I realized he was telling me that he had given up and completely run out of hope.

I fumbled out some lame, patronizing answer like, "It's going to get better. Read the *Daily Word* I send you every morning…ask the Lord for help and forgiveness…try to get some exercise…and talk with your doctors." But I knew helping him was way beyond my capabilities or theirs. No one had ever been able to really help him with this illness. Helping him seemed way beyond all of medical science's capabilities. Helping him seemed impossible, because he had finally had as much of the mental torture as he could bear and was giving up. He didn't need to say it that way either. His eyes told me he had reached his end.

In mid-December, a few days after his visit, I received a call from his roommates, a lovely Israeli couple with whom he boarded. Surprisingly, they told me he had sold *all* of his gun collection, as everyone had been urging him. He was going to use the money to buy himself some new clothes and some Christmas presents for the few people he knew. They were thrilled with his turnaround and told me he was looking forward to visiting his niece again. Despite my having some reservations, this news was encouraging.

∞

A few days after I heard this good news, though, Chris called me. It was late on a weeknight during the height of the Christmas season. He was very agitated, and the conversation was brief.

"I need to borrow some money…now. One thousand dollars."

I knew he had a healthy allowance from my mother's trust and that all of his bills were paid by her trustees. I also knew that the money he wanted was most definitely for drugs. He used and abused cocaine often after our mother's death.

"I'm in trouble, and I need it now," he said.

I said I couldn't lend him the money and that he should call his trust fund trustee and ask him. My brother responded with a loud "F--k you!" and hung up. It was not the first time that this had happened. But it turned out to be the last. Those were his final words to me.

On Christmas Eve 1990, at around 6:00 p.m., I answered the phone to the Los Angeles paramedics. They asked me if I was related to Christopher Corday. I told them I was his brother. After the shortest of pauses, they explained why they were calling. That pause still echoes in my mind today, like the click before the gunshot my brother heard as his final sound. He had saved one old Colt .45 revolver, an 1890s classic, and used it to take his life.

Was this an act of great courage in the face of doom or the act of a terminally lost man without a compass? It mattered not. It was such a sad and tragic end to a great life begun and then gone. He was supposed to be my forever Eagle Scout. I was his Life Scout.

I spent years trying to find closure with his death, and even today there are many moments when I'm not totally sure I have. But to me, he is a hero. Bipolar disorder, then called manic depression, was an incurably frustrating mess in those days. My brother was a hero because he was dealt the most difficult hand in life—a terminal illness with no chance of knowing when the end would arrive. And he bravely lived with that burden for as long as he could continue to bear it and fight it.

∞

We scattered his ashes at sea off the Santa Monica coast on a very bright and clear morning shortly after the New Year. I attached a small cork to an old Boy Scout compass we had shared and lowered it into the ocean. It would be something to help him find his way. We lovingly laid flowers on the surface of a calm and windless sea. Then we prayed aloud and in silence. A single pelican circled our boat. It made a few circles over us, paused as if to see what we were doing, and then flew on.

To this day, during my tenure as executive producer, we have never told or even dealt with a story about suicide on *Days of our Lives*. Suicide is the loss that never goes away. It is just too difficult and too personal… for me and for many in the audience.

> Fly on my sweet Angel,
> Fly on to the sky…
> Fly on my sweet Angel,
> Tomorrow I will be by your side.

—From "Little Wing" by Jimi Hendrix

CHAPTER 20

I NEED A HERO

A beautiful woman, a devoted fan of *Days of our Lives*, happily married with two children, once told a research panel that she watched the show because, in her words, "When Bo looks into Hope's eyes…I could die."

Another equally well-adjusted thirty-year-old housewife from New Jersey said that even though she loved her husband, and even though she knew Patch was, at one time, an incorrigible bad guy, she would love, for just one night, to have Patch's boots *under her bed*!

Women all over America love real men who are real heroes. They love a heartthrob. Always have…always will.

Whether that hero is blond, blue-eyed, and unshaven, or dark, tall, and clean-cut, it matters not. If these guys know how to kiss and cry and flex their pecs, but above all, how to light the fire in their women's hearts, they will be forever adored. Big or small, tall or short, loud or soft…if they are strong and real and truly loved by their heroines, they are the special men among men. They are our heroes.

In the history of *Days of our Lives* there have been many such men. However, I can name the Magnificent Seven who have enduringly appeared on the show during its forty-four years. These seven characters were and are still the best of the role models on *Days of our Lives*. They are heroes for all to admire.

∽

First and foremost, and father of them all, was MacDonald Carey, who played Dr. Tom Horton. Even though Mac has been dead for more than ten years, his spirit is still with us and the show, both on and off camera.

Mac Carey was a remarkable human being and a humanitarian. He amounted to a great deal more in his personal life than in his illustrious professional career, simply because he cared and gave so much of his time and himself to his fellow man and community.

He was almost holy in his last years. Much as he had been a sinner in his earlier ones, he became a recovering alcoholic sponsoring other alcoholics. He was an acclaimed author and poet, and he was one of the highest placed laymen in the Roman Catholic Archdiocese of Los Angeles. The archdiocese allowed him the privilege of giving communion to Catholics who were unable to leave their homes to go to Mass, whether due to old age or infirmity. Mac was always there for these poor unfortunate souls, with a blessing, good word, and his own special, soft, and kind personal touch.

Mac was also a published author and poet, with a prodigious personal library of more than fifty thousand books, many of which were first editions. He was a classy guy and one hell of a dancer. Even in his sixties, after having two hip replacements, he could still "give 'em the old soft shoe."

MacDonald Carey was also wry and comical, much as his costar Frances Reid, but there was a very deep and warm spirituality to his personality that touched everyone he met. Even fans of the show, when visiting the set for the first time, would run up to him and say, "Oh, 'Dr.

Horton,' it is so great to meet you!" These fans were unable to make the separation between Mac and Tom Horton. The two were one and the same.

I remember many nights when Mac hosted poker games at his home in Benedict Canyon. The old-guard actors—such as Joe Gallison (Neil Curtis), Jed Allan (Don Craig), Mark Tapscott (Bob Anderson)—and little "old" me would get together with Mac in his library to smoke cigars and play cards until the wee hours.

Mac would regale us with stories of *his* good old days, when his weekly poker games were attended by William Holden, Broderick Crawford, Forrest Tucker, and other famous celebs of the '40s and '50s. They would each bring their own fifth of whiskey, either Johnnie Walker or Jack Daniels, and finish drinking the entire bottle by the end of every night's game…and then drive home through Mulholland Canyon. The times were different then. Mac was a man's man all the way. He was also the only man—or more appropriately, "lead actor"—to ever win an Emmy in that category for *Days of our Lives*, which he did in 1967.

There have been many great men on the show over the years, but Mac was the first…and maybe the best. He was "old-school cool," just like Gary Cooper, and underplayed everything. To the greatest effect. Everyone loved, admired, and trusted MacDonald Carey, and thus, Dr. Tom Horton.

∞

Bill Hayes is the same sweet "most beautiful guy in the world" as his character Doug Williams is. Bill was part of the first super couple of *Days of our Lives*, with his costar and eventual wife, the beautiful and alluring Susan Seaforth Hayes, who plays Julie (Olson Banning) Williams.

Like Doug, Bill is soft and strong and even-tempered. Most of all, he is so nice to everyone he meets or knows, and he just seems to love everyone. I believe this is because he has such a love of life and a special spiritual quality. He is a good Christian and a role model to many of the younger cast, much as his father was to him. But "still waters always run deep." Bill has a depth of age that few will ever fathom, and yet he is always smiling at life.

My first memories of Bill, professionally speaking, were working with him in 1979 on the *University Hospital Variety Show*, which he wrote and choreographed for many of the cast to showcase their variety of talents by singing, dancing, and acting in comic sketches, all in the name of charity.

I was one of six musicians in the small orchestra playing live off-stage, and Bill gave me the responsibility of throwing a large rubber chicken onstage every time someone said the "secret word" during a Marx Brothers skit. I would blow an Acme siren whistle and then wing that rubber bird at Bill, Frances Reid, or Robert Clary, and we would all crack up with laughter. Tears of laughter.

But such is Bill Hayes. He is a very talented, lovable, and funny man and, above all else, one you can always trust and who trusts everyone. Most importantly, he is a fine actor, always honest and was the first to embody a new, romantic sexiness on the show. He is our Frank Sinatra, Bobby Darrin, and Tony Bennett all rolled into one.

∞

Mac and Bill were followed by Josh Taylor, who played the role of our first blue-collar hero, Chris Kositchek. Josh also returned many years later in the late 1990s as the last, or third, incarnation of Roman Brady.

Besides being my close friend and godfather to my son, Josh is the most honest actor I've ever had the pleasure of watching. Every performance he gives is the same in its consistency of character, which comes not only from his acting talent but also from his keen ability to find the subtleties under the dialogue he is given and deliver in his best

Midwestern accent. He is the perfect "hero," both as a character and as a man. The great detective. I could go on and on about Josh, but the most important thing is that he and the viewers love the characters he has played, and the proof is in his daily performance.

When you call his home and get his answering machine, the message is simple and testifies to the man. The recording goes as follows: "You have reached the home of Josh and Lisa Taylor...Go!"

However, he was once a self-avowed and unabashed ladies' man. He was a bachelor for almost thirty years, following an early marriage and divorce after his graduation from Dartmouth. At his second wedding ten years ago to his beautiful second wife, Lisa Marie, I was one of a few best men.

We all joked with Josh about finally getting "hooked" after living the devoted bachelor's life. But all any of us really wanted to know was what had become of his infamous "little black book"...the one with countless names and addresses of his past paramours. To this day, no one has ever been able to find it. It's a secret best left undiscovered. Knowing Josh, he probably burned it. But none of those ladies ever forgot Josh. The first of his kind. Big-armed, warm-hearted, and filled with countrified sex appeal.

James Reynolds (or Jim, as he is known to his friends) has played Abe Carver for the past thirty years. During that time, Abe has been a police detective, captain, and commander, as well as mayor. Jim is the most well-spoken member of the cast, uttering his lines in impeccable English with a superior baritone softness.

I admire Jim almost to the point of reverence, not only because he is a great role model for *Days of our Lives* but also because of his amazing past. Jim served in the U.S. Marine Corps during the Vietnam War. He was a journalist and a radio news announcer during his service after pulling a tour in combat. He was awarded the Purple Heart, and his valor behind enemy lines can be seen in the scar over his left eye. It also can be seen in his reticence to discuss the particulars of how he was stuck behind enemy lines for many days after being separated from his platoon. Only through his sheer will and heroic nature was he able to make it back in one piece.

That soft-spoken quality of valor makes the man so strong and, in turn, makes Mayor Abe Carver the heroic character he is. The man embodies a force against evil who truly must be reckoned with if you are on the wrong side of truth, justice, and the American way.

As an actor Jim has great depth and sureness in his portrayal of Abe Carver, as in any of the other characters he portrays in the many local theatrical productions he does in Los Angeles and at his own Pasadena playhouse. You have to believe Jim. He always speaks the truth.

A Kansas native, a wonderful father to his son, Jed, and loving husband to his wife, Lissa, Jim made his "bars" the hard and honest way…he earned them all. And the love of his life on screen, Dr. Lexie Carver (played by Renee Jones), shows how easy it is to love this man. Jim Reynolds also exemplifies a superlative role model for all African Americans, whether actors or real-life heroes.

Beloved as well is Peter Reckell, who plays Roman Brady's younger brother, Bo, once a detective and now police commander. He was introduced in 1983 as the first antiheroic, angry young man on *Days of our Lives*. Bo's hidden qualities and heroism emerged and then were brought to the surface by the love of his beautiful costar, the girl from the other side of the white picket fence, Hope Williams Brady, played by the gorgeous Kristian Alfonso.

Peter and Bo are one and the same—cool men, whose looks not only belie their years but, even more so, make female viewers gush and gaggle at such a hunky man and smart blue-collar detective. Who wouldn't want Bo Brady on their case? But for those of us who know him, Peter is a real "pussycat." He's humble and soft-spoken, even in his occasional criticism, born of good conscience, of the way his character should be written. He protects Bo's values and good qualities with the same quiet fervor that he protects all of Salem's citizens.

Peter is also a practicing environmentalist. His entire home is built on the concept of having the least possible negative environmental impact, and it's a beautiful place to live. He is globally conscious and hip. His means of transportation is a bicycle or, for long commutes, a fifty-miles-to-the-gallon hybrid car. He cares about the world and what it will be like for his daughter.

But more than anything, Peter is a good man whose "karma" seems so clean that Bo Brady can't be anything less than the man who makes him real. Bo is a hero because of Peter Reckell's heroic qualities. He's not only a ladies' man, but also a man's man. As an actor, he is marvelous, and few actors in daytime are as well grounded when the camera's tally light comes on. But don't ever try to get the drop on him. His right cross will nail you before you can even unholster your gun. Then, he'll go right back to holding his beer bottle in the most unique way that has become Peter's signature. Manly and cool.

Days of our Lives has had another antihero, the James Dean of brooding leading men, in Stephen Nichols, who plays Steve "Patch" Johnson. Stephen himself is as enigmatic as Patch. He is always very deep into his work. He cares so much about Patch and his accompanying baggage that he will always find a producer or writer to talk with regarding staying true to his character, by being either good or bad. And Patch has been both good and bad throughout the past twenty-plus years, even though he was "dead but not really buried," for more than ten of those years.

Stephen started as a day player, a short-term character, who was discovered by our producer, Shelley Curtis, while he was working in an actors' workshop. Patch was supposed to have a very short run on *Days of our Lives* playing a bad guy who held Hope hostage while tying her to a chair with a bucket of dripping hydrochloric acid suspended over her head.

Patch was *not* a nice guy, but the actor "owned" the character so much that we kept Stephen under contract for many years after that incident. He went on to become the infamous "one-eyed" antihero who played the blues harmonica—a perfect foil for Bo and the perfect match for Bo's younger sister, Kayla.

Stephen Nichols's quiet surface and long stride are in direct contrast to the volcanic fire that burns in this actor's proud heart. He is *always* unpredictable in his working method, and that's what makes the character of Patch so riveting. The element of surprise!

Stephen once told me that he grew up as a foster child, and that explained a lot about his streetwise, tough exterior. Now, as a devoted husband and father, he is a real sweetheart of a guy. As an actor, he is always dynamically dramatic and fiery, passionate, and perfectly suited to be the one-eyed good guy or dark force for good. He may not be in Salem at the present time, but we will never see the "end" of Patch. He'll be back…and when you least expect it.

Finally, the hunkiest of them all is Drake Hogestyn, who portrays superhero, ISA operative, and millionaire John Black. This Iron Man–like character is married to Dr. Marlena Evans Black (Deidre Hall), his beloved "Doc," and they were and are perhaps the most fervent of the super couples on the show.

Drake's John Black is like Superman in his ability to defy gravity, leap tall obstacles in a single bound, and seems both faster than a speeding bullet and more powerful than a locomotive. All at once. Much of that is because that is really who Drake is. He is a role model for all daytime heroes.

Drake is what makes John go. Drake has his own small gym in his dressing room, where he lifts weights for hours a day, and he is tireless in keeping his body in superhero shape. A devoted father and husband for more than twenty years, he once had all the earmarks of becoming a professional baseball player. He played third base in the minor leagues for the New York Yankees, and were it not for one bad pitch, he probably would have eventually gone to "the show" and played with the big-league Yankees.

Unfortunately for baseball and fortunately for *Days of our Lives*, he was hit in the head on a rainy afternoon by a very fast and soggy baseball thrown by future big-league pitcher Lee Smith. Drake lost most of his hearing in one ear—and subsequently his job in baseball—because of that dizzying injury. The Yankees' loss was our gain.

"Hogey," as we call him, is an all-world golden man…Old Spice and old-fashioned. He is a conservative titan in life who brings that quality of "I could have been president of anything" to all that John Black says and does. He's the guy you want standing next to you when the fight breaks out in the bar. He's the one who seems to eventually emerge unscathed, no matter how much crap has hit the fan. Even his character's name, John Black, evokes a Wild West gunfightin' man. Drake is a superb actor and the show's John Wayne.

But more than anything the viewer sees on camera, we behind the scenes know that Drake is so admirably a man to be loved, respected, and wanted as a friend. Our heroes don't come any better, and I wish the good Lord would make more new souls like Drake's. We, and the world, would be much better off for a gift like that.

He created the mold for many of our current younger and new heroes such as his son, Brady, Rafe Hernandez, and Dr. Nathan Horton.

But they have a long way to go to reach "John Black" status. Don't call 911, call Drake Hogestyn.

Many more wonderful male actors and accompanying heroic characters have been and are in place today on *Days of our Lives*, as there will be in the years to come. But over the last forty years, these seven men—especially Mac Carey, in his guardian angel–announcer role—have exemplified what every woman wants or what any one of us wants when we say, "I need a hero!"

In many classic Greek dramas, a hero is portrayed as a "sympathetic character, up against insurmountable odds, in order to achieve a worthy goal." That's the quality that makes our heroes on *Days of our Lives* or any heroes, for that matter, so admirable.

Besides being "eye candy," these men, their actions, and their characters are nourishment for our souls. And that is what makes them truly our heroes.

CHAPTER 21

THE GAY NINETIES

Life at the end of the twentieth century, from 1990 to 2000, couldn't have been better. The economy was booming, there was a new young president, Bill Clinton, lots of dot-commers were building sudden vast amounts of wealth, and the United States seemed a better place to live than ever.

The same held true for Salem in the 1990s. Even though Marlena was possessed by the most evil of darkest entities and another of our heroines, Carly Manning, had been buried alive for a week by the wicked Vivian Alamain, Salem was enjoying the fruits of its previous decades of growth. Ratings were high...NBC was rolling.

As the decade came to its peak, so did the level of youthful enthusiasm in both the viewers of *Days of our Lives* and the show's new characters. This was most clearly evidenced by a new demographic—female viewers between the ages of eighteen to thirty-four—in the Nielsen ratings, the gold standard by which many daytime television shows are now judged. Viewers between the ages of eighteen to forty-nine still accounted for the baseline of judgment, but this new interest in not only the young but also the future generation of viewers generated an amazing amount of heat for NBC and *Days of our Lives*. It was the time of *Seinfeld* and *Friends* on "must-see TV," and NBC was absolutely clobbering the competition.

Days of our Lives won four People's Choice Awards and two TV Guide Awards (the only two ever given out in the category of Daytime Drama), complete with national prime-time special broadcasts and acceptance speeches. And the show won almost every Soap Opera Digest Award possible.

I was never nervous or, thankfully, without the right words when given the chance to stand onstage in front of millions of television viewers and accept these awards. My feet would hit the stage, I'd find my "mark," my mouth would open, and the right words always seemed to come. It was as if both of my parents were sitting on my shoulders, whispering my lines into each ear. I would walk offstage, award in hand, and ask my wife or fellow producers and cast if I had made any sense. They would always effusively say that I was great, even though I had absolutely no recollection of what I had said on all of their behalf in my acceptance speech. Those were glorious award shows, and I'm sure that my parents were watching and with me.

The best reward of all took place at the People's Choice Awards in 2002 when Julia Roberts won an award for Best Actress and asked to be seated with the cast of *Days of our Lives*. She was, and her mom still is, a huge fan of the show. *Days of our Lives* won the award for Best Soap Opera, and as I stood looking out at the applauding audience, I saw her incandescent face and the smile that has lit up so many movie screens with its sheer beauty. She loved seeing us win and rushed backstage to celebrate with our cast. Those were some of the very best days of our lives.

∽

Jim Reilly's wildly successful and outrageous tenure as head writer had begun in 1993 and spawned many of the aforementioned outrageous and successful stories. Then, in 1999, our producer, Tom Langan, started writing the show, and we set out to secure the future of *Days of our Lives* with the next generation of Hortons and Bradys.

My mother had always believed that the show had to be "watered" with the blood of a new generation every five to ten years. By the end of the '90s, that time had come again. So in the course of one amazing year came the introduction of many new vital and young characters.

They were the class of 2000, the "Scooby-Doo" gang, as they were jokingly referred to by the cast and crew. The attendees of the Last-Blast Dance at Salem High School were Shawn Brady, Belle Black, Philip Kiriakis, Mimi Lockhart, and Chloe Lane. Brady Black and Nicole Walker were there as chaperones. What a marvelously talented young ensemble, all cut in their parents' traditional or nontraditional molds, but very much their own individuals.

There was something special about this newest generation. They were different from any previous good or bad characters on *Days of our Lives* in that they reflected the new society from which they had been spawned. Many were social misfits or rebellious "Generation X-ers." And their dialogue sounded new and different—"Like, you know, oh my God!"

Chloe Lane, played by the exquisitely beautiful Nadia Bjorlin, was so weird, introverted, and "goth" that her high school classmates called her "ghoul girl." Belle Black (Kirsten Storms) was so squeaky clean and pure that both of her parents, John and Marlena, seemed to pale in her youthfully exuberant light and called her "Tink." Shawn Brady (Jason Cook) was just like his once-bad-boy father, Bo, only potentially even darker and more threatening.

Mimi Lockheart (Farah Fath) brought new meaning to "lower class," coming from a family so poor that they lived in a box and eventually had their home provided by a Habitat for Humanity story line. Philip Kiriakis (Jay Johnson) the son of Victor and Kate, was so good-looking and such a spoiled, filthy-rich kid that he didn't give a rat's ass about anyone or anything unless he was the center of attention.

And Brady Black (Kyle Lowder), son of John Black and long-deceased Isabella Toscano Black, was a dark, brooding artist and poet, who was more the phantom of the opera than the soap opera star! He even had conversations with his ghost of a mother, played by Staci Greason.

Together, these kids entered and ripped asunder that which had made *Days of our Lives* so great in the '80s but had begun to grow a bit long in the tooth when the twentieth century came to a close. In the '90s their stories were the new "must-see" stories of *Days of our Lives*. Their virtues, or lack thereof, were different and fresh and totally relatable to our new and rapidly growing audience.

Even today, as the next generation of Salem's new characters wait in the wings of the future, this special group of actors and characters, the once innocent Scooby-Doos, but now adult "Screw-me-do's," carry the weight of the show squarely on their young, broad, and vibrant shoulders. Their stories are still the ones that bring viewers of all ages, especially those eighteen to thirty-four, to the television every day.

But into every life a little rain must fall, and the storm of the new millennium was just around the bend in the Salem River.

We were in transition by adding these new characters and doing what has always been so important to *Days of our Lives* as the decades went on. We were having fun, the show was running successfully, and all seemed very happy as the twentieth century came to a close. These new, young characters were portrayed with such authenticity that they—or more truthfully, I—never saw the storm approaching.

CHAPTER 22

"THE BARBARIANS ARE AT THE LEVERAGED GATE"

*Look out, Kid! It's something you did. God knows
when, but you're doin' it again...*
　　　　—Bob Dylan, "Subterranean Homesick Blues," 1965

In the first line of the movie *Gladiator*, as the barbarian hordes emerge from the forest to attack, Maximus says to his chief legionnaire, "When will they ever learn?"

These were my exact feelings as I girded my own loins in 2001 to once again go into negotiations with NBC, this time for the renewal of *Days of our Lives* due in March 2002. This battle became very long, very confusing, and, for me, very disrespectful, almost to the point of insulting. But as all the smart lawyers and business-affairs executives from Sony Television and Corday Productions constantly would remind me, "It's just about business, Ken. It's all about the money."

The powers in control at NBC did not seem to care or respect the fact that by this time *Days of our Lives* had been on for thirty-seven years and was not only still winning its own time slot but also still the first- or second-highest-rated show with women eighteen to forty-nine and constantly number one with women eighteen to thirty-four. NBC still claimed they were overpaying for the licensing of the show from Corday Productions and Sony Television. They seemed to be saying, "The hell with the past and all that went with it."

Their model for the financial future of *Days of our Lives* dictated cutbacks and downsizing but, most importantly, asserted their right to ultimate creative input and control. That was something that my parents and then I had *never* given to the network. The network's job was to buy the show from us, work with us, promote it, and find a way to profit from it through the sale of advertising revenue…which meant how much they could charge for every minute of commercial time they placed in the show. In the one hour that is *Days of our Lives*, every day more than twenty minutes—more than one-third of the show—is devoted to commercials. Yet the network claimed that it was losing advertising revenue based on the sale of those commercials. They claimed that the advertising CPM's (costs per thousand viewers for a commercial) were now being sold at a lower rate than they had been five years previously, at the time of the last contract renewal for the show.

Now, I would not then, nor will I ever, bite the hand that feeds us, meaning NBC. But this was coming from a company that was a division of the General Electric Corporation, whose annual gross revenue was in the billions. This was coming from a television network that would soon purchase—or take over, to be more precise—a movie studio, Universal Pictures, for 1.6 billion dollars.

Days of our Lives was losing the network money? Who were they trying to kid? Unfortunately, they weren't kidding, and they had facts and numbers to back it up, or so they said. Brinkmanship is really *blinks*manship. He who blinks first loses. It's all in the bluff.

So into the fray I jumped, accompanied by my friends at Sony Television, specifically Steve Mosko, its formidable, visionary president of television, and my brilliant attorneys, Barry Felsen and Ken Ziffren.

After the first six months of talks, from January to June 2001, things hadn't moved. It was like trench warfare. Back and forth, back and forth, nothing changing, and time was on their side. The longer it took to make a deal, the more leverage they believed they had.

One day we'd make a move and take a step forward, and the next day NBC would fire back and we'd retreat, all the while ready to try to close a deal another day. Meanwhile, all five hundred or so of the dedicated people—the cast, the crew, the production staff, and countless others who were attached at the hip to the show and who made it the fine daytime drama that it was—were waiting to find out if they would still have jobs by March 2002. Worst of all, there was no other qualified buyer. Neither CBS nor ABC wanted or could afford to buy *Days of our Lives*, and we all still wanted to be on NBC, our "mother" peacock. We were stuck but good.

Much as the pressing pawn slowly but surely makes its way across the chessboard to become a queen, a new player in the game shifted everything that had been a preamble to the final completion of the new deal. That chess piece was James Edward Reilly, the former outrageous and widely and weirdly talented head writer of *Days of our Lives*, and then head writer and creator of NBC's only other soap opera at that time, *Passions*.

This was the same Jim Reilly who had brought *Days of our Lives* to eminence in the early '90s with utterly sensational and unbelievable story lines, such as Marlena's possession, Carly being buried alive, and the five personalities of Kristen. He was a fine writer to be sure, but one who was now writing and owned his very own show in *Passions*.

The rub, as they say in gambling parlance, was that NBC had decided that Jim Reilly would be not only capable of but also perfect as the new head writer of *Days of our Lives*, as well as continuing as head writer on *Passions*. In other words, they believed he was the answer to all of our problems (What problems? we wondered), and capable of writing two soaps at the same time, more than five hundred shows a year. That's five hundred separate, serialized, and individual episodes, and NBC thought he could do it with major aplomb!

I told them I thought it was impossible. How could anyone believe that any one person was capable of such a Herculean feat, let alone capable of pulling it off with gusto and glee instead of sheer monetarily driven avarice? NBC believed! And, of course, Jim Reilly did, too.

And so in late June a deal was struck. The show would be picked up for five more years with two conditions: First, Jim Reilly would head-write *Days of our Lives* for the next five years guaranteed—with no "out" clause. Second, the show would take a large reduction in pay—known in the business as a "haircut."

Now, we at *Days of our Lives* were absolutely willing to take a little shave to save the show, but we were concerned about the long-term commitment to Reilly. He would have to bring something really great to the show, or else I would look like a fool for accepting such a ridiculous deal. If we weren't able to pull everything off perfectly, the barber's razor could cut our throats, and we'd all go down, sinking, not swimming, in a pile of retreaded stories and audience disapproval.

The most overlooked person in all of this was our head writer at the time, Dena Higley. She had been the head writer for only six months but had been part of the writing staff for nearly two decades, and the show was flourishing under her pen. We had been getting good, consistently solid ratings and staying in the front of the soap opera pack. She was writing a successful show, and I couldn't understand why she was being replaced. But there were other powers at play. Words were said and negotiations made behind closed doors at NBC, which I will never know or fully understand.

This was a done deal, but the fallout would prove to send the show, my father and mother's golden legacy and the viewers' adored daily one-hour appointment, into a huge tailspin, from which we could only try to correct and fight hard to recover.

CHAPTER 23

"BANG! YOU'RE ALIVE"

For Jim Reilly's first story on his return to *Days of our Lives*, he planned to introduce his imprimatur, or personal signature, with the most amazing piece of "stunt" storytelling ever told on this previously well-rooted, Midwestern, family-oriented, romance-filled soap opera. Yes, we occasionally had done some sensational storytelling, but nothing like this.

Jim's first big story would kill *ten* major cast members over the course of six months! The last of the "victims" would be our beloved matriarch, Alice Horton, who would choke to death on one of her own famous homemade doughnuts. And the Salem Stalker, the killer of all these great characters, would unbelievably be revealed as Dr. Marlena Evans…once the Goddess of Beauty, Wisdom, and Light and now the Salem Stalker, a serial murderer!

When I heard on our initial conference call with Jim what his long-term story for all of these characters was, I simply put down my pen and pad and for the next hour or so listened in shocked amazement as he painted every sordid detail of this story…complete with the reveal, halfway through, at the end of the figurative first act, that Marlena was "the killer." Then to act two, wherein Alice was the last to die, and then

Marlena was shot and killed by the police in pursuit. And then in act three they all reunite in a heaven-sent look-alike "Salem Place" called "Melaswen" (New Salem spelled backward) where the audience finds the dead are all still living!

Totally preposterous, right? Sure, some would say, "Hey, it's just a soap opera!" But now it was Reilly's soap opera, wherein no one ever really dies. How would the viewers ever trust us again?

So we "killed off" most of our veteran cast members at the hands of Dr. Marlena's despicable "Mr. Hyde." She shot, bludgeoned, slashed, and stabbed them all to death over the next six months, from Halloween to Easter. What a way to enter 2004…new contract or not!

Ten dead in six months…and strangely enough, the ratings climbed and climbed during that time. The viewers were thoroughly disgusted by the brutality and totally shocked, but though they threw their lunches at the television sets, they never changed channels.

Unfortunately for me, over those next six months I had the ugly and lonely job of telling each of the ten veteran actors that their characters were going to die. Their run of twenty or thirty years had come to a close. All that was left to do was have a "good-bye" cake on the set on the day of their last performance, ask them to give a thankful speech, and then say, "Adios!"

All of those wonderfully talented and eternally loyal actors listened to my news of their tragic end with great dignity. With much chagrin, each hugged me good-bye and then a few weeks later stood in front of the cast and crew, all assembled like some funeral cortege to say their final good-byes to everyone.

That was the most challenging and, at the same time, most depressing send-off I or any of these actors had ever known. Why? *Because I was sitting on "the secret."*

However, *I think most of them knew*. Not from my words or tears…not from a wink of the eye or a tongue in cheek. No, they knew that there was more to this than what seemed to be a mass slaughter of the cast. They knew that something bigger than all of its parts was afoot. There had to be more to this picture.

Of course, there was more. Every day I would come to work with this festering yet exciting secret and have to lie and cheat and deal with it in a professional way. I was so tempted to just come right out and say to each actor I was firing, "It's really one giant hoax!…Sssh!" But I never had to go that far. Each and every actor seemed to know that I was acting a little too thick-skinned for me, for someone they had worked with for so long. "This is just not like Ken to be so impersonal and matter-of-fact about something so big."

Whether from the hints and clues I would drop, such as an inscription on Jim Reynolds's golden carriage clock: "Whenever we may have the chance to work together again," or all the other subtle innuendo and "between-the-line" readings in my farewells, I acted the part well and kept it to myself and from the soap press, the cast, staff, and crew. But for those who were "killed off," I did my very subtle best to let them know, as Gilbert and Sullivan say in HMS *Pinafore*: "Things are seldom what they seem, skim milk masquerades as cream."

However, the exception to all this mayhem was Frances Reid. I knew I had neither the heart to hurt Frances nor the ability to pull the wool over her eyes with the news of Alice's impending death. So one afternoon, I visited her home with roses and a box of chocolates. I told her that Alice was going to die on the show and how it was going to happen. Her response was, "Oh, he's never liked me anyway" (meaning Reilly). But after convincing her otherwise about Jim, and hemming and hawing, I finally got around to telling her that it was all really a ruse.

Once the dust had settled and she agreed to be in on the secret with me, we played it to the hilt. On her "last day" on the show, I presented to her, on bended knee, a fabulously expensive diamond ring from Tiffany's and thanked her for all of the time she had given us. There wasn't a dry eye in the house. Frances was brilliant.

I think many of the cast knew, and I knew they knew the real truth, but none cried foul.

∾

In the end, Tony DiMera would be revealed as the real one behind not only his own death but also those of the rest of the characters. The largest prank ever told, or pulled on the cast and crew and the viewers, was about to be played out.

In the week before the script was to be delivered to the cast and crew revealing that Marlena and Alice (as well as all the other "dead" characters) were alive and well, talking on a park bench in "Melaswen," I secretly talked to each of the actors whose characters were dead and let them in on the switch at the story's end, in which they were all found to be still alive. Thank God, each of them agreed to come back to the show. That was the biggest risk that Reilly took with the entire payoff of this preposterous story.

I also asked them if they would each agree to keep the secret for a few days, after which time we would surprise the company, cast, and crew at a predesignated time and place. They also all agreed to this astonishingly bold request. But this was such a *huge* secret…how could it be kept by so many? But they all promised…and delivered.

Two days later I called for a mandatory meeting of the entire cast and crew to be held on the set at the midday lunch break. This was something I had rarely done in the past, so everyone knew it was important to be there.

The entire production company and cast and crew gathered. To everyone's knowledge, the show's contract had still not been renewed, and the feeling onstage was extremely tense. No one knew what the announcement would be; it could be bad news or even cancellation.

I took my place on the set in front of them all. I lit a small, white candle that Thaao Penghlis, who played the dashing and evil Count Antony DiMera, had brought me from the Nazarene monks on his recent travels to Israel. I played the moment for all it was worth. I asked everyone if they were sick and tired of all the needless slaughters in Salem.

"Yes," they murmured. I repeated the question. A louder "yes" was heard. Then I said, "I can't hear you!" and that was met with a vicious, resounding, "Yes!"

"Well," I said, "then are you ready for it to stop?"

"Yes!" they shouted again. "Well, so am I," I retorted, "and it's going to stop now!" Huge reaction! "Yes!"

The next few moments are so clear to me that I can play them back in my mind exactly as they happened. "Well, guess what?" I asked. "They're all still alive!"

Total shock. Silence. *What did he just say?*

One by one they made their entrances…in order of their untimely deaths, each of the "dead" actors emerged from an upstage door as I cryptically reintroduced them to the completely astonished cast and crew. One by one…Jim Reynolds (Abe Carver), Matthew Ashford (Jack Devereaux), Suzanne Rogers (Maggie Horton), Peggy McCay (Caroline Brady), Alexis Thorpe (Cassie Brady), Thaao Penghlis (Tony DiMera), Josh Taylor (Roman Brady), Bill Hayes (Doug Williams), Frances Reid (Alice Horton), and finally, Deidre Hall (Marlena Evans Brady).

They all stood there alive as you or me. Everyone was either crying over or applauding their entrances. One after the other, the dead were alive. They all stood there together. Ten living, breathing icons.

Then I asked Drake Hogestyn, who was in the midst of the shock, what I had told him he'd say to me during the previous few weeks (before the secret was out). He yelled, "Ken, you're such an asshole!" He meant it. The cast and crew felt it, but everyone understood why it had been played out the way it had. Everyone laughed and hugged, and on we went.

Reflecting on this experience from a more serious standpoint, and knowing how hard it was to have kept secrets from beloved cast members, I realize the amazing grace with which the actors handled it, and that reinforces for me the sense of family on *Days of our Lives*.

I also know the story line seriously eroded our fans' trust in the show. Jim's story had created a new stigma for the show in that it told the viewers that no one is ever *really* dead in Salem. How could they trust us now? We would have to win back their trust…and that would take quite awhile.

CHAPTER 24

BEHIND THE SCENES

In television, as in film, the director refers to the "fourth wall" as the part of the set that is never seen, that line that is never crossed. It is before the front-row seat, the invisible part of the set that represents, and is, the audience's point of view.

Crossing the imaginary line of this wall is strictly a no-no. It is called the "proscenium" in the theater, or more easily spoken, the very front of the stage, the line upon which the opening curtain rests. If an actor addresses the audience while onstage, that is called "breaking the fourth wall."

In traditional Greek and Shakespearean theater, actors would often break the fourth wall by speaking directly to the audience, whether as the entire Greek chorus or as Puck does in a sweetly comedic way at the end of William Shakespeare's *A Midsummer Night's Dream*.

In soap operas this never happens. If every single part of *Days of our Lives* takes place in "fictitious" Salem, then the characters can never speak directly to the audience. They can never break the fourth wall. Yes, they can and do talk to themselves, but they never talk directly to the viewer. They never look directly into the camera.

But what the fourth wall is to the viewer, the other three walls are to the characters and Salem. Sometimes what happens behind those three walls is more interesting and, yes, more baffling to the actors than anything their characters could ever play onstage. It is what's commonly known as what goes on "behind the scenes." The secret stuff, the good stuff.

∞

There has always been a genuine feeling of family throughout the entire cast and crew on *Days of our Lives*. When something goes right or something goes wrong, we celebrate or endure it together. I shall not preach any further, but I know that a special, warm and fuzzy, happy feeling permeates the hallways, makeup rooms, dressing rooms, and control rooms of NBC Studios Burbank, and that feeling is one of being protected and loved. Almost "watched over."

There are multitudinous funny stories about what goes on behind the scenes at *Days of our Lives*, such as when Wayne Northrop lowered Robert Clary's doorknob on his dressing room...by two feet! (Lovable Robert Clary was, and is, "Robert LeClair" and is all of about five feet tall in his song-and-dance shoes.) Or the countless times a leading lady has slipped while dramatically entering a scene in her high-heeled shoes, looking very ungraceful yet hilarious as she stumbles to gain her footing or fall on her derriere, and her cast mates start howling with glee.

But it's the special stuff that really goes on behind the scenes that no one but a few of us know about. Those moments have become a bit historic around the set. And they aren't ever on camera. Well, almost never.

Most of all, they are all magical, truly magical. For example, our fans never figured out how we made Deidre Hall float above her bed when Marlena was at the peak of the possession story line. Or how we made her eyes look so demonically yellow. Well, the truth is that David

Copperfield helped us pull off that floating trick by giving us his magical hydraulic "T-bar" apparatus that he uses to float people. We built the walls and bed of Marlena's set around the apparatus and then proceeded to levitate her, dressed in a billowing, wind-blown chiffon nightgown. Andrea Levine of Body Tech, who created similar lenses for Brad Pitt in *Interview with a Vampire*, gave us Marlena's yellow contact lenses, which had their own special glow…if you know what I mean.

There is far greater magic than that, though, magic moments that happen only in a show that has a great backstage like *Days of our Lives*. And those few moments are the ones that last a lifetime in our memory. These are but a few of those stories.

∞

Everyone and anyone who knows *Days of our Lives* knows the evil and all-powerfully dark character Stefano DiMera. Most of all, we know the sound of his voice…deep and resonant and definitely Italian cosmopolitan. What most viewers don't know is that Joseph Mascolo, the actor who plays Stefano, does not have an Italian accent. Joe speaks without a trace of any accent, except perhaps that of a well-spoken native of Connecticut.

What is amazing about Joe, however, is the remarkable commitment he has to his character. He patterned Stefano's accent after Rossano Brazzi's in *South Pacific*. Joe never breaks character from the time he arrives on the set in the morning until his scenes are done. At the studio he *is* Stefano. He speaks with that pseudo-Italian accent offstage as well as onstage. So imagine anyone's surprise upon meeting Joe away from NBC Studios, or even as he is exiting the stage, and finding that his accent is gone. We all have gotten used to it around the set, but in more than twenty-five years I have never seen Joe out of character, "out of Stefano," at the studio—not once! Amazing and strange. Dedicated. Methodical.

∞

One of the loveliest behind-the-scenes moments happened in the early *Days*. In the mid-'70s, Doug and Julie, played by Bill Hayes and Susan Seaforth, were *the* most popular couple, bar none, on *Days of our Lives*, and in most of daytime, for that matter. They were the forerunners to all of the super couples on the show and, as I previously mentioned, were featured on the cover of *Time* magazine in 1976. Theirs was, however, a romance born of all the wrong intentions.

Doug Williams had come to Salem to run a scam on Julie's mother, Addie Horton. Instead, he fell in love with Addie, married her, and was changed into a good man by her love. They also had a baby daughter, Hope. But Addie died shortly after Hope's birth. Doug suffered through her death but was consoled by Addie's full-grown daughter, Julie.

Over the course of the next six years, Doug and Julie's story blossomed on-screen, as head writer Bill Bell wrote the brilliant plot twists and turns of these two star-crossed lovers. They shared their first on-screen kiss in 1970, and following that the couple grew hotter and hotter and more popular with each passing year, until Doug finally married Julie in 1976.

At the time, what few people in the audience knew was that the love between Bill Hayes and Susan Seaforth was also growing offscreen, at an even more rapid and torrid pace than that of their on-screen characters. Everyone around the set knew that these two actors had fallen in love, but no one knew to what extent their love had grown. One day in 1974 their sweet secret was played out.

At a romantic high point in Doug and Julie's relationship, "the big script" had arrived at the studio and called for "the big kiss" at the end of the episode. The control booth rolled tape, and as the scene came to a crescendo of "I love you's," "I always have," and "I always will," the camera pushed in for an extreme close-up as the two finally melted into the kiss for which the audience had eagerly been waiting.

It wasn't a "big wet one," much as we have become accustomed to today. No, it was just one beautiful kiss, two beautiful profiles, and a very hot and steamy moment. We froze the camera on their smoldering lip lock, and after a few poignant beats the stage manager called, "And we're out!"

But Bill and Susan kept on kissing, and the cameras kept on rolling. For quite a long time, the cameras rolled...and still they kissed. Now everyone in the crew started to feel a bit uncomfortable with this public display of affection that was way over the top...way off the page! Finally, when it was time for someone to clear his throat or say, "Excuse me," Bill and Susan both turned directly to the camera, broke the fourth wall, and in unison exclaimed, "We're married!" Everyone applauded, cheered, laughed, and cried tears of glee. No one knew that they had been secretly married a few days before in a small, very private ceremony.

Producer Jack Herzberg had a wedding cake on the set for Bill and Susan within a few hours. My mother was a bit miffed that they had kept such huge news a secret, but everyone was ecstatic for the new Mr. and Mrs. Hayes. When all was said and done, two years later in 1976, their characters, Doug and Julie, "tied the knot" in Salem and actually used the same wedding vows that Bill and Susan Hayes had pledged to one another when they secretly married. Bill and Susan, as well as their characters, Doug and Julie, became a classic example of art imitating life and love conquering all.

Today, more than thirty years later, Bill and Susan's love for each other is still a shining example for all. For the airing of that one show, we cut their prolonged hot kiss down to a slow fade to black. But behind the scenes, their love still burns bright.

∞

Everyone knows the less formal word used for any faithful viewer is "fan"...and that "fan" is short for "fanatic." Our *Days of our Lives* fans are among the most, if not *the* most fanatic (and fantastic) fans in all of daytime. There have been times when our fans have reacted in ways we never expected. Three specific instances come to mind that were newsworthy but never seen on the air, only behind the scenes.

In 1982 Marlena Evans (not yet Brady or Black) was being stalked by the lethal Salem Strangler, a serial killer named Jake Kositchek, played by Jack Coleman. One Friday the climactic scene in the show left us hooked to our television sets and also left Marlena dead on the floor of her apartment, the latest victim of the Salem Strangler. The fans were outraged!

The next Monday morning we arrived at work to the sight of hundreds of picketers outside the NBC lot. They all were carrying signs that said they were boycotting *Days of our Lives* because we had killed Marlena…an unthinkable act in those days. They all wanted her back, and they were equipped with bullhorns and holding signs with very angry slogans.

What they didn't know, and what eventually gave them a false sense of accomplishment, was that the person who had been strangled on Friday and left dead in Marlena's apartment was, in fact, not Marlena, but her sister, Samantha Evans, played by Deidre's real-life identical twin, Andrea. When Marlena appeared alive, magically, in Tuesday's broadcast, the fans, thinking they had swayed the writers of *Days of our Lives* and NBC, happily packed in their picket signs and victoriously went home.

We had never expected hundreds of picketers in such a short time, nor had they, these picketers, expected to settle the dispute so amazingly fast. In the end, it gave our fans a feeling of hope that they did have a say in changing the stories of their favorite characters, even though they never knew that the switch had been videotaped weeks earlier.

Our fans are most involved with their favorite couples, more than any single character, especially if those couples become triangles. A woman torn between two men is the classic romantic fantasy for any female viewer…and there have been many great three-way love affairs on *Days of our Lives*. In 1999 young stars Kyle Lowder, Nadia Bjorlin, and Jay Johnson were the pillars for Tom Langan's classic high school *Phantom of the Opera* meets ghoul girl meets rich boy romance.

Philip loved Chloe, but so did Brady. Chloe, who had been transformed from spaced-out, introverted ghoul girl to high school beauty queen, loved both men. But in different ways. Very different ways.

The fans were completely divided in their allegiances, and their numbers grew as the letters poured in from all over the country. *We love Brady and Chloe…"Broe" forever! We love Philip and Chloe…"Phloe" forever!* And writer Tom Langan hadn't yet really decided whether Chloe would eventually pick Brady or Philip as her lover. Both were worthy lovers and friends to her.

So we milked it for all it was worth and stretched out the story of these three young lovers for many months. The letters kept coming in, and the fans, for one of the few times in the history of *Days of our Lives*, were equally divided. The "Broe" fans versus the "Phloe" fans…and who dreamed up those conglomeration of names? The fans did…and still do!

Then one day two extremely large cardboard boxes were delivered to the set. They each contained more than a thousand rubber balls: blue ones that said "Broe," and pink ones that said "Phloe." Two thousand balls from the fans! But what were we supposed to do with so many balls? How could they have thought they would sway the writers with this stunt? But it did show the writers the deep love the fans have for the show…especially their most adored couples.

The most memorable frightening backstage moment, though, was in 1984. We were riding the peak of the first wave of Bo and Hope's popularity. Peter Reckell and Kristian Alfonso were young, new actors with their fingers on the pulse of our nation's young, hot youth movement of the '80s. He, the rebel, star-crossed with she, the good girl. Their only major obstacle, besides the differences in their characters, came in the form of Larry Welch, professional scumbag and extortionist, who was sent by Maxfield Hathaway to thwart Bo's love and also happened to leer at the object of his extortion, Hope Williams.

Larry was played with great sinister effect by Andrew Masset, a fine actor whose good looks helped his sneer seem a little less dismal and made him almost sympathetic. But a bad guy is a bad guy, and Larry Welch was heartless. He tortured Hope emotionally and blackmailed her into agreeing to marry him to save Bo from harm, even though Hope was in love with Bo. Larry's evil ways played out through much of that year as the sexual tension between Bo and Hope grew in perfect juxtaposition to his ramped-up threats toward Hope.

Off set, though, it became difficult for Andrew Masset to go almost anywhere in public, for he was always given dirty looks by anyone who watched *Days of our Lives* and loved Bo and Hope and wanted them together. He grew more and more uncomfortable on every new trip to the supermarket. The checkout stands even had his picture on the soap magazines as the most reviled person in all of Salem. He was once accosted in the vegetable department by a woman brandishing a large zucchini!

Then one day it all came to a head.

Andrew walked into my office one morning looking as though he'd seen a ghost...his ghost. He was as white as the proverbial sheet and had broken out in a cold sweat. His hands were shaking, and they held a letter. The letter was addressed to him, Andrew Masset, as well as his character, Larry Welch. It was not a typical, friendly fan letter. It was, plain and simple, a death threat.

The text of the letter described "a man" who was going to hunt Andrew (Larry) down and, when he found him, was going to make sure he never harassed Hope again. To do so, he was going to shoot Andrew in the leg, then cut off a very sensitive body part, then feed it to him, then shoot him in the other leg, and then finally cut off his head. Nice letter, huh? And all this was going to be done when the letter writer was finally released from where he was. Soon. At the bottom of the handwritten letter was the man's name…and address:

[Name withheld]
Care of: Cell Block 15
Folsom Federal Penitentiary

Andy handed me the letter and said he was really scared. Of course, he didn't know what to do, where to go, or if he should still be on *Days of our Lives*, for that matter.

I contacted our attorney, who then turned the letter over to the FBI. Death threats made by mail and sent over state lines constitute a serious federal crime, especially if perpetrated by a convicted felon who is in jail!

When confronted by the FBI, the inmate at Folsom who had sent the letter never tried to deny his authorship; instead, he reassured the federal authorities that he was sincere in "carrying out his threats as soon as he was paroled, unless the evil Larry Welch got his point and stopped harassing and blackmailing Hope. Or else." At his next hearing, they sentenced him to three more years in prison and denied his parole. Not a very nice, typical *Days of our Lives* fan to say the least.

∞

My favorite behind-the-scenes story took place in 1994. MacDonald Carey had passed away in March of that year, and losing Mac and his beloved character, founding father Dr. Tom Horton, was a huge blow and a loss to us all. Mac's death left a hole in the fabric of the show that will never be mended. His voice still resonates in the opening couplet, "Like sands through the hourglass…so are the days of our lives." Even though he's been gone for more than fifteen years, his voice is and always will be the voice of *Days of our Lives*. He was our father figure.

We all were missing Mac so terribly, and when we got around to doing the Christmas show that year, the one in which you could always count on Tom and Alice, and all the Horton clan, to hang the Horton Christmas tree ornaments, it was just not the same without Mac. His absence weighed heavily on the entire cast and crew, especially Frances Reid, Tom's beloved wife, Alice Horton. We were having a hard time letting him go and getting on with the show.

We finished the Christmas show in early December, and on the day that we wrapped that show, Deidre Hall was one of the last cast members to leave the studio. The show wrapped. The lights on the sets were turned off, and the stages sat empty.

As Deidre walked through the stage to go to her car, she stopped to say happy holidays to our prop man, the late, lovable Bob Bateman. She and Bob were talking in front of the Horton living-room set, which, of course, held the famous Horton Christmas tree. As they said their good-byes, they noticed something peculiar.

On the mantel above the fireplace sat a large framed picture of Tom Horton (Mac), with his ever-present, gentle smile. The last scenes that day had been played out in the Horton living room, and they noticed that a spotlight that had been left on was shining on Mac's picture.

Bob thought the lighting directors or engineers had forgotten to turn off this "pin" spot. When he and Deidre walked into the set and up to the picture to admire Mac's face, it was awash in light. But when they looked up at all the set's lights, they were astonished to see that not one was lit. They were all off. There was no source for the light shining on Tom Horton's face. But his face was lit by a bright light from somewhere. They looked at each other, hugged, and reverently walked out of the studio, and they both knew the source of that light. It was Mac.

When Deidre told us this story after the holidays, no one doubted her word. On the contrary, it was what we needed to hear to keep us going. And it is proof to us that Tom Horton and MacDonald Carey still watch over us every day, in that studio, in front of the camera and behind the scenes. And no one in the cast and crew ever doubts that.

∞

Years later, Frances Reid (Alice) was taping the climactic scenes in Jim Reilly's outrageous Salem Stalker story line, in which she knew the evil Dr. Marlena Evans was coming to visit her in her kitchen in the Horton house to bring about Alice's inevitable death by doughnut. The script called for Alice to have a long monologue while sitting at her kitchen table awaiting Marlena's entrance. Even though Alice's speech was a monologue, spoken to her dear, departed husband, Tom, and even though she was the only one in the scene, the scene was neither a monologue nor set with just one character.

As we rolled tape and started Alice's good-bye scene, an "I'll be with you, soon, Tom, dear" monologue, the director immediately called, "Cut!" A glare or reflection was coming off the kitchen table right in front of Alice and the empty chair to which she was speaking. It was distracting, to say the least.

The prop man sprayed down the surface of the table to stop the glare, presumably caused by the onstage lights. We repositioned the table and chair a bit, and the camera, and started to roll tape on a second take. This time all went well, and Frances started singing Alice's "swan song" with fervent sentiment. We were starting to reach for our boxes of tissues when again the director yelled, "Cut!" The glare or glow or strange blue reflection was now on the chair, the empty chair to which Alice was directing her lines. Again the prop man was dispatched to alleviate the problem, and with his trusty spray can (much like hairspray), he covered the chair and, for good measure, the table again.

We set up and rolled on the third take, which, by the way, was the one that aired. All was going smoothly as Frances tugged at our heartstrings, talking to Tom as if he were in the room, as well as waiting for her in heaven. Then it happened again. Where there had been no glare or light reflection, there it was again and brighter in its blue hue. It was not seemingly attached to either table or chair.

Everyone in the control room saw it on the monitor for camera three. Everyone on the floor of the stage saw it on the stage TV monitor, although it was not actually visible in the set. There was a light, a presence, seen on camera that was not seen off camera in the same set. It was Mac, or Mac's spirit or presence, and we all saw it. The director kept the tape rolling…all the way to the end of the monologue and the end of Alice's "last scene." And if you looked very closely, you could see "it," that aura, when the edited show finally aired three weeks later. An inextinguishable glow.

That's some of what happens behind the scenes. We love our fans, for without them we're nothing, but with them and their viewership and support we flourish. The next big milestone was a result of their devotion to our *Days of our Lives* family. A devotion and loyalty that began in the space age and has stretched into the second decade of a new millennium.

CHAPTER 25

"FORTY YEARS, TEN THOUSAND EPISODES, AND GROWING"

The fruits of one's labors are measured in the fruits of the future years of good crop.

In that great proverb lies the secret to the success of *Days of our Lives*. It isn't the flower; it's the tree. It is the hub, more than the many spokes and rim, that makes the wheel work and, at the same time, makes it different and unique.

In 2005 *Days of our Lives* achieved two of the greatest milestones that any television show—whether early morning, midday, prime-time, or late night—could ever dream of achieving.

First, we taped episode ten thousand on February 1, 2005. Ten thousand shows! Unbelievable, and so exciting. Getting caught up in such landmark success and its excitement, and prodded by Jim Reilly, I agreed to play the "hanging judge," Judge Shay, who presided at a criminal hearing for Billie Reed in that historic episode.

After a quick laugh and a number of takes, we got the scene in the can. I'll never forget the look in Peter Reckell's and Julie Pinson's (Bo's and Billie's) eyes when I, their employer and executive producer, in the place of the stand-in who had been hired to front for me as part of the gag, popped up on the bench as Judge Shay. Bo and Billie were speechless as I pronounced her sentence. Then everybody onstage cracked up!

Of course, I continually botched my lines. I am not now, have never been, and never will be an actor. After five takes our director, Roger Inman, came out and kindly said, "I think we probably have enough to make it work, Ken." Whew, get me out of here!

My mom and dad had said, "Never, ever end up on the wrong side of the camera." And I had...but only for that one special show. I will always respect our actors so much more for having had that experience. Their jobs are the toughest.

For the ten thousandth episode of anything...even waking up... one should be able to put on a show and throw a party. And party we did. From the ten thousandth episode cake—represented by a one followed by four zeroes...five different flavored cakes in all—to the fortieth anniversary of *Days of our Lives* on November 8, 2005, nine months later. A tribute and celebration of forty years of romance, super couples, serial killers, switched babies, love triangles, evil twins, bad hair...and miracles.

We held a huge bash at the Hollywood Palladium. It was a real doozy of an affair, complete with the Rat Pack and the Fab Four sound-alikes to entertain. The party's theme was an evening from the '60s. Many of the well-known cast from the past, even John de Lancie and Arleen Sorkin (Eugene and Calliope), were there. Matt Ashford (Jack Deveraux), in his Haight-Ashbury finest, was dancing with his wife and his ten-year-old daughter, who were dressed like hippies. Steve Wyman, co-executive producer, was dressed like a Willie Nelson–esque biker dude. And Deidre Hall made her typically late, beautiful Hollywood entrance on the arm of her twin sister, Andrea, and everyone gasped, "Who the heck was who?"

I was sitting at a table next to Bill and Susan Hayes, and as the

Rat Pack played "Mack the Knife," I whispered to Bill, "I love this song…but who wrote it?" He just paused, winked, and as if history were echoing and resounding with that brilliant composition of lust and misplaced heroism embodied in "Mack the Knife," he just said "Oh, yeah…right…it's Kurt Weill…from *The Threepenny Opera*."

That play typifies much of what makes *Days of our Lives*, and soap operas in general, so successful. *The Threepenny Opera* is a story about the stormy antihero Macheath, or Mack the Knife, who is a murderous, womanizing gigolo, loved by all the downtrodden, especially those most in need of love, even though he is despicable. Mack is finally sent to the gallows, only to be saved at the last moment by a random gracious act of the mayor. All of his female admirers cheer and applaud as he is freed from his executioner and returns to them.

So as all of us at *Days of our Lives* heard the song, something dawned on me in that moment. The antihero, the bad boy, is always attractive and interesting. But nobody really cares about him and roots for him unless his lovers, his female admirers, do. That's what separates the men from the menaces. That's what makes soap operas "operatic," as in *The Threepenny Opera*, and everyone can attend for free…on NBC.

They can say it's only a soap opera…but is it? Soap operas reflect our society as viewed through a lens of beauty and curiosity and doubt.

Make them weep. Make them wait. Then make them victorious! The heroine and the villainess at odds. The lioness and the hyena. Who will win out? Who will make the kill and, in so doing, save her pride? That is what keeps us coming back to the story again and again.

That night all I remember is counting my blessings. I was grateful that we were all living in better times, and that the sands had run through the hourglass for forty years!

CHAPTER 26

THE DIRTIEST HALF DOZEN

The villains and villainesses. We hate them, we hate them, we hate them…but we *love* to hate them! No hero is a hero without a villain to throw rocks at him. No heroine is a heroine without a bitch or a she-demon to vex her and make her life hell.

Villains and villainesses are the creators of all the impossible odds that must be overcome by our good guys and girls. Wretched, slimy, sociopathic, or even homicidal, our villains are the *key ingredient* for drama on *Days of our Lives*. Despicable and hated by all, they drive our stories. And if deftly written and portrayed, they keep us glued to our televisions…to watch the next horrid, foul, unlawful, or just plain putrefying act they will commit. And we just can't look away.

We seldom ponder why they do all the terrible things they do. They will always offer their own self-fulfilling, preposterously awful reasons. However, there is one constant in their hate and spite and unleashed hell. *They do what they do for the love of their families.* It is the quality that humanizes their characters and helps the viewer understand their hubris. It shows us there is still a glimmer of faint hope that someday they may see and understand their evil ways…and repent. But seldom, if ever, do they change. Most of the time, as our show grows year to year, so, too, does their raging, despicable behavior.

Incorrigible is the word that best describes our ne'er-do-wells. Beyond repair…or are they? The formula is really simple: "Make your villain or villainess somewhat lovable or sympathetic, no matter how absurd their reasoning may be, and the audience will watch and be entertained by all the crap they throw, all the hearts they break, all the homes they wreck, and even the lives they take."

Today six such despicable souls prowl the canvas that is *Days of our Lives'* Salem. I call them "the dirtiest half dozen," all of whom are living the villainous life and represent the forces of darkness that threaten to extinguish the light of love, goodness, and mercy that our heroes and heroines possess.

∞

First and foremost is Stefano DiMera, the darkest of them all. A cross between Don Corleone and Darth Vader, with a little Pavarotti thrown in.

In 1981 head writer Pat Falken Smith created Stefano DiMera, Salem's own Machiavellian resident villain, with a bit of a twist. He lived in a mansion (our first!), where, even though he was a sociopathic scourge, his evil personification was balanced by an overbearing yet undying love for his children.

Stefano will do anything to protect his children, even if they don't want him to or disagree with his methods. Stefano has been "dead" to his children so many times I've lost count, but in the end they all realize that everything he did was out of love for them. A parent's instinct is to protect, and no one is more devoted to his children and grandchildren, no one will go to more lengths to protect them, no matter how nefarious those lengths may be, than Stefano DiMera.

He always plays a dangerous game of chess with their lives and everybody else's in Salem…and he is always ten or twenty moves ahead of them. Stefano's chessboard is actually a centerpiece in the DiMera living room. His obsession with the game has even inspired him to nickname other characters. John Black was his brainwashed "pawn"; Marlena Evans, his caged "Queen of the Night." Stefano treats all those he both loves and hates as pieces in a chess game. And what makes it so scary to us, the viewers, is that he literally plays both sides of the board at the same time as he acts his way through any scene in that set.

To top it all off, Stefano never has someone else's blood on his hands. He is above all that gruesomeness and hands-on skullduggery…meaning he leaves the dirty work, always one undetectable step removed, to his countless minions, soldiers, hit men, or mad scientists. Who could ever forget the sadistically brilliant and theatrical Dr. Rolf, played by William Utay? Stefano pulls all the strings, and his puppets do the dirty work.

But Stefano's monstrous character also has its warm side. He sheds countless tears, weeps aplenty, and even has an occasional heart attack, diabetic shock, or massive stroke over his children. They believe him, and we believe him. He cries these crocodile tears that keep his kids, grandkids, and wives believing in his innocence, but all the while he is plotting how to best run the world his and only his way. A megalomaniac. Maybe the best villain Salem has ever had. Enduring and perennially surprising.

The list of all of his transgressions is legion, too legion to mention all of them here. Suffice it to say that if you just watch *Days of our Lives* for any short period of time, now or in the future, you will immediately be caught up in the spider web of another of Stefano's sinful plots. He is our Big Bad Wolf…yet he is so Teflon. He always finds a way of having the blame roll off his shoulders. "The Phoenix," Stefano DiMera, continually rises from the ashes. The eternal question he poses is whether he will ever find his humanity or continue to be the monster he has to be.

I've known Joseph Mascolo, the actor who plays Stefano, for almost thirty years. Even though he has come and gone from the show for periods of time, like a good, dark red wine, the actor and the character he plays only grow better and more robust with age. My mother told me that when Joe auditioned for the role of Stefano, his reading was so extraordinarily impressive, and the writer and producers were so astonished, that he immediately got the part. Joe told me the same story. He said it happened because he knew and "owned" Stefano DiMera long before he auditioned and, because of that self-confidence, was able to put the producers at ease, gain their confidence, convince them, and garner the role. He hasn't let us down.

Joe and I share a mutual love of classical music and can speak in the language that only musicians know. It was Joe's idea to always have Stefano listening to opera when he's alone. Few know that Joe played the clarinet professionally and is an absolutely devoted lover of great opera. He was close friends with Luciano Pavarotti, one of the greatest operatic tenors of all time, and there is always a lyrical and musical lift to the way Joe delivers his lines that makes his dialogue seem almost operatic (as in soap "operatic"). He seldom just says no. He most often says, "No, no, no, no, no…"

Joe knows Stefano better than anyone, because he cares about the character, knows all the inner flaws and strange forces that make Stefano tick, and will defend his character to the very end (not that I'm expecting an end to Stefano anytime soon).

Joe Mascolo is a devoted husband and father, and a sweetheart of a human being. The cast all love him and respect him and are always on their toes, knowing all of their lines, when they work with such a professional.

Joe is a wonderful man, but Stefano is not. Stefano will eternally hate the Bradys. But we who know him will always love Joe.

✁

Kate Roberts, played by Lauren Koslow, is our reigning resident bitch and all-around bad-to-the-bone mom. The perennial black widow… you know, the kind that eats her mate alive after seducing him.

But what is so startling about this villainess is her "look" and the way she carries herself. She may try to kill Chloe with a poisoned apple, but she does not in any way resemble the wicked, ugly witch in *Snow White*. She doesn't seek to be the fairest in the land, because she knows she always looks gorgeous.

She only seeks to protect her sons, Philip and Lucas. And in doing so, her warped perception and angst over their choice of the women in their lives sets her off on wicked and sometimes murderous tangents. But we see and understand her misdirected reasoning in "protecting" her sons and exacting revenge for any wrongdoing done to them.

She failed with her two other children, Austin and Billie, so she overcompensates with Philip and Lucas. Her vulnerability as a mother makes us almost forgive her ludicrous schemes. We may totally disagree with and hate her for what she does, but we are engrossed in her devious plots and compelled to watch them being played out. She is dangerous, yet organic and real.

Like Lauren Koslow, the actress who portrays her, Kate Roberts has a classy, dangerously seductive look with a beautiful face, sultry dark eyes, gorgeous skin, and high cheekbones. Kate is ageless, as is Lauren. Lauren Koslow's beauty balances and distracts us from Kate's true evil presence. Do those flaming nostrils and perfect high cheekbones belie her cold, calculating ruthlessness in running her family's lives? Yes, they do.

Lauren Koslow makes Kate work. She makes Kate the embodiment of the most sophisticated of schemers, with the ability to mete out poison and exact revenge from any outside threat to her and her family and look great while she's doing so. And now that she is Mrs. Stefano DiMera, the sky's the limit! No telling what these two "hellers" will do now that they are together and their self-justifying forces of evil are doubled, or even squared. Shakespeare couldn't have invented a darker king and queen in any of his dramas. They are the finest "love to hate" couple to have ever hung like the impending sword of doom over the heads of all the characters we love in Salem.

Conversely, Lauren Koslow, who has played Kate Roberts for the past fifteen years, is a sweet, soft-spoken, and warmly intelligent woman. Her smile, off camera, is so genuinely different from her on-camera smile that I always feel instantly comfortable in her presence, although a bit enraptured and unnerved by her beauty. She, like Kristian Alfonso, is classically beautiful, and it's damn near impossible for the camera to take a bad picture of her...at any angle.

And as you might expect, Lauren is the opposite of her character, Kate. She's gentle, quiet, and smiles a lot. She is a happy soul. Lauren is really an angel, but her Kate Roberts is always dressed in wolves' clothing and in some beautiful styles. Kate is all about style. No one else in the cast can pull off wearing her wardrobe.

Lauren's dark and brooding portrayal of Kate Roberts is the antithesis of the actress's authentic human qualities of grace and graciousness. Lauren is so benign and endearing; Kate is so malevolent and calculating. Lauren leaves herself in her dressing room, becomes a horrid bitch on camera, and then returns to being herself as soon as she is out of makeup and costume and back in her dressing room.

An amazing transformation, from zero to bitch in sixty seconds. She is the object of many of our male viewers' hidden desires. Whether eighteen to forty-nine or older, men can't look away from Lauren's undeniable beauty. Like Kate's many victims and conquests, they are pulled like helpless flies into her tangled and deadly web.

I admire Lauren, but I enjoy despising Kate. Her adoring fans even show up at *Days of our Lives* events wearing "Team Kate" T-shirts. They love Kate...they love to hate her.

❦

Of all of Stefano DiMera's progeny, only two still remain: Lexie Carver and E. J. DiMera. Lexie was able to overcome her DNA's pull toward the "dark side," but the same glowing accolades cannot be made for Stefano's only son, E. J., played by James Scott.

I met James on the set shortly after we cast him in the role of Elvis Jr., Stefano's long-lost son. I was immediately struck by James's intelligence, his refined accent, and his mastery of the English language. At six feet, six inches tall and with his extremely good looks, he has an almost noble bearing; he made me, as a person, feel a bit ill at ease. Yet as a producer, he made me eager to know what was at the core of this actor who makes E. J. tick and march to a different drum. For quite some time thereafter, James remained an enigma to me. A new darker force in Salem, E. J. experienced an immediate rise in popularity.

It was only after the Writers' Strike concluded two years ago that I realized the depth of his caring for his character and the show. We sat for quite some time in the actors' lounge and discussed the changes and new direction in the writing of *Days of our Lives*. We were both excited by the potential for growth in both the show and E. J.'s character. We delved deeply into what James felt made E. J. so dark and yet so popular.

James possessed a staunch belief that E. J. was doing all he could to be a better man and not follow in the footsteps of his father, Stefano. James saw E. J. as a man who wanted to be different, who wanted to be redeemable, which for the youngest and sole heir to the DiMera empire seemed almost impossible. Unspoken in that conversation, understood by both of us, and seen in each of his performances was the fact that his lifelong battle would be the struggle against his DNA and Stefano's stranglehold of misdirected love. Would he wither under it all, and would being a DiMera eventually choke all the goodness from his soul?

But we also both knew that E. J. is not a megalomaniac. Deep down, he wants to be a good man, a good husband, and a good father. He is a man whose heart is in the right place, but whose head and ego get in the way of letting it run his life. E. J. is obsessive and compulsive in his drive to be better and smarter than anyone else in Salem, even if that means not listening to his heart and using his vast wealth, power, and intelligence to win out, no matter what, no matter who may get in his way, or who in his family may suffer the consequences.

Even though he shares two children with Sami Brady, he cannot open his heart to her without question, judgment, doubt, and usually bitter remorse. Poor E. J. If only he would let himself be vulnerable. But each time he has in the past, he has been burned or disenchanted with the result, so his first and most overriding impulse is to exact revenge instead of asking for or receiving forgiveness. E. J. thinks he knows what's best for everyone, but somehow, magically, it's only best for him.

I applaud James Scott as an actor, for he has to walk a very fine line between good and evil and always has us wondering which way he will fall. James always makes it all so palatable and utterly engrossing to watch.

Victor Kiriakis grew up on the docks of the Salem River and made his bones the hard way. He paid his dues through the school of hard knocks, which taught Victor his incredible street smarts and always insightful judgment of other people's character. He left Salem as a young man after a torrid affair with Caroline Brady who bore his illegitimate son, Bo, who never knew he was Victor's son and was raised as a Brady. Victor returned to Salem many years later as a very wealthy and very shady Greek tycoon, and the truth came out. He was a changed man, yet unchanged as a villain.

Victor is a very evolved man and, therefore, a very evolved villain. He is not as warm and fuzzy as some of our other baddies. Why? Because Victor doesn't really care what the rest of the world thinks. Victor is also funny, and it is his humor that makes him accessible as a villain. Yes, he's cold and cruel, but he's not so wrong in his perception of all the folks in Salem. We know he's right, and he knows it, too. Victor is the ultimate truth teller. He comes into a scene and speaks the truth.

So what makes him so bad? The answer is that he sets aside morality for whatever capricious reason he wants to. He says, "It's for family," but it is all self-serving in the end. Victor never ultimately takes any action that's not in his own best interests. Yet there is a stoicism to his character that we adore watching. He has a million emotions yet never changes his expression.

Interestingly, there is no "Victor" in the actor who brilliantly portrays him, John Aniston. John is a real teddy bear. After work he can be seen walking around the halls of the studio in a cardigan and driving moccasins, never the same as the buttoned-down, seriously dressed, and arch-mannered character he plays. He is so accessible, so genuine, so lovable.

John and I have always had a running gag every time our paths cross. We always act the part of our "real selves" as we quizzically look at each other and repeatedly say, "Don't I know you? Umm…yes, you're the guy who plays…who is it?…ah yes!" Then we stare at each other like long-lost friends and resume whatever conversation we were having, even if from months before.

He is recognized as Victor by all of our viewers, but those of us who know him never see him as his character. He is just the nicest, most endearing person in real life, and the complete opposite of the all-powerful Titan he portrays. A wonderfully talented actor with years of experience in daytime television, John brings that special color to his character that can only come from "wearing" him for such a long, enduring time. John always sails into the scene as Victor. He "owns" Victor and wears him like a glove, but he is able to shed Victor's skin and leave him in the studio every time he returns home to his wife and son. Like the Kiriakis dynasty he has created, Victor is a living legend, but John Aniston is what makes Victor royal.

As my mother often taught me, great characters are the direct result of great writing combined with great acting. Our head writing team, which included Sheri Anderson, Thom Racina, and Leah Laiman, created Victor, and many head writers since have written him through a myriad of plot twists and turns. But John Aniston is the constant. The one and only actor to have ever played Victor, he has played him with amazing power for twenty-five years. Even though Victor can occasionally be defeated, he can never be destroyed.

∽

Then there's Vivian Alamain, played by Louise Sorel, or "Loo-Loo" as we jokingly call her. Vivian is just plain scary nuts. She is a completely off-the-wall villainess, full of huge panache and largesse, yet inside that exterior of flighty craziness lurks an utterly vicious and highly dangerous beast of a broad. She is the scorpion, compared to Kate Roberts's black widow. Her penetrating eyes are a window into her psychosis.

Her actions are utterly ruthless and often completely macabre. Who will ever forget her burying Carly Manning alive and then dancing on her grave? How can this completely scary villainess ever find her humanity while being the monster she has no control over? Just look at Vivian's hands…her fingers are like long talons, with the brightest blood-red, polished fingernails. She reads like a character from an Edgar Allan Poe nightmare.

I believe, as a producer, that Vivian and Louise are very similar. And I might be the object of the actress's wrath in saying so, but Vivian is more focused than Louise. Vivian would never have thanked our head writer, Jim Reilly, on national television upon winning her first Soap Opera Digest Award as Best Villainess by saying, "I don't know what he's smoking up there!" However, Louise did, because that's just her uncanny way of being glib and direct at the same time, without meaning to hurt the object of her comments, or herself.

Yet, as Vivian Alamain, Louise is the most passionate of the *Days of our Lives* villains. She is *always* completely committed to the passion of the moment. If we were to do an "aura check" on her, she would read the "hottest" of all our evildoers.

Yet her enigma as Vivian is her strength. She has had the wildest roller-coaster ride of all our villains and villainesses, but she always wants to get back in line and wait for the next mortifying thrill ride. Wherever Vivian wants us to go, we go. She always commits herself totally to her malevolence. She is our shining example of someone who throws herself off the ledge without ever worrying about the landing.

Louise Sorel is also an enigma to me. She has a great love of dogs and all *choses Françaises* (French things). She even painted her dressing room to match French Impressionist artwork. She is full of wild energy and always seeks to make her character consistent and authentic, even if it means constantly questioning our producers or directors. She cares deeply for her character.

I truly admire Louise and find her not only a complete hoot but also a very smart lady, an actress who is able to bring all of herself to the part in making Vivian a great character and villainess. She has a "watch-and-learn-what-else-I-can-do-to-surprise-you" quality.

Louise's drive to make Vivian the best that she can be, as well as an insight into Louise herself, can be illustrated in the following true story. After winning one of her many Soap Opera Digest Awards, Louise was riding high and mighty. Her attention to every detail in Vivian's character became obsessive and, at times, a bit overbearing. Yes, to her great credit, she cared immensely, but her very presence sometimes drove our producers and staff into a state of fear.

In one instance she was constantly "looking for" Greg Meng, our executive in charge of production, high and low throughout the day. Day after day. One late evening after the show had wrapped, she ran through the halls calling his name, "Gregory...Gregory...?" He, of course, heard her coming toward his office. With no visible means of escape, he pushed back his chair and hid from her...*under his desk*. But Louise, being Louise, simply walked right into his office and marched around behind his desk. When she found him cowering underneath it, she matter-of-factly asked, "Good heavens! What are you doing down there?"

There's no getting around Louise Sorel, and there's no getting around Vivian. She's tenaciously dedicated to what she loves the most, just being herself and letting the fur fly. And that's why we love her.

∞

Finally there's Nicole Walker DiMera, lusciously played by the beautiful, fascinating, and alluring Arianne Zucker. Nicole was the porn star with the heart of gold. Now she's the baby kidnapper with the heart of gold.

Yes, she has done many horrible things, yet she always comes across as a victim. She drives the story in a villainous way, yet she always clearly disguises that she is the one responsible.

Even our viewers write in and ask, "Why is everybody being so mean to Nicole?" Amazing! After all the wicked, conniving, scheming, devious plots she has hatched, the audience doesn't hold her responsible. The audience gives her a free pass.

In the hands of any other actress, Nicole wouldn't be able to pull the wool over everyone's eyes, but Arianne Zucker, or "Ari," as we call her, is the perfect example of how our casting director hit pay dirt. She is just one amazing actress, pure and simple. And she has grown so much in the time she's been in Salem, just like her "television" ex-husband, E. J. (James Scott), has. We still don't know how high up is for this talented actress (or is that how low she can go?). Excellent writing coupled with top-notch acting makes for great characters.

Our *Days of our Lives* viewers watch the show for iconic, complex, and compelling characters. Nicole Walker is all of the above. Nicole's self-worth is nil, a product of a horrible past that was beyond her control, but somehow she is not self-destructive. She's a survivor. That's what we want to watch. She digs and digs and digs her own grave and then magically jumps out of it.

She does everything she does out of love for her man, whether that's E. J. or Brady, but she is always shooting herself in the foot before she can get to dance with them. So she resorts to switching babies, stealing babies, coupling lie after lie with startlingly convincing ease. And even when she's busted, even when she's behind bars or justifiably slapped silly in retaliation by all her victims, *we feel for her*. She is an amazingly well-rounded, multidimensional character, whose evil ways are always justified by flashing us that one meek look...that "Why me?" look that makes a villainess sympathetic. We believe Nicole even when we know she's dead wrong.

Ari makes it work. Somehow Ari's Nicole knows that we, the audience, can be charmed by a bad person. It's not a pretty thing; it's not politically correct, but it's true. We love to watch her do her bad, bad things. It is so entertaining.

Arianne Zucker and her husband, Kyle Lowder, who played the first Brady Black, fell in love after being on *Days of our Lives* for only a few years. They are currently married. They are both stunningly attractive people, and their marriage continues the tradition on the show of life imitating art. Bill and Susan Hayes, Crystal Chappell and Michael Sabatino, and now Kyle and Ari have found love on and off the set...and Kyle and Ari are the proud parents of a baby girl born in December 2009.

Arianne is an actress cut from the mold of the great divas in the golden age of film noir like Rita Hayworth, Lauren Bacall, and Maureen O'Hara...all bigger than life. With her soft, big green eyes and long legs and blonde hair, Arianne makes a striking impression on anyone who sees her on or off camera. In time, as with her costar James Scott, I will get to know her more closely. But for now, curiosity is the quality that she brings out in me and our viewers. What makes Nicole so special and so different? Perhaps it's tied to her ability to keep deep secrets from her fellow characters while projecting her inner turmoil to an entranced, sympathetic audience. Only time will tell.

∞

Villains are just so much more interesting than the rest of us. It was Emerson who said, "As there is a use in medicine for poisons, so the world cannot move without rogues."

Here's to our scoundrels.

CHAPTER 27

LIFE AFTER FORTY

Doctors used to believe that you grew until you were twenty, had the prime years until forty, and then you were over the hill. But it's a whole new world now. Today's forty is like yesterday's thirty. Today's fifty is like yesterday's forty, and so on. We grow more vital with each new generation.

After the show passed its fortieth birthday in 2005, I did not in any way expect it to succumb to a short period of decay and eventual death—that is, cancellation. Not on my watch. We were still young! There still had to be great new stories to tell with romantic vistas unforetold.

The show must go on. And on we would go, sailing into what would prove to be our greatest storm, an adversary we had never dreamed of facing. Weathering this one would prove to be our greatest challenge.

∞

By 2005 the global information and entertainment market had expanded in quantum leaps never before seen or even expected. We found ourselves, and the tradition and standard of once-great network television, becoming a smaller and smaller island in a growing sea of alternative entertainment. We had been a giant iceberg forty years ago, but now the global warming of all worldwide webs, cable, and satellite transmissions had left us, and NBC, a shrinking icon, seemingly soon to be melted down and overtaken by future alternative entertainment.

But neither we nor NBC would go pleasantly into that long and lonely night. We would stand up and fight! And what a fight we had and have on our hands.

In 2005 NBC and all the other networks were facing the loss of many of their top-rated shows due to an unwillingness, or more aptly put, a willingness by those shows' actors and producers not to make any more episodes after a long, illustrious run on prime-time television, which translates to many constantly rerun episodes and the prize of syndication.

So as *Seinfeld, Friends, Frasier,* and other great series said good-bye in their closing episodes, the world knew we would see reruns of these wonderful network television icons in all kinds of different, syndicated marketplaces. But this future would not put any food on the table of Mother NBC.

Trouble began more imminently brewing because NBC had no great replacement programming. *Will & Grace,* as lyrically funny as it was, could not hold up an entire Thursday lineup, like "must-see TV" had done over the past ten years.

Now it was a matter of not only convenience, but also necessity, to fill the prime-time lineups with easier-to-make (meaning much less expensive) programming. Reality shows and game shows saw a return to popularity never before experienced. From *The Weakest Link* to *Who Wants to Be a Millionaire* to *The Bachelor* to current raves such as *American Idol, Survivor, Deal or No Deal, Dancing with the Stars, The Apprentice,* and *The Biggest Loser,* real people, meaning nonactors...nonpaid contestants, filled the airwaves with the classic formula of art imitating life or art making fun of life. The only big expense in producing these shows was the cost of the celebrity hosts and the cost of one big set for all the scenes. The audience and contestants were the stars.

Reality television had knocked scripted dramatic television out of the box, and the primetime ratings for these new shows, although nothing like the decade before the dwindling occurred, were sufficiently high to make the young lions running NBC feel proud. No more moral lessons in classic dramatic form. No more big action shows; just keep it simple. Why pay more for something you can have for almost nothing and still sell for almost as much?

NBC has created some real lemons in the various lead-in shows to *Days of our Lives*. From *Passions* to *I-Village* to the *Bonnie Hunt Show*, we just couldn't seem to get any traction from what precedes us every day. Even today, in many markets we are preceded by one-hour infomercials. Not having a consistent lead-in makes the odds for success tougher on us.

Believe me, I am not bitter about this turn of events over the past five to seven years. Everyone has to accept reality when faced with its glaring truth and sometimes has to make lemonade out of lemons. The sad news facing all daytime dramas was, and is, that as prime-time ratings slide, so do those of the morning talk shows, the late-night talk shows, and everything in between…meaning soap operas. We needed to help ourselves.

Once again, desperate times called for desperate measures. Despite the early ratings success, eventually Jim Reilly's stories were more alienating to the viewers than attractive. By June 2006, ratings were way down and I knew it was time to make another huge change. Of course, the network daytime programmers totally disagreed at first. But after pointing out to NBC president Jeff Zucker how we had been taking it on the nose both in the ratings and from the viewers for the past two years because of Jim's lack of romantic and riveting stories, Jeff finally agreed with me.

I know it took a lot for Jeff to admit that his daytime programmers, who had issued an ultimatum in 2003 that I hire Jim or they would cancel the show, had been wrong. (My mother had been right... "Watch out for temporary people making permanent decisions, especially if they don't know what they don't know.") To his credit, Jeff cleared the way for me to change head writers, and he gave me his full support and encouragement.

NBC approved my choice for a new head writer in Hogan Sheffer, who had distinguished himself by winning four Daytime Emmy Awards for Best Writing in his first five years working for our competitor, CBS's *As the World Turns*. But the network would still exact a price for allowing *Days of our Lives* to go forward with a new visionary writing team. Their price, which they could justify because of the softening of their advertising revenues, would be to reduce our license fee again, this time by almost 30 percent. Now *that* was really brutal.

But the show must go on. We sailed into the hurricane of huge production cutbacks in not only cast and crew sizes but also salaries. *Days of our Lives* became a much leaner and meaner machine. A little too lean, as a matter of fact. The "lemonade" we made out of the lemons we were given had to be made without sugar, and the sugar substitutes we were using did not do justice to the once-glorious tradition of our sweet, lushly produced, and ambitiously promoted daytime drama.

We were starting to show not only our age but also our budget. We were not playing the veteran (meaning more highly paid) cast, and the absence on screen of characters like John, Marlena, Patch, and Kayla, coupled with giving much more airtime to a lot of newer and less expensively paid younger characters, was taking its toll. Our tried-and-true faithful viewers were not seeing a *Days of our Lives* they were familiar with.

Then we were hit with a huge shock. Because the network television industry was still in a tailspin, Jeff Zucker suddenly announced in early 2007 at the National Association of Television Program Executives Convention in Las Vegas that *Passions* would be canceled in September and that NBC probably would not keep *Days of our Lives* on the air after the show's contract expired in March 2009.

But March 2009 was two years down the road. Why would he drop the ax now? Was Jeff merely firing a shot across our bow to warn us that "nothing is forever"…even *Days of our Lives*? Was this Jeff's way of sending me the message that like all network television producers, I had to make a better show than before even though I was given less with which to make it?

To make matters much worse, in November 2007 the Writers Guild of America went on strike. The strike brought much of the television and film industry's production to a screeching, devastating halt. Prime-time went into reruns, as did late-night, with Jay Leno being an exception. Yet *Days of our Lives* had to go on. And on we went, without the services of our head writer and without a clear road map of future story lines.

It was insult added to injury. First a severe license fee reduction and the loss of production value, and then a strike that almost crippled our ability to churn out 260 one-hour scripts each year. But somehow we got through it all. It was a "somehow" that is known only to me and a handful of talented producers, directors, and daytime programmers. We found a way. We kept the show running while many others faltered or failed. "That which doesn't kill you makes you stronger," according to an old saying. And when the strike ended and the smoke cleared, we were still humming along.

∞

In 2008 we received a blessing in the form of head writer Dena Higley. Ironically, she had just been hitting her stride as a head writer on

Days of our Lives when she was replaced by Jim Reilly five years earlier in the debacle of 2003. But now, in 2008, *Days of our Lives* needed a transfusion of great new stories to pull us out of the doldrums created over the previous few years from a lack of exciting and romantic storytelling and the aforementioned strike. So when the strike ended, Dena quickly hatched a plan to return Salem to its place of prominence in the highly competitive arena of daytime dramas. It was time to renew *Days of our Lives* by revisiting what had worked wonders for us in the past.

Hogan Sheffer had reset the once-great feud among the Bradys, the Kiriakises, and the DiMeras by bringing back that oh-so-villainous bunch of villains. Stefano, Tony, Victor, all of their evil machinations, and all of their henchmen (like Dr. Rolf) returned, as well as mixing in the newest of this family's prodigal sons, the fascinating character of E. J. DiMera, Stefano's son, played by that oh-so-dashing Brit James Scott.

The backstory of the Bradys and the DiMeras returned to the present *Days of our Lives* like the prodigal son. Viewers were excited again by the return of the DiMeras and the front-and-center inclusion of the core members of the Brady family—Bo and Hope, John and Marlena and Roman, Patch and Kayla, and Shawn and Caroline—all involved in bringing a close to Stefano's wicked generational vendetta.

Working with Hogan Sheffer, and then using the road map that he had left when the strike began, Dena showed her masterful touch as a writer, which was best played out as we watched the past unfold with the tragic gothic romance between Santo and Colleen, Stefano's father and Shawn Brady's sister. That was the match that lit the fuse decades before that started the war between the Bradys and the DiMeras. And then viewers watched the death and transformation of John Black, a man without any memory of the past!

Finally there was a tragedy in the aftermath of this backstory, played out in a plane crash that left *Days of our Lives* without Grandpa Shawn Brady, who sacrificed his life by giving Bo his oxygen mask as the plane went down. Those shows were among the finest we had ever produced as a cast, crew, and staff as we fought for our "lives."

All great things must return, in time, to their roots. *Days of our Lives* was reinventing itself again, much as it had to do many times in the past to stay fresh, new, and most importantly, vital enough to be on the air for years to come. Seeds that had been planted more than twenty-five years earlier by head writer Pat Falken Smith were now the huge family trees of good and evil, locked in an eternal struggle for the future of Salem. The fruits of these trees were being harvested by Dena Higley and a talented staff of writers, actors, directors, producers, and tireless crew.

By late summer 2008 the cast and crew took note of these winds of change and were also newly excited and challenged by it all. When the cast and crew are loving it, that comes through on screen. No more fear on the set or behind the scenes. People are talking again. "Have you seen *Days of our Lives* recently? It's getting really good...again!"

"Where there is fear, there is only confusion, but where there is love, there can be no fear." Two hundred and sixty shows a year.

CHAPTER 28

LIFE SUPPORT

Once in a while my father used to take me after school to the CBS Television Studios in New York City to watch a "table reading" of *As the World Turns*. It was a special treat and a glimpse into his professional life. I was ten or eleven at the time, in third or fourth grade, but smart enough to know I was being granted a privilege few ever had and provided with the opportunity to see the inner workings at a soap opera's core...to glimpse and absorb how it all came together and stuck.

I would sit unobtrusively off to the side, while my father, the director, and the cast for *As the World Turns* would rehearse the next day's episode. The actors would sit around a long table with only their scripts, my father at the head of the table with his script and watch, and they would run their lines for the next day...a "table reading." It was done to the clock, meaning that my father timed every scene with his chronograph or stopwatch, the same one he'd had for many years, dating back to *The Guiding Light* on the radio in 1948. The cast would run their lines and only stop when he would say, "And we're out."

He would occasionally stop the reading mid-scene and give an actor line notes or deeper acting notes dealing with their subtext in a scene or what their blocking (physical movement) was going to be the next day on air. They would all respectfully listen, understand, and then go on.

While I was quietly sitting there and listening one day, I distinctly remember Don Hastings (Bob Hughes) and Helen Wagner (Nancy Hughes) stopping mid-scene. After a moment they heatedly asked my father why they were saying almost the same lines they had said the day before in almost the same scene.

I remember that my father did not answer them at first. In his understated and sharply intelligent way, he simply took the red Mark Cross pen that he used to mark his director's script, calmly stood up, and wrote across the wall in that small conference room in big red letters: "Zat was Zen. Zis is Now."

The cast was impressed and silenced. Then he quietly sat down, and they all resumed. He seemed to have quieted the cast's burning question. But more so, in that act he revealed his own deep understanding of the soap medium and his philosophy of life…that life is full of changes. In his own life he had changed countries, changed careers, and changed beliefs. He had lived through the changes brought by the Great Depression and World War II and embraced the opportunities that were presented.

He tried to never dwell on the past. He would always say, "Yesterday is history; tomorrow is a mystery. All we have is today." Not necessarily the eternal optimist, but always the eternal realist.

Every chapter in this book has, thus far, been a total joy to write, no matter how challenging, how painful, how revealing, or how true. But this one is extremely difficult.

The only thing certain in life is that things change. How we deal with change defines us as individuals, as a people, and as a show.

∞

Even though our story lines were stronger than ever, in 2008 change was upon us again. This time it was change that the entire world would have to learn to deal with. The economic problems caused by bad real-estate loans, too much debt, and other excesses crippled our economy (and the world's), and the world has recently experienced the greatest economic downturn since the Great Depression. Since the recession began in late 2007 and early 2008, more than seven million Americans have lost their jobs. The recession happened faster and is deeper than most of us were prepared for. I know the readers know this and don't want this news shoved at them again…especially the jobs lost. But *Days of our Lives* is a reflection of real life, and real life has real problems that can't be ignored.

I, too, was caught totally off-guard. The *Days of our Lives* contract with NBC was due to expire again in March 2009, so I met with NBC president Jeff Zucker in New York in June 2008. Jeff is a very bright and talented programmer, an inspiring leader, and a great example of "living strong." Not only was it a cordial, pleasant meeting, but also he assured me that despite what he had announced before, *Days of our Lives* was very much a part of NBC's future plans and we were in good stead with him and the network. Not exactly a written pick-up, but a very reassuring handshake and a vote of confidence. I returned to Burbank believing it was a perfunctory matter to dot the *i*'s, cross the *t*'s, and nail down another three-year deal with NBC over the next few months, even at the much reduced rate that we were then working for.

To give perspective, we had already agreed to a stiff 30 percent pay cut in 2006 to accommodate NBC's loss of advertising and sales revenue. We had cut the budget of our show to reflect this pay cut, and there was no fat left to burn. We had changed our production format in 2006 so that one week a month we would do six shows instead of five, thus picking up an extra twelve shows or more every year. This kept studio overhead and production costs down. Additionally, we all took pay cuts, and we downsized our cast, crew, and staff. We were forced to lay off people, shorten work hours, and reduce pay, all while NBC expected to get the same product. And…it worked.

We started playing fewer stories every day, putting up fewer sets every day, and using fewer actors every day. We got it done, and everyone worked to the bone. We changed the way we did business while trying to make everyone happy, both in front of and behind the cameras, and most importantly, all of our viewers at home.

We were a leaner, meaner fighting machine, and I was proud that our *Days* family was still able to produce a high-quality show in spite of all the sacrifices we had made.

Despite my positive conversation with Jeff Zucker in June, by September 2008 we still did not have a signed renewal contract with NBC. We knew why. As the economy further deteriorated, so did the advertising dollars on which NBC counted to pay our license fees. Indeed, General Electric, which owns NBC, lost more than 60 percent of the value of its stock by year's end, and the economy continued to collapse in a never-before-seen (other than the Great Depression) rapid free fall.

September crept into October and then October into November, and there was still no deal to renew *Days of our Lives* beyond March 2009. All of our employees, cast, and crew grew extremely ill at ease. Would we all still have a show in less than six months?

NBC was being very close-mouthed about the whole negotiation, but they finally made us what we thought was an offer. It involved a further cut in our license fees that was so ridiculously low it would necessitate our reinventing the *Days of our Lives* wheel if we accepted. The warm and fuzzy feeling I'd had in Jeff Zucker's office in June was replaced by the anxiety that precedes cancellation. In a few short months things had taken a drastic turn for the worse.

Never before had I been so unsure of our future. And to make matters worse, there were not only rampant rumors of our cancellation in the air and in the press, but we also had proof that a new talk show was being readied to take our place in March 2009 if we wouldn't agree to NBC's offer. The fans were extremely concerned. And outside of staying upbeat, I had no real answers for our employees as to the fate of our future.

As Election Day approached, Steve Mosko, the president of Sony Pictures Television (our distributor), met with Marc Graboff, NBC entertainment cochairman, in a last-ditch effort to make a reasonable deal and prevent the cancellation of *Days of our Lives*. NBC was definitely ready to pull the plug if we didn't accept their unbelievably difficult lowball offer…and even then, none of us, including Steve Mosko, was really sure that a deal could be made once we got into the details.

Few of us at *Days of our Lives* were getting much sleep, and our *Days* family's eyes were not only looking at the future with doubt but also to the near future for a new job. My mother had always told me that nothing lasts forever, and "everything has a beginning, a middle, and an end." I seriously wondered if that time had come for *Days of our Lives*.

In that now well-known meeting between Steve Mosko and Marc Graboff, Steve declared that he did not want to be known as the Sony president under whose watch *Days of our Lives* had been canceled. Ben Silverman, chief NBC programmer, felt the same way. But business is business. NBC was holding its cards very close to its peacock-feathered chest. They were not budging; in fact, they were more than ready to retract and pull the deal, leaving us without a home, a network, or a future.

According to Steve, in his meeting with Mr. Graboff, he almost got down on his knees and begged NBC to pick up the show…to keep *Days of our Lives* on the air. For a man of Steve's stature to go to such lengths reflects his and Sony's profound dedication and commitment to the show.

Finally we received our answer. NBC would renew *Days of our Lives* in March 2009 for one and a half years, followed by an additional automatic pick-up for another year after that, based on our ratings performance. Most of all, they insisted that we take an onerous astronomical cut in our license fee…again. General Electric and NBC were losing even more revenue from their advertisers and could guarantee us no better offer.

So we had a solid pick-up for eighteen months followed automatically by another year if the show performed well. But here was the catch: The license fee would be reduced by another whopping 40 percent, with strings attached in their favor, if we bombed in the ratings anytime during the two-and-a-half-year term.

Including the 30 percent reduction we received in 2006, we would now go to less than half of what we were being paid three years before. But what could we do? CBS and ABC didn't want to, or couldn't, buy the show. NBC was the only game in town. So Steve Mosko negotiated, Marc Graboff finally acquiesced, and we were guaranteed to still be on the air come March of the next year, 2009, through at least September of 2010.

∞

To produce the show with a 40 percent smaller budget, we all knew that *Days of our Lives* would have to reinvent itself and do it mighty fast over the four months from November 2008 to March 2009. So reinvent ourselves we did. But at such a sad and enormous cost to so many faithful cast members, staff, and crew.

The three months following our pick-up were the most difficult I had experienced in the previous thirty years of my association with, ownership of, and guardianship of *Days of our Lives*. In 1979 I had started my career at the show by answering fan mail from mostly content and happy viewers. Now, thirty years later, the fan mail I was personally getting was so hateful and hurtful that some days I just wanted to pull the covers over my head, stay in bed, and not go into the office or studio to deal with so many layoffs, firings, and top-to-bottom cuts in all aspects of production. I tried not to feel self-pity. We were, after all, still going to be on the air! But how could we do it for so little? How could we ever mount the show every day for those dollars?

The challenge seemed so enormous and formidable; the odds were against us. But thank God it was not impossible. We were blessed with a new, innovative co-executive producer, Gary Tomlin, who ironically had been in New York with me, Al Rabin, and co-head writer Michelle Poteet Lisanti in 1980 when we all saved the show from the brink of cancellation. He had saved us as a writer then. Now he would be saving us again by working extremely hard as he got together with head writer Dena Higley, associate head writer Christopher Whitesell, our executive in charge of production, Greg Meng, producers Janet Rider, Noel Maxam, and Mary Kelly Weir ("M. K."), and yours truly to forge a plan.

The plan was that all of us would take a huge cutback in our salaries, once again, and would trim all aspects of production to the bone. We would try to do so without changing the look of the show. But we would have to let many great employees go, and that meant many of the popular cast members who had been on the air for decades. There was no other way to produce our show, balance our books, and move onward and upward into the future.

On Election Day, Tuesday, November 4, 2008, America elected a new president, Barack Obama. That day I also elected to make the difficult decision to no longer delay implementing the major changes I knew were coming. That afternoon I called both Deidre Hall and Drake Hogestyn to tell them that their beloved characters of John and Marlena were going to have to leave Salem, albeit happily reunited, for the foreseeable future. We weren't going to kill their characters, but we would have to "rest" them. However, there was no way around it: I was letting them go.

My pain before and during those phone calls was enormous, but nothing compared to their own unfathomable pain. We had to reduce the cast size and cost, and they were the first of many of the old guard and the new to exit. I cannot remember a more painful time of change on *Days of our Lives*, yet we had to preserve the show.

Over the next few weeks I delivered the same gut-wrenching message to Stephen Nichols and Mary Beth Evans, who had created and played the characters of Patch and Kayla for many years, as well as to Thaao Penghlis, who had portrayed Tony DiMera with amazing love of character, class, and aplomb for more than twenty-eight years. They were all being written out.

We had to make the choice of who would now carry heavy story and who wouldn't. We had no other choice but to pare down to survive. We would give the limelight to Peter Reckell and Kristian Alfonso, the enduring Bo and Hope. With Alison Sweeney, James Scott, and Arianne Zucker (Sami, E. J., and Nicole), we put a classic "double-switch" baby story on the front burner. At the same time, we retained and enhanced our younger cast, such as Philip Kiriakis and Stephanie Johnson, Melanie Layton and Nathan Horton (a more recent addition to the Hortons), in fresh, new story lines that would sow the seeds for future *Days of our Lives* blossoms. And we would still give the popular Stefano, Victor, Kate, Caroline, and Maggie a prominent presence in the show.

All of these cast reductions were implemented at the same time we reduced the size of our production staff and crew. Overall we let more than a quarter of our *Days of our Lives* family go. Those who stayed were asked to work for much less.

What a profound testament to their allegiance to *Days of our Lives* in keeping the show on the air that so many agreed to stay on, work harder, and make less, all to save the show and keep the sands flowing. They are a blessing. Suddenly I realized through my pain that there was a positive to all of this.

Days of our Lives has been a show of many firsts: from being the first to broadcast in color to now creating a new model for the production of a daytime drama at a dramatically reduced cost. We would survive and lead the way for other daytime dramas to thrive in such difficult economic times. We would succeed.

We now produce one and a half shows a day. We have reinvented the wheel behind the scenes, but not the scenes themselves. They still have the magic that has always kept the viewers tuned in. Amazingly enough, after having painfully cleaned the canvas and our house, at the same time we find ourselves and our loyal fans stronger than ever. With the return of some wonderful and legendary cast members, such as Justin and Adrienne Kiriakis (Wally Kurth and Judi Evans), Carly Manning (Crystal Chappell), Vivian Alamain (Louise Sorel), Anna DiMera (Leann Hunley), and Calliope Jones (Arleen Sorkin), we have reinvigorated Salem.

In April 2009 the show received thirteen Daytime Emmy nominations, more than we have ever received in any of the previous forty-three years. The show grows rather than withers. The audience adjusts and stays tuned. *Days of our Lives* is now generating the biggest year-to-year viewer gain of any daytime series on the major networks and is one of only two daytime dramas up in women viewers ages eighteen to forty-nine!

We're not doing it with smoke and mirrors, like some midway magic act. Our success, as always, is dependent on great writing and fine acting. We are doing it with new production efficiency and a renewed passion. Who says an old dog can't learn new tricks?

I do not see an end to the show anymore. I see this as a new beginning, as if the hourglass has been turned over again and the sands are flowing anew. No matter what happens, love, respect, traditional values, and faith in goodness will always pull us through, along with massive amounts of talented hard work to accompany these morals.

∞

Life for me at *Days of our Lives* is wonderful. As each week comes to a close, I look back and know that I have tried to do my very best. I remember my father once telling me that Friday evening is the holiest evening of the week and Sunday morning is the holiest morning of the week. What comes before and after is what you do, but what comes in between is what you dream of doing. "Reach for the heavens," he would say, "and if you do, you get the stars thrown in."

∞

Thinking back, I realize the palm reader was right. I have been blessed to be able to do one thing and to do it well. That is to keep my parents' dream and legacy alive; to keep hundreds of people gainfully employed; and to keep the millions of viewers entertained, enthralled, and excited, looking forward to their one-hour appointment, their special time, with *Days of our Lives*, every day. Most of all, I have been blessed to have been able to work with so many talented, loving, and dedicated souls—the *Days* family. They have nurtured my mother and father's dream and vision into a living legacy, each and every day of our lives.

We are all so blessed. So very, very, blessed. I am deeply grateful, and I know those who have gone before us, who worked on, or watched or loved the show, would be proud of us today. And as sure as I am that my mother and father, Ted and Betty Corday, reside in the Lord's house, I am also sure they still have part of their souls in every episode of *Days of our Lives*, now and forever.

> *"Like sands through the hourglass,*
> *So are the days of our lives."*

May the sands run for many years to come.

EPILOGUE

It was the first time I had been left entirely to myself for over a year. I went to the Pacific Ocean in Ventura, California, to ceremoniously say a last good-bye, or more appropriately, an "until we meet again" to my brother, Chris. I placed an old picture of us in the sand at the edge of the ocean. I lit three sticks of incense, put them beside the photo, and prayed for my brother's place and soul in heaven. I sat on the sand in my wetsuit as the afternoon grew pale and cold.

After a while I cast a line out with my fishing pole to far beyond the breakers. The hooks were too large for a small fish like a perch or halibut, and each was baited with an entire squid. They were anchored to the ocean floor by an eight-ounce lead sinker, exactly as my brother had taught me. Then I forgot about the fishing and meditated on my brother's life from day one.

I had recently been told by another psychic in a five-minute session, done as a novelty at someone's birthday party, that I needed to clean up my past karma and say a final good-bye. Offer forgiveness to the one who had left me behind, and let him go. I knew the psychic meant my brother.

So on that shivering afternoon I sat on the beach next to our photograph and thought of the precious time Chris and I had shared and all I had learned from him during those glorious early years growing up together in New York and spending our summers in Southampton. How much we loved to go fishing in our little sixteen-foot boat runabout, aptly named the *Cobro*. I thought of the times when, early in the morning, we would sneak out to troll the inlets and canals of Peconic Bay for striped bass and bluefish. Those many special moments. I really loved those summers more than anything else in my youth. I recalled how Chris helped me grow up and was there for me after our father died.

Unfortunately, I also recalled that nightmare on Christmas Eve, fifteen years before, when the paramedics had informed me of Chris's suicide. How when I arrived at the scene the paramedics were sensitive enough to prevent me from seeing my brother lying dead from his self-inflicted gunshot wound. Thankfully I wouldn't have to witness or remember that horrible image.

As my quiet and soulful afternoon on the beach unfolded, I finally made peace with what my brother had done. Whatever emotional and intellectual torture Chris had endured, it must have been far too overwhelming for him to deal with day by day. When he looked in the mirror that one last time before he decided to pull the trigger, I hope he saw the face of courage looking back at him.

I sat on the shore thinking about my brother all those years ago and remembering times I hadn't thought of for decades. The sun was setting. I had been on the beach for about an hour and had forgotten about the fishing line I had cast way out past the breakers. The rod was resting in its holder, some ten yards up the beach.

Suddenly I caught sight of the fishing pole bent over like a piece of bamboo in a high wind. The line was singing off the reel so fast that the fishing rod, all twelve feet of it, was about to be pulled out of the rod holder and launched toward the surf.

I scrambled to my feet and started sprinting toward the pole. But after only a few strides, I felt a sharp pain and then a "pop" in my left hamstring. It was as if I had been stabbed in my thigh. I was almost knocked to the ground by the pain as my forward momentum carried me straight toward the severely bent fishing pole.

I got to the pole just in time to free it from the surf spike and back the drag off the reel to keep the line from breaking. The pain in my leg was intense. I couldn't decide whether to rub it or chase after the fish I had hooked.

My decision was made simpler by the fact that I had already lost one hundred yards of line in less than a minute, and the fish, whatever it was, was still swimming straight out west past the surf break...and traveling fast. So I had to "stop it or pop it," which meant tightening the drag on the reel as much as I could and running into the surf to get a better angle on the line to stay with this fish when and if it decided to stop its initial run.

Two hundred yards of line had been peeled off the big Penn reel, and I was now up to my armpits in the cold surf, hooked up to one hell of a fish. The bracing ocean water felt good on my burning hamstring. Even so, I had to move with a limp as my torn hamstring muscle shot a searing pain through my leg. I knew I had to stay with the fish but, at the same time, not get over my head in the surf and lose my footing and pressure on the line.

I had just fifty yards of line left on the reel. I used my thumb to apply all the extra pressure the line could stand on that fish. Suddenly it stopped its run and, after a brief pause, turned and started moving back in toward the surf. Then it began another furious run, but this time directly at me. Smart fish...it must have been hooked before.

I picked up line as fast as I could reel. After regaining almost half of it, I realized that this was going to turn out to be a pretty fair fight, one that I could even win were it not for my damaged leg and my inability to move up and down the beach while standing in four feet of cold, churned-up water.

The fish stopped its run and then starting swimming north outside the waves. So it went for the next half hour, never gaining or giving more than a few yards of line at a time, as the fish stayed out more than a hundred yards offshore and slowly, steadily, swam north outside of the surf. Its pull was very heavy, and it now swam without panic…a very deliberate move up the coast way out past the breakers. The fish wasn't hooked to me; I was hooked to the fish.

My leg was numb from the cold, salty water. My will was being tested. Would I be able to pull on this fish at the same time I was side-stepping through the surf? Why not just break the line and give this fish everything: hook, line, and sinker?

Because I had to see it. What was this fish I had hooked? I had caught many fish at this beach…mostly perch, halibut, skate, and leopard sharks, but this one reminded me of the few rare stingrays that I had encountered here over the years. None of those had been more than fifty pounds, but this one seemed to "own" all of them. If it were truly a stingray, it would be able to swim faster, stronger, and longer than any other fish in these waters.

After an hour the fish turned around and started swimming southward, back to the place it had taken the bait, now almost half a mile down the beach. And slowly it started moving closer to shore. It was as if I were walking a dog back down the surf line. It wouldn't pull on the leash, but it also wouldn't heel to it. It just swam back to where it had been hooked.

Night was falling, and this fish seemed to be feeling more comfortable with the steady drag of the line. Unfortunately, I was feeling worse. I definitely wasn't going to prolong this fight into the night, when the fish would gain a distinct advantage. Dusk is an uncomfortable time for fish, big or small. If this happened to be a giant stingray, it would be foolish to try to fight it in the dark.

As I was thinking this, the creature made another bold run into the surf. Now was a good time to try to bring it through the breakers and land it. Killing it was out of the question, since I was all alone with neither friend nor gaff to help take this monster.

But maybe I wasn't alone. For the past hour, I had felt a familiar presence with me and this fish. It was as if my brother, Chris, was fishing beside me, silently encouraging me and offering the strength and resolve to finish the fight: "It's you or the fish…decide!"

As I and my friend, this really big fish, got closer to the point where we had first crossed paths, I noticed a few surfers sitting on their boards and waiting to catch the evening's last waves. The stingray broke into one final, furious run and moved out again away from the surf line. I had to back the drag way off on it, and just as I released the tension, the fish responded and showed itself for the first time.

Rising out of the water and jumping high into the air, the stingray had to weigh more than one hundred pounds. It flew free, straight above the surface like a kite, and crashed back down into the water, leaving a wake and startling quite a few surfers. What a huge fish! How was I ever going to catch it?

No matter. Having seen it, I knew it was bigger than anything I had ever caught. Now I *knew* my brother was with me.

The tide had started to rise, and now as it washed in, the fish came with it. Maybe it was just hungry and wanted to eat again. Maybe it, too, wanted to see who was at the other end of the line. Or maybe it just wanted to prowl the surf. It sure wasn't tired. Nevertheless, the fish was coming to me now, just fifty yards of line separating us. As it floated to the top of a large wave breaking far from shore, it was suddenly flipped over on its back. Disoriented, the huge stingray tumbled through the large breakers and landed upside down like a surfboard tossed to shore.

Thrashing in three or four feet of churning water and in the undertow, the stingray was unable to right itself. Its own weight moved against it as I reeled in the slack line. It glided with the tide on its beautiful olive-green back toward the glazed shore and the sand that would serve as an anchor. The beach was not what the fish had bargained for.

As I closed the gap between us, I could see the stingray's massive underside through the water. How white it was in contrast to the ray's dark olive-green back! There were patches of black tar stuck to it in a few places, souvenirs of the oil derricks that dot the Santa Barbara Channel between Ventura and the Channel Islands. I saw its great, long, whipping tail, as thick as a broomstick tapering to a bullwhip.

One crack from that barb at the end of its three-foot tail, or even worse, a stab from the spike that pointed up at the base of the tail, would no doubt knock me on my butt before the anaphylactic shock from its poison set in. It could cause a heart attack. It had been known to happen. Fisherman and stingray, both found dead on a rock jetty the next morning.

Dusk was spreading. The fish was being pushed ashore by the softly moving incoming tide, all the while flailing on its back, disoriented and rendered helpless. I picked up the last twenty yards of line, got the fish above and to the side of me in the surf, and on the next incoming wave, pulled with a few sharp, short strokes and finally beached the great stingray.

What a wondrous sight…it was four feet across and furious now at being taken totally out of its element. Its tail whipped wildly back and forth in the few inches of water above the sand, seeking to inflict enough of an injury to convince its captor to relent. But all in vain. It had been landed.

I retrieved the leader and hooks, the latter with great care, and now was left with a big problem: how to release this fish back into the deep water unharmed.

The surfers had gotten out of the water and were onshore watching all this with great interest. One approached and offered to help flip over this sea creature using his surfboard. So together we tried to manage the task of turning over the stingray, but with no success. It kept slipping off the surfboard.

By now night was upon us, and the rising tide was making everything much more difficult to deal with. He and I couldn't flip this fish over, and it was getting more and more tired. It was heavy and I was injured, which made it seem hopeless for us to try to turn it over and help it back into the ocean.

Just as we were about to give up, a man came jogging down the beach. By now the fish was suffocating under its own beached weight. The jogger was wearing a California Highway Patrol T-shirt and immediately recognized the intensity of the situation. He asked to help, and with the addition of his strong arms and the aid of a beach towel as a "stretcher," the three of us turned the massive stingray on its stomach. It, in turn, immediately flapped its huge wet wings. And even though it was starting in just a foot or so of seawater, the stingray made a swift exit from the shoreline and faded back into the deep.

It was gone...released, unharmed. We were all exhausted. The jogger looked at me and said that he had pulled a lot of big people from car wrecks, and that fish weighed more than most people he had saved.

"Must have weighed over two hundred pounds," he said, matter-of-factly. "Big heavy fish...maybe you just threw back the world record."

Reflecting on all that the afternoon had brought and what it all meant, I simply answered, "I couldn't kill him...he was too courageous."

But in truth I was talking about more than just the stingray. I was talking about my brother, with whom I had spent the afternoon.

So I closed the door and let him go. I picked up our picture from the sand, grabbed my tackle bag, and folded up my surf rod and holder. Then I trudged back up the beach toward home feeling less like Santiago, the old man in Ernest Hemingway's novel, and more like a new man. A man without guilt, self-pity, or remorse for a life begun and gone, or for all that might have been had my brother lived. I had released the fish and, with it, my brother's soul.

SPECIAL THANKS

To my beloved parents, Ted and Betty Corday, who made *Days of our Lives* one of the greatest of all soaps and blessed me with its legacy.

To my wife, Sherry, and my children, Amanda, Kimberly, and Teddy, who continually show me that love is all you need and are the four greatest treasures in my life.

To Margot Hawley and Jim McMackin, who started my education at Trinity School in New York City, and to Lou Harrison and Ron Elfving, who moved it along in college.

To my valued cocomposer, bass player, and great friend, Brent Nelson.

To Jeff and Deborah Herman, who believed in this book and shepherded it to publication.

To Peter Lynch, my Sourcebooks chief editor, for his kind guidance and insightfulness.

To Barry Felsen, my attorney for the past thirty years, whose sage advice always inspires me and who is the one I trust most to watch my back and get the big deals done.

To Greg Meng, our executive in charge of production and senior vice president, for his present, steadfast, and enduring dedication.

To Andrea McKinnon, our publicist, for all her tireless devotion to our show and this book.

To my associate editor, Angela Anderson, who never let me quit writing this book, inspired me, and kept my feet to the fire.

To Mike Russell, for his spit-and-polish editing approach in helping me make this an easier book to read.

To Kathy Edwards, my copyist, typist, friend, and general chicken-scratch interpreter, for all of her cogent patience, serenity, and wisdom.

To all the cast and crew, who tirelessly gave and continue to give of themselves each and every day in a peerless and priceless way to keep the sands of *Days of our Lives* running.

To NBC and all of its affiliates, for broadcasting *Days of our Lives* for forty-four amazingly blessed years.

To Steve Mosko and Sony Pictures Television, for distributing *Days of our Lives* in twenty-two countries worldwide, and also to Steve for being a wonderful partner, protector, and friend.

Finally, most of all, to the viewers who have stayed tuned and have been faithfully entertained for more than eleven thousand episodes and without whom *Days of our Lives* would have remained only my father's dream.

BIOGRAPHY OF
KEN CORDAY

K en Corday was only a teenager when his parents, Ted and Betty Corday, first created NBC's daytime drama *Days of our Lives* in 1965. A year after the show's inception, Ted passed away, and it was up to Betty to carry on the show. Ken became his mother's support system as she taught him everything he would need to know to continue the family legacy.

Ken received his bachelor of arts in music from the University of California, Santa Cruz, before receiving a master's degree in music composition from San Jose State University.

Prior to taking over *Days of our Lives* as executive producer in 1985, Ken worked on the show for almost ten years, first as a composer, then as assistant producer, and finally as producer.

Ken's first love is still music, and in addition to his role as executive producer, he continues to compose all of the original background score for the show.

He has received two Emmy Awards for music. The show has also received eight nominations for an Emmy Award for Best Daytime Drama. *Days of our Lives* won the Emmy Award for Best Daytime Drama in

1975, and Ted and Betty Corday received a Lifetime Achievement Emmy Award in 1988.

In addition, *Days of our Lives* has won four People's Choice Awards, two TV Guide Awards, and ten Soap Opera Digest Awards: four for Favorite Show and six for Outstanding Daytime Serial.

Ken Corday lives in Los Angeles with his wife and three children.